◄ Tombstones
at Highgate
Cemetery, London

▼ Bagan temples
at sunrise,
Mandalay, Burma

GUIDE TO THE WORLD'S
SUPERNATURAL
PLACES

More Than 250 Spine-Chilling
Destinations Around the Globe

SARAH BARTLETT

WASHINGTON, D.C.

CONTENTS

◄ A voodoo shrine in the national cemetery of Port-au-Prince, Haiti

▼ The Inca ruins of Machu Picchu, Cusco, Peru

INTRODUCTION

FROM THE BARREN DESERTS OF SOUTHERN PERU to the dark valleys of central Europe, mysterious forces have wreaked havoc, instilled fear, and evoked wonder and awe in people throughout the centuries. For thousands of years, people have reported seeing ghosts, feeling disturbed by malevolent spirits, and being graced by mystical powers. Restless spirits and sinister legends continue to captivate, while lost cities and ancient ruins inspire with their spiritual treasures. Myths and legends replete with heroes are as numerous in modern-day South America as they were in ancient Greece, and mystical places are widespread—some are as exhilarating in their natural beauty as Uluru (Ayers Rock), situated in the Northern Territory, Australia, others as mysterious in their purpose as the Carnac Stones found in Brittany, France. In defiance of scientific explanation, such supernatural places have fascinated and perplexed in equal measure. Many contemporary indigenous peoples believe that a spiritual realm exists alongside the apparent "real" world, and some—including the Wanapum of northwest North America—believe that journeys can be made back and forth between the two of them.

> For thousands of years people have reported seeing ghosts and feeling disturbed by spirits.

Supernatural beings pervade the beliefs of every culture. Predatory vampires are believed to have inhabited not only ruined castles and chapels but also quiet villages, remote jungles, and busy cities. The *loogaroo* of Grenada, the *pontianak* of Indonesia, and the shroud-eating vampire of Venice are as terrifying as Romania's famed Vlad the Impaler and the legendary Mercy Brown, hungry for blood in her Rhode Island grave. Ghosts are said to haunt ruined medieval castles across Europe, American cemeteries, the desert lands of South Africa, deserted towns, battle sites, abandoned mental asylums, and islands all over the globe. Although numerous in the American Southwest, reported UFO sightings have also been registered as far afield as the Burragorang Valley in Australia and San Clemente in Chile.

▶ *The Kiss of the Vampire* (1916), oil painting by Bolesław Biegas

Wherever they are located, be it the Tower of London, England, the Versailles Gardens in France, or Sleepy Hollow in New York, haunted places are not necessarily evil—they are sites of human tragedy, loss, or some horrifying event that has left an indelible memory. Disembodied souls, trapped between the material and the spiritual world, may haunt places where earthly business needs to be resolved before they can find peace. Such restless wraiths can be spiteful, mischievous, or sorrowful, and their negative energy may be felt, seen, or heard. Perhaps they create the atmosphere of the places in which they are said to occur, or perhaps they have been invented to rationalize a disturbing ambience. Houska Castle in the Czech Republic is reputedly built over a Hellmouth; Bhangarh Fort in India was abandoned, it is said, because of a wizard's curse. Many ancient monuments seem to have an unearthly atmosphere, possibly because their original purpose has been lost in the mists of time. Visitors report an eerie air among the standing stones at Stonehenge in England. The *moai* effigies on Easter Island in Chile are often said to have a disquieting effect. Travelogues tell of a sense of unease around the temple at Tikal in Guatemala. Some places, such as Mount Shasta in California and Mount Fuji in Japan, seem to be sources of divine power in themselves.

> Disembodied souls may haunt places where earthly business needs to be resolved.

Shakespeare's Hamlet famously said to his skeptical friend that "There are more things in heaven and earth, Horatio, than are dreamt of in your philosophy." Whether searching for the answer to a universal mystery, hunting a ghost, or trying to assess the likelihood of a UFO report being credible evidence of life in other worlds, this book is your ticket to uncharted territory. The realm of the supernatural never fails to intrigue, mystify, and enchant, and the *National Geographic Guide to the World's Supernatural Places* will introduce you to more than 250 spine-tingling locations. Haunted castles, vampire lairs, houses of witchcraft, sacred sites, UFO hot spots, and legendary places of tremendous spiritual power are all to be found within the pages of this extraordinary book.

◀ The prehistoric stone circle at Stonehenge, England

▲ A 19th-century engraving of a couple strolling through haunted woods

HAUNTED

PLACES

EDINBURGH CASTLE SCOTLAND

A phantom drumbeat haunts the battlements, while mournful piping drifts through secret passages.

▲ Dusk gathers over the craggy outline of Edinburgh Castle on Castle Rock.

WHEN TO VISIT

Come on a winter afternoon just before sunset, when shadows create a sinister atmosphere.

PERCHED HIGH ON A ROCK OVERLOOKING the city of Edinburgh, this foreboding Scottish stronghold has many supernatural associations. A haloed hound is believed to preside over the castle's entrance, while apparitions of prisoners loom in the dank dungeons and the ghost of a headless drummer beats a morbid rhythm on the battlements. According to legend, this drumbeat warned the Scots of an English attack in 1296 when King Edward I of England captured the castle after a three-day siege. It is said that drummer was the first man to be slit from ear to ear by an English sword.

In the 17th century, secret tunnels were discovered running from the castle to the city center. According to legend, a young piper sent to investigate the tunnels—playing his pipes so those above could follow his progress below ground—disappeared without trace. Some say his pipes can still be heard within the castle as his ghost wanders the passages beneath.

On the esplanade below the castle, hundreds of so-called witches were burned at the stake in the early 16th century. Among them was Janet Douglas, Lady of Glamis, accused of using witchcraft in an attempt to murder King James V of Scotland. On walks along the esplanade, some have claimed to see her screaming in the flames, while others have described a feeling of being scorched by fire. As evening falls over the gray towers, her weeping ghost is said to search for her son, who was sent to watch her horrific death. ◆

GLAMIS CASTLE ANGUS, SCOTLAND

Among the cadre of ghosts at this atmospheric Scottish castle is an earl who gambled with the devil.

IN DEEPEST WINTER, icy winds blow across the rooftops and howl through the courtyards of Glamis Castle. Crows gather here on dry winter days, and at night a barn owl shrieks in the distance. Dating back to the 14th century, the castle is the historic seat of the Bowes-Lyon family, the ancestral line of Queen Elizabeth The Queen Mother. Numerous ghosts are rumored to wander through its rooms and grounds.

It is said that specters tiptoe behind the visitors with the kindest hearts in the hope of warming their own chilly souls. The Grey Lady, considered to be the spirit of Lady Janet Douglas (see p. 14), has been seen in the chapel and above the clock tower. Ever searching for her son, she runs like a burning shroud up the stone staircase, then disappears, leaving a trail of ash.

A woman with no tongue is reputed to run through the parkland, pointing at her mutilated face in horror, while a young boy, the ghost of a black servant who was badly treated in the 18th century, haunts a stone seat by the door of the queen's bedroom.

One of the most notorious ghosts is Earl Beardie, the Earl of Crawford, once a castle guest. After a heavy drinking session, he returned to his room in a drunken rage, demanding that someone play him at cards. If not, he said, he would play the devil himself. Then a man, hooded and dressed in black, knocked on the castle door and offered to play with Beardie. Allegedly, a nosy servant peeping through the keyhole of the door where the game took place was blinded in one eye by a bright light, and the next morning Earl Beardie had disappeared. It is said that his ghost still lurks in a secret room, and reports of swearing, loud voices, the rattle of dice, and clinking glasses are evidence of his pact to gamble with the devil for eternity. ◆

> Searching for her son, she runs like a burning shroud up the stone staircase.

▲ The arrival of a hooded man in black at Glamis Castle led to the disappearance of Earl Beardie.

See Also: Versailles Gardens, p. 22

TOWER OF LONDON ENGLAND

Trapped in the earthly realm by unfinished business, several royal wraiths prowl this iconic landmark.

THERE MAY BE AS MANY GHOSTS haunting the Tower of London as people who have lived or died there. Behind its somber battlements, a host of restless souls are reputed to infest its turrets and chambers. Constructed by William the Conqueror in 1078, the Tower claims to be the most haunted building in England.

> Anne Boleyn's spiritual footprint wanders restlessly through the towers.

Tears are said to stream down Lord Guildford Dudley's face as he haunts the Beauchamp Tower, reliving his final moments before facing the executioner in 1554. The pale specter of his wife, Lady Jane Grey, kneels beside a wall on Tower Green, just as she did on the scaffold when facing her own execution moments after Dudley.

One who refused to kneel was Margaret Pole, beheaded on May 27, 1581. On the anniversary of her death, her screaming ghost is said to run across Tower Green. Seventy-two-year-old Margaret was executed in reprisal for her son, Cardinal Pole, who denounced Henry VIII's claim as Supreme Head of the Church of England then escaped to France. Defiantly spitting at the executioner, Margaret ran across the Green, where the axman hacked her to death. Another victim of the ax was Anne Boleyn, Henry VIII's second wife,

▼ The Tower was the scene of royal executions and imprisonment.

ENTRY TO THE TRAITORS GATE

PRINCES IN THE TOWER The dimly lit Bloody Tower is said to be haunted by two children dressed in white nightgowns, who clutch each other in terror. They are known as the two princes, the sons of Edward IV. When Edward died in April 1483, his 12-year-old son Prince Edward was destined to succeed him. Before the coronation could take place, however, Edward and his brother Richard were declared illegitimate by Parliament and their uncle ascended the throne as Richard III. The boys were staying at the Tower of London in preparation for Edward's coronation, and were often seen playing in the grounds. Two months later they mysteriously vanished—widely supposed murdered on Richard III's instruction.

who was accused of witchcraft and adultery. Anne's orb, or spiritual footprint, is reputed to be as vibrant and mesmerizing as the young queen was in life. It wanders restlessly among the towers, forever hoping for redemption.

Meanwhile, the phantom of melancholic Henry VI reportedly paces back and forth in the Wakefield Tower. Some believe he was murdered by the Duke of Gloucester just before midnight on May 21, 1471. His unhappy ghost appears as the clock ticks toward 12; on the last stroke, it fades back into the stone walls and rests peacefully for another year.

The oldest building in the Tower of London is the White Tower, where a group of schoolchildren witnessed an unexplained incident in the 1970s. The children were visiting the infamous Bloody Tower (see panel above), when they heard bells chiming. Glancing across the courtyard to the White Tower, one girl saw a woman with a white veil billowing around her shoulders at one of the slit windows. She appeared to be sobbing. The girl called the other children over, and as they looked the woman waved, as if to say good-bye, and then vanished. Knowing the Tower's history, their teacher was convinced it was the ghost of Lady Jane Grey. ◆

▲ Sir John Everett Millais's 1878 painting of the two princes. Two skeletons discovered under a staircase in the Tower in 1674 were thought to be their remains. They were reburied in Westminster Abbey.

See Also: Chase Vaults, p. 42

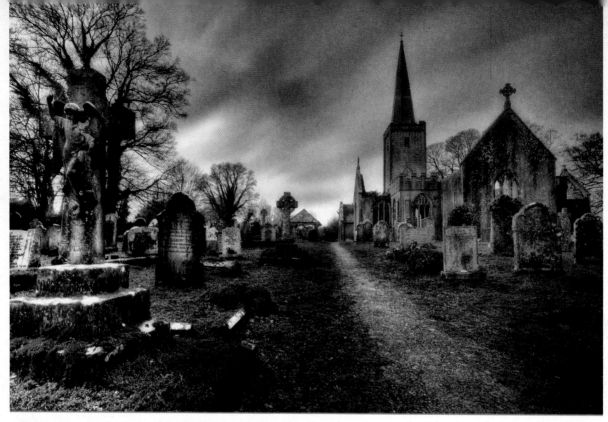

BUCKFASTLEIGH CHURCHYARD DEVON, ENGLAND

A ghostly red light emanates from a shadowy tomb in this abandoned English graveyard.

▲ The ivy-covered graves of Buckfastleigh Churchyard, home to the tomb of Richard Cabell

WHEN TO VISIT

Come after nightfall to experience the menacing atmosphere of Cabell's tomb.

GUTTED BY FIRE IN 1992, Buckfastleigh Church draws a congregation of crows by day and owls by night. But it is the ivy-covered graveyard rather than the desolate ruins of the church that sends shivers up the spine of locals. A strange little building just off the path houses a tomb encased by heavy metal bars. Known locally as the sepulcher, it is the Cabell family tomb.

A mysterious white slab covers the stone tomb, as if to imprison its contents forever. Inside are the remains of Richard Cabell, a monstrously evil 17th-century squire reputed to have murdered his wife and sold his soul to the devil. In July 1677, Cabell passed away and was laid to rest in the sepulcher. That night, it is said, a ghostly pack of hounds raced across the moors and howled outside his tomb. Cabell's ghost then rose, left the sepulcher, and led the phantom hounds on a night-long hunt, snatching and tearing to pieces every living creature in their path. In an attempt to lay his soul to rest, the villagers set iron bars around the sepulcher and placed a slab on top of Cabell's grave. Some claim to have seen a red glow emanating through the bars, while others report demonic beasts circling the grave.

According to legend, if you run around the tomb seven times and then stick your hand through the bars, either Squire Cabell or the devil will bite your fingers. ◆

JAMAICA INN CORNWALL, ENGLAND

A stranger's phantom returns nightly to this historic smugglers' pub on a bleak Cornish moor.

SET HIGH ON THE BLEAK and treacherous Bodmin Moor, Jamaica Inn was both a coaching house and a meeting place for smugglers in the 18th century. The setting for Daphne du Maurier's famous novel of the same name, the inn has a reputation for supernatural sightings, especially of phantom smugglers and menacing spirits on the moors.

There are many disturbing stories. One account concerns a roughly dressed foreign man who was drinking a tankard of ale at the bar. Beckoned outside by another stranger, he left his beer unfinished, went out into the dark and windy night, and never returned. The following day, locals found his disemboweled corpse on the moor. Who murdered him and why has always been a mystery, but a supernatural sequel to the tale presented itself on a January night at the end of the 19th century. According to the story, a strange man sat on the wall outside the inn at closing time. As the landlord took out his key and bade him farewell, the man stood up, raised his tankard, and ran past him to the bar. Rushing after him, the landlord saw a disemboweled figure glugging down a beer before vanishing into the smoky gloom. Since then, landlords and visitors at the inn have heard footsteps along the passage as the ghastly apparition returns to finish his ale.

Outside the inn, the clatter of hooves and cart wheels are sometimes heard, as phantom smugglers make their way to London with their booty. According to legend, anyone hearing the rumble of iron wheels will be cursed with financial ruin. ◆

> **Many landlords have heard footsteps along the passage to the bar.**

▼ Inaccessible by land, Cornwall's hidden bays made it a favorite haunt of smugglers in the 18th century, as depicted in this engraving of 1793 by George Morland.

NEWSTEAD ABBEY NOTTINGHAM, ENGLAND

A Black Mass—dubbed the Goblin Friar—is thought to be a harbinger of doom at this historic abbey.

ONCE THE HOME OF THE romantic poet Lord Byron, picturesque Newstead Abbey nestles in rolling green parkland. Yet it harbors a dark secret. A ghost seen by Lord Byron and immortalized in his epic poem "Don Juan" is said to watch all visitors. In his poem, Byron tells how a black shapeless mass would roll from the bed onto the floor and vanish.

Although known as the Black Friar, Byron referred to the ghost as the Goblin Friar in "Don Juan." He claimed the apparition would appear to members of the Byron family before any unhappy event and was seen shortly before his own disastrous marriage to Anne Milbanke.

> The apparition stalked the abbey at midnight, terrifying all who stayed there.

The American writer Washington Irving brought more ghostly experiences to public attention when he stayed at Newstead at the end of the 19th century. He recounted the story of the ghost of a heavily bearded ancestor of Byron. Descending from a painting above the drawing-room fireplace, the apparition, he said, stalked the abbey at midnight, terrifying all who stayed here.

Often reported wandering the gardens reading a book is the White Lady, the phantom of an orphaned deaf girl named Sophia Hyatt, who visited the abbey as one of Byron's greatest fans. ◆

▼ Fanciful depiction of Byron, his daughter Ada, and dog in a hand-colored line engraving of Newstead, dating from 1836

LOFTUS HALL COUNTY WEXFORD, IRELAND

A lovesick ghost and her demon lover forever play hide-and-seek in this isolated Irish mansion.

ON THE REMOTE HOOK PENINSULA of County Wexford, a solitary mansion stands starkly outlined against the skyline. Built at the end of the 19th century, it replaced an earlier hall occupied by the Tottenham family. According to local legend, in the late 18th century the daughter of the house, Anne Tottenham, became infatuated with a young visitor to Loftus Hall. The stranger had been shipwrecked at sea during a storm.

As they played cards one night, Anne bent down to pick a card up from the floor and noticed the man had a cloven foot. She immediately fainted, and the man disappeared through the roof in a blaze of fire. Afterward she refused to eat or drink, and sat gazing across to the sea, her knees tucked under her chin, hoping her stranger would return.

When Anne died in 1775, she was buried in a sitting position, for it was impossible to straighten her legs without breaking them. Her death triggered poltergeist activity in the house, and various priests were summoned to perform exorcisms. It is still believed that Anne's ghost and that of her demon lover roam through the mansion's empty hallways, chasing each other in an endless game of hide-and-seek ◆

◄ In folklore, a cloven foot is associated with the devil, as in this engraving of 1879.

LEAP CASTLE COUNTY OFFALY, IRELAND

Impaled corpses are believed to be the source of a terrifying force field in this somber Irish castle.

SOMETHING TERRIBLE is thought to haunt Leap Castle, for centuries the seat of bitter clan rivalries and vengeance. The menacing force is said to emanate from the oubliette—a deep dungeon only accessible by a trapdoor.

In the castle's early days prisoners thrown into the oubliette were impaled on iron spikes, where they suffered a slow and agonizing death. In the 15th century, clan member One-Eyed Tadgh is supposed to have drugged 40 members of a rival clan and then flung them one at a time onto the dungeon spikes.

In the 20th century, workmen found the skeletal remains of 150 people in the oubliette. The ghosts of the victims are said to have created a horrific, vengeful force field known as "the elemental." People who have experienced this mysterious energy say it brings a terrible sense of dread and fear. They also report an overwhelming urge to throw themselves into the dungeon, as a sacrifice to the pit's victims, who long to rest in peace. ◆

▲ The so-called Bloody Chapel in which the trapdoor to the oubliette is located

VERSAILLES GARDENS FRANCE

Casualties of the French Revolution wander the gardens, accompanied by the spooky sound of music.

LOST IN THE GARDENS OF VERSAILLES in 1901, two Oxford academics, Anne Moberly and Eleanor Jourdain, claimed they felt an eerie presence. They saw strangers, some fearsome, others melancholic, all dressed in 18th-century costume.

Three months later, Anne mentioned she had also seen a woman sketching by the lake. As the two friends compared accounts, they felt sure they had been surrounded by ghosts or fallen into a time warp. Convinced that the lady sketching had been Marie Antoinette, they wrote a book about their extraordinary experience. Its publication caused a sensation.

It is claimed Marie Antoinette still wanders the gardens behind Petit Trianon, her miniature château in the grounds of Versailles, and contemplates the world from her Grotto. It was here that she would draw and write during her lifetime, reflecting on the course her life might have taken.

> The ghost of Marie Antoinette leans wistfully against the Temple of Love.

Some say Marie Antoinette's execution at the guillotine in 1793 left her spirit restlessly wandering the gardens, in search of her children or a tranquil spot in which to relive her life before the French Revolution. She sits alone on the Belvedere and leans wistfully against the columns in the Temple of Love. Many visitors have reported hearing the sounds of ghostly chamber music, laughter, and lovers giggling in the grottos and beside the fountains.

Other phantoms associated with the Palace of Versailles include Louis XV, who is seen dancing through the Orangerie with his mistress Madame de Pompadour. His other paramour, Madame du Barry, who died in terrible fear at the guillotine, has reportedly been seen gazing across the gardens from the Hall of Mirrors. ◆

▼ The spirit of Marie Antoinette is reputed to haunt the lakeside in front of the Queen's Cottage in the gardens of Versailles.

MORTEMER ABBEY EURE, FRANCE

This creepy abbey known as the "dead pool" is haunted by a queen, a werewolf, and spectral monks.

BUILT BY HENRY I OF ENGLAND IN 1134, this abbey gets its name from the surrounding marshland known as the *morte mare*, or dead pool. On misty winter mornings, ravens swoop between the bare trees while wraith-like shapes rise from the abbey's gardens.

Henry I of England imprisoned his daughter Matilda here, to stop her from colluding with rebels after the death of her husband, the emperor of Germany. Her ghost is said to drift through the ruins on moonlit nights. If she is wearing white gloves it's a good omen, while black ones signal doom.

At the beginning of the 16th century, nearby villagers accused a local woman of being possessed by the spirit of a wolf. The monks exorcised the woman, but the wolf took its revenge by killing a local poacher's wife and inhabiting her spirit instead. During the full moon, the beast is said to roam the grounds, howling for her husband.

During the French Revolution, the few monks remaining at the abbey were butchered as they tried to escape. Revolutionaries chopped off their heads, threw the corpses into the abbey's cellar, and then drank the monks' blood mixed with holy wine. The monks' spirits are said to wander the abbey at night and flee through the abbey gates by day. ◆

▲ The skeletal ruins of Mortemer Abbey

THE REIGN OF TERROR On July 14, 1789, rioters stormed the Bastille in Paris, marking the beginning of the French Revolution. From May 1793 until July 1794, the Reign of Terror, led by Robespierre, condemned up to 40,000 "enemies of the Revolution" to death, either by the guillotine or other forms of execution throughout France. The power of the aristocracy and the church was overturned forever.

POVEGLIA ISLAND
VENETIAN LAGOON, ITALY

Once a mental hospital overseen by a twisted psychiatrist, this somber place is forbidden territory.

▲ The prewar interiors of the mental hospital still contain the original furniture, including the iron beds to which the mentally ill were chained.

WHEN TO VISIT

Officially the island is closed to visitors, but boatmen will take you there for a steep price.

ACROSS THE VENETIAN LAGOON, far from the elegant city of Venice, lies the ghostly island of Poveglia. Uninhabited, overgrown, and out of bounds to the public, the island has a disturbing history. Originally a quarantine station for 18th-century travelers who might be carrying bubonic plague, it quickly became a mass death pit for plague victims. The plague raged through Italy at the end of the 18th century, and more than 160,000 people were thrown into mass graves or piled up on bonfires on Poveglia Island. Fifty percent of the island's soil is thought to consist of human ash.

In the 1920s, the authorities built a mental hospital on the island. According to local stories, the psychiatrist in charge tortured and murdered his patients until going mad with guilt and throwing himself from the bell tower. The doctor is said to have survived the fall but was immediately asphyxiated by a ghostly mist that rose from the ground.

Scaffolding stops the building from crumbling away, but weeds ramble over the windows, preventing any light from penetrating the lower floors. From the turret of the bell tower where the doctor threw himself down, a beautiful view extends across the lagoon. Ghost hunters claim to have heard the doctor's screams echo inside the tower, smelled burning corpses in the rooms, and witnessed the ghastly cries of the mentally ill bound to their beds. ◆

COLOSSEUM ROME, ITALY

The bloody phantoms of slain gladiators are said to relive their final battles in this famous arena.

MANY DISEMBODIED SPIRITS are said to populate this well-known heritage site. Tales abound of slaughtered gladiators who return by night to reenact their final combat, while invisible chariots rattle across the long-vanished sand. Visitors describe hearing Latin spoken or seeing Roman guards silhouetted against the sky.

Countless victims of religious persecution met a grisly end in the jaws of lions and tigers here, but more horrors lay in the underground vaults where prisoners died from their wounds. The sounds of weeping slaves, swords clashing, and animals howling have all been reported. Some visitors claim to have seen figures cheering in the stadium and the ghosts of corpses rise from the ground. In the first century A.D., one of the church fathers,

St. Ignatius of Antioch, was martyred here, ripped apart by lions. His ghost is said to wander the arena every night in search of his mutilated hands so that he can continue writing his epistles and letters to the Romans.

In A.D. 404, a Christian monk, St. Telemachus, tried to stop a gladiator fight and was stoned to death by the crowd. The emperor was so enraged by the massacre that he stopped all gladiator sports in Rome. Many visitors to the arena have reported seeing a saintly figure crying for help. Some who may never have heard of St. Telemachus and his terrible story have also reported a sensation of being stoned alive. ◆

▲ A vicious and bloody sport

FEMALE GLADIATORS Not all those who died and suffered in the arena were men. Ethiopian female gladiators appeared in the first century A.D., when Emperor Nero sought to impress King Tiridates I of Armenia. The brave women, who had to train just like the male gladiators, would fight one another to the death or hunt boars, with spear in hand and breasts exposed.

5 CREEPIEST CASTLES IN GERMANY

Germany has a plethora of eerie-looking castles—multi-turreted fortifications guarding wooded valleys and river bends—bristling with supernatural phenomena.

1 WOLFSEGG CASTLE, REGENSBURG: Hidden deep below this medieval castle is a limestone cave where restless specters are rumored to rise at night to stalk the castle grounds. A phantom woman in white is believed to be Klara, the wife of a medieval knight, who began an affair with a local nobleman. When her husband found out, he had the pair murdered and their bodies tossed into the cave.

2 STOCKENFELS CASTLE, BAVARIA: This castle is said to be haunted by the souls of publicans who, in life, cheated customers by diluting their beer. Here, upon a Satan's ladder reaching into a bottomless well, the publicans must hand up buckets of water to Satan perched at the top. At midnight, Satan pours the water into the river below. Many have heard the gushing of phantom water, and the devil laughing.

▼ The craggy outline of Eltz Castle, the haunt of militant Lady Agnes

3 NORDKIRCHEN CASTLE, WESTPHALIA: When the miserly debt collector who lived in this 16th-century castle died, his terrifying specter returned to haunt it. Local folk prayed for deliverance, and one night a carriage stopped at the castle gates before lurching off into the dark. The ghost was not seen again, but on moonlit nights a black carriage can be seen racing past the castle entrance.

4 PLASSENBURG CASTLE, KULMBACH, BAVARIA: In the 15th century, a widow named Katharina fell in love with a prince. He vowed to marry her "if there were not four eyes between us," meaning his parents. Misunderstanding him, she murdered her two children. Her horrified lover fled, and she was soon found dead. Her ghost is said to roam the castle, longing for her children, who fear her every step.

5 ELTZ CASTLE, MÜNSTERMAIFELD: Patrolled by the souls of medieval knights, Eltz stands on a rocky hilltop in a forested valley. The sound of laughter, the clatter of goblets, and the clink of armor echo in its courtyards and towers. The armor and battle-ax on the wall of the Countess's Room were worn by Lady Agnes, who died defending the castle from invasion. Her ghost is said to pace the room.

DRAGSHOLM CASTLE ZEALAND, DENMARK

The ghost of a nobleman chained to a pillar for ten years haunts the courtyards of this Danish castle.

Once a prison for noble traitors, Dragsholm Castle stands on an island in Denmark's Zealand archipelago. Phantoms of a White Lady and the Earl of Bothwell are reputed to stalk its staircases and courtyard in the chill northern air.

The White Lady is thought to be the lovelorn daughter of a draconian former master of the castle. According to legend, when her father discovered she loved a commoner he was so angry and ashamed that he cut her throat and bricked her up in the castle walls. During the 1930s, workmen repairing the walls found a skeleton shrouded in a tattered white dress imprisoned inside. Many people claim to have seen the White Lady weeping as she walks through the castle at night; by day, she is sometimes spotted counting the petals of a flower as she waits for her lover beside the castle walls.

King Frederick of Denmark imprisoned the sinister Earl of Bothwell on suspicion of the murder of Lord Darnley, the husband of Mary Queen of Scots. Not long after Lord Darnley's demise, Bothwell had married Mary himself, with the aim, it was thought, of becoming Scotland's king.

Unable to decide his fate, Frederick kept Bothwell alive in appalling conditions. Chained to a pillar with a circular groove in the floor to drain off excreta, he went insane after ten years and died at the age of 44. Many people claim to have seen his ghostly figure riding across the courtyard of Dragsholm as he relives his dream of wearing the Scottish crown. ◆

▲ A portrait of the Earl of Bothwell. When his body was exhumed after his death, it was found to be mummified.

▼ A deceptively peaceful pen-and-ink drawing of Dragsholm Castle

PALACIO DE LINARES MADRID, SPAIN

Behind the grand facade of this Spanish palace the souls of a tragic couple search for salvation.

▲ A tale of incest and murder lies behind the reported hauntings in the Palacio de Linares.

WHEN TO VISIT

Take the first guided tour of the day to hear the sound of whispering children.

THIS EXQUISITE PALACE dating from the mid-19th century is known for its beautiful architecture, sweeping staircase, and tormented ghostly couple. Many visitors to Palacio de Linares claim to have seen apparitions—either a man or a woman, or both—dressed in 19th-century clothes.

The Marqués Jose de Murga was the son of a wealthy noble. When he fell in love with a poor tobacconist's daughter named Raimunda his father sent him to England to forget her. But on his father's death the Marqués returned to Madrid and married his lover. A few months later he found a letter from his father, revealing a horrifying truth: Raimunda was Jose's half-sister, the result of his father's secret affair with the tobacconist's wife.

Now aware of their incestuous marriage, the couple vowed to the church that they would live together in chastity. Yet their passion was too powerful, and a few years later a baby daughter was born. Their guilt was so great that to avoid a scandal they had the child murdered and bricked up behind the walls of the hallway in the palace. Within a few months the Marqués had committed suicide and his wife had died of remorse.

The child's ghost is rumored to wander the great rooms of the palace, singing lullabies and calling for her parents. The guilt-ridden spirits of the Marqués and his wife wander the palace too, hoping for deliverance from their eternal damnation. ◆

SLEEPY HOLLOW NEW YORK, U.S.A.

Home of the infamous Headless Horseman, this quaint town is immortalized in American literature.

THIRTY MILES (50 KM) NORTH of Manhattan lies Sleepy Hollow, a small village originally known as North Tarrytown. Its name was changed in 1996 in honor of Washington Irving's story "The Legend of Sleepy Hollow," a supernatural tale inspired by the local legend of the Headless Horseman. The author is buried in Sleepy Hollow Cemetery, where his amiable ghost is said to roam.

The legend that inspired Irving was based on the real-life discovery of a decapitated body—thought to be a German sharpshooter from the Revolutionary War—in the Old Dutch Burying Ground. According to the legend, the terrifying ghost of the Headless Horseman appears to unwary travelers at night.

Irving's story centers on three men's love for a young woman. One of her suitors, a teacher named Ichabod, meets a cloaked rider in a swamp. As the mist clears, he sees that the rider's head is not on his shoulders but on his saddle. Frantic to escape, Ichabod rides for his life close to the Burying Ground, where, according to legend, the headless rider should vanish. But Ichabod's experience does not fit with the legend. Instead, the horseman follows him, hurling his head at Ichabod's face. By the next day, Ichabod has disappeared, his spirit forever roaming the hollow in search of his lost love. ◆

▲ Lithograph of the Old Dutch Church in Sleepy Hollow, dating from 1867

HEADLESS HORSEMEN In Celtic myth, the "dullahan," or dark man, is a headless spirit that rides a black horse and carries his head under one arm. He gallops through the night for eternity; if he stops, a death occurs—the dullahan will call out the name of the victim. Another headless horseman of Celtic myth, the "gan ceann," can be frightened away by wearing gold, or casting gold objects in his path.

BILLOP HOUSE NEW YORK, U.S.A.

A murdered girl and phantom redcoats relive Revolutionary War events in this manor house.

IN THE 1770S, A COLONEL BILLOP LIVED in what is now known as Conference House, on Staten Island. In 1776, during the Revolutionary War, a peace conference was held at the house. The colonists seemed near defeat and British Lord Howe offered to end the war if the Colonies would swear allegiance to England. However, Benjamin Franklin refused, so the peace talks collapsed and the war intensified.

From then on, Billop's home was secretly used by the British redcoats as a safe house, with the kitchen often used as a temporary hospital for wounded British soldiers. Those who died were hastily buried in unmarked graves in the grounds.

The colonists suspected Billop of helping the British, and after many arrests Billop became

> If you turn your back to the staircase, you may feel her hands clawing at your legs in the last moment of life.

convinced there was a spy in his house. He discovered a 15-year-old servant girl placing a lamp in a window and became convinced she was signaling to patriots in nearby St. Peter's Church. In a rage, he threw her down the stairs and killed her. He buried her in the grounds and fled, leaving the spirit of the accused girl to stalk his former home.

Many visitors claim to have heard a man shouting, a girl screaming, and then the sound of a body falling down stairs. If you turn your back to the staircase, you may even feel hands clawing at your legs. Meanwhile, phantom redcoats are said to restlessly wander the gardens and kitchen of Conference House. ◆

▲ A ghost of a young woman carrying an oil lamp is said to haunt the staircase of the house.

GETTYSBURG PENNSYLVANIA, U.S.A.

The spirits of thousands of fallen soldiers are reputed to haunt this Civil War battleground.

OVER THE DECADES, hundreds of people have seen ghosts in this national military park, and supernatural activity is repeatedly investigated. Many visitors report phantom cries of wounded soldiers and ghoulish apparitions. The undeniably creepy atmosphere even affects many skeptics.

The Battle of Gettysburg was a turning point in the American Civil War. After three days of intense battle, ending on July 3, 1863, thousands of Union and Confederate soldiers lay dead, and tens of thousands more wounded. The three-day bloodbath changed American history forever. When the cannon smoke cleared, the Union soldiers were victorious, but thousands of men and horses lay dead or dying on the battleground.

Many of the Confederate soldiers never received a proper burial, and their restless spirits are rumored to roam Gettysburg still, both on the battlefield and at sites around the town. The ghostly forms of soldiers are said to crouch in the undergrowth, ready to attack, while others move stealthily behind bushes. You may hear someone whistling a tune or smell tobacco. While some spirits seem to wander aimlessly, unable to move on, others relive their final agony.

Near the battleground, Daniel Lady Farm served as the Confederate army's field hospital. Some soldiers recovered here, but many died. The ghosts of General Isaac Ewell and more than 10,000 troops are reputed to haunt the farm. Meanwhile, Gettysburg Hotel in the town claims many hauntings. In the hotel ballroom, for example, a ghostly woman is said to dance, longing for her soldier lover to return from battle. Reportedly, when she discovered he had been fatally wounded, she drank herself to death. ◆

▲ Portrait of Private Andrew Blakeley, a Confederate soldier in the Washington Artillery

▼ Confederate soldiers lie dead after the Battle of Gettysburg, 1863

HULL HOUSE CHICAGO, ILLINOIS, U.S.A.

An evil presence in the attic of this town house inspired the novel and movie *Rosemary's Baby*.

AFTER THE WIFE OF CHARLES HULL, the first owner of Hull House, died here in 1860, her ghost appeared in every room. But a more malevolent spirit is also said to lurk here, a fearsome presence that inspired Ira Levin's famous 1967 novel *Rosemary's Baby*.

When, in 1889, Jane Addams and Ellen Gates Starr bought the property and turned it into a refuge for European immigrants, Addams immediately sensed a supernatural presence. Stories of hauntings proliferated throughout the decades. According to one story, in 1913, in a local Chicago bar, a drunken man shouted in front

of many witnesses that he would rather have the devil in his house than the picture of the Virgin Mary that his pregnant wife had put on the wall. When their child was born it had pointed ears, horns, scaly skin, and cloven feet. The mother took the devil baby to Hull House, where it was locked in the attic and later died. Addams denied the story, but many believed it. It was said that cloven hooves tiptoed over the floorboards and menacing baby eyes stared from dark corners. Today, they say that if you hear the devil baby gurgle or cry, you will be cursed with bad luck. ◆

◄ Late medieval woodcut depicting the birth of the Antichrist

INDEPENDENCE HALL PHILADELPHIA, U.S.A.

Considered one of the most haunted cities in the United States, Philadelphia is full of spooky tales.

THE GHOST of Benjamin Franklin himself wafts through Philadelphia's Independence Hall, or so it is said. According to a local tale, one winter's night, just as a national park ranger was locking up, the security alarm rang in the clock tower. As the ranger turned the corner, he saw a man dressed in 18th-century costume—identifiable as Franklin—vanish into the walls. Other ghostly sightings in the building include orbs near the staircase and in the Assembly Rooms.

Unwilling to leave this earth for the afterlife, Franklin's spirit has been seen lurking elsewhere in Philadelphia, including Christ Church Cemetery, where he was buried.

Other ghost stories feature writer Edgar Allan Poe, the master of the macabre, who lived in Philadelphia. His mysterious ghost is said to inhabit dark corners of his house on N. 7th Street, sending shivers down visitors' spines. The spirit of the founder of the Province of Pennsylvania, William Penn, is seen materializing from his statue on the lawn in front of Pennsylvania Hospital and then walking around the grounds and halls, and at the Academy of Music, there have been reports of mysterious impressions on empty theater seats and pinching and hair-pulling in the upper balconies. ◆

▲ Independence Hall, the haunt of Founding Father Franklin

BELL WITCH CAVE TENNESSEE, U.S.A.

Unexplained noises, ghostly whispering, and physical phenomena disturb this ancient cave.

▲ The entrance to Bell Witch Cave, believed by some to be a portal to another world

WHEN TO VISIT

Go in summer and take the last tour at 4:15 p.m., when spooky phenomena are said to begin.

THE CURIOUS BELL WITCH CAVE sits atop a Native American burial mound overlooking the Red River in Adams, Tennessee. It forms part of the former property of the Bell family, 19th-century farmers who were menaced by a malevolent spirit known as the Bell Witch.

The first hauntings on the farm began in 1817, with unexplained knocking and scratching and the sounds of dragging chains and stones dropping on the wooden floors. The family could also hear gulping and choking noises. To begin with, the terrified Bells told no one, but when the torment became unbearable they invited their neighbors to witness the strange phenomena. Soon a committee was formed to investigate what was happening, and before long people from miles around arrived to experience the forces terrorizing the Bell home. Eventually the spirit started to whisper, revealing that she was Kate Batts, an alleged witch who had died many years before.

Over the next three years, the Bell Witch is said to have persecuted the family almost daily. She pinched, scratched, beat, and stuck pins into daughter Betsy, and cursed the father, John Bell, whose body grew unaccountably thin and weak. In December 1820, John died. As soon as he was gone, the spirit of the witch seemingly left the farm and returned to the cave. Some ghost hunters believe the cave is a spiritual portal, and that the Bell Witch will return to terrorize anyone about to discover this secret gateway to another world. ◆

CHARLESTON SOUTH CAROLINA, U.S.A.

Creepy stories abound in the grand old buildings and gardens of this steamy Southern city.

CHARLESTON'S HISTORIC DISTRICT claims many haunted locations. One of its most famous spots is the site of the Cooper River Bridge, the scene of a tragic family accident. In 1946 the bridge collapsed when a ship rammed one of its pillars. A car carrying a family of five plummeted into the river and all the occupants drowned. In 2005, Arthur Ravenel Bridge replaced the old bridge, but the tragic associations live on. Motorists sometimes report seeing a ghostly family in an old 1940s car. The apparitions stare across the river, then scream, and disappear.

Battery Carriage House Inn in Charleston claims several ghosts. It is said that a roofer leaped to his death on seeing a headless phantom, while female guests in room No. 10 sometimes describe seeing a well-dressed young man who touches their hair and then fades away. It is thought to be the spirit of a jilted man whose girlfriend married his best friend. In desperation, the man committed suicide; his ghost forever haunts the inn looking for Miss Right.

Another tale concerns the ghost of Dr. Joseph Brown, who built a successful medical practice in Charleston in the 1780s. On meeting a man named Ralph Isaacs, Brown moved into his lodgings at 59 Church Street owned by two elderly sisters. The women came to adore their lodger and his happy whistle as he bounded up the stairs. But Ralph was jealous of him, and their rivalry culminated in a duel. While Brown fired his pistol into the air, not wanting to harm his friend, Isaacs aimed at Brown's legs just below the knee, intending to cripple him. Within a few weeks Brown was dead. Some claim to hear his tuneful whistling and footsteps still outside 59 Church Street. ◆

> Motorists crossing the bridge report seeing a ghostly family sitting pale and lifeless in an old 1940s car.

▲ With its Spanish moss and crumbling masonry, Charleston makes an atmospheric setting for ghostly tales.

MYRTLES PLANTATION
LOUISIANA, U.S.A.

Restless spirits roam through this plantation house, while a phantom corpse swings from an oak tree.

THIS ELEGANT PLANTATION HOUSE hides a dark secret involving jealousy, fear, and murder. It was originally inhabited by Judge Woodruffe, a notorious womanizer who seduced one of his slaves, Chloe, and made her his mistress. Fearing she might lose the judge's affections, Chloe spent every possible moment eavesdropping on her master to see if he favored another slave. One day, Woodruffe caught her at the keyhole and sliced off one of her ears. From that day forward, Chloe wore a green turban.

To win back the judge's affection, Chloe decided to mildly poison the judge's wife and daughters during a birthday celebration and then miraculously cure them. But her plan went wrong and they died. Fearing a backlash, the other slaves hung Chloe from an oak tree and then threw her body in the Mississippi. It is said that a green-turbaned woman and sobbing children haunt the site. At sunrise, as light plays between the trees where Chloe was hung, her corpse reportedly appears upside down like a vampire bat. Smiling, she pulls witnesses closer so that she can possess their souls. ◆

◀ Trees used for hangings are often said to be haunted.

WINCHESTER MYSTERY HOUSE
SAN JOSE, CALIFORNIA, U.S.A.

This house is a maze of secret passages and dead ends, designed to trick any house-hunting spirits.

ONCE THE RESIDENCE of Sarah Winchester, widow of gun magnate William Wirt Winchester, this rambling house is the product of a mind deranged by grief. Sarah believed that the house was haunted by the ghosts of victims killed with Winchester rifles. She thought she could prevent them from settling in the house only by constantly adding to and altering the property, so from 1884 until Sarah's death in 1922 construction work was continuous.

Sarah incorporated many features to trap or confuse the spirits. Doors lead nowhere, windows look inward rather than outward, and twisting hallways have secret passageways. Sarah would slip through these to confuse any mischievous ghosts that might be following her. She even had her own seance room to encourage and communicate with benevolent spirits, as well as her late husband and a baby daughter who had died when she was just six weeks old.

The number 13 carried spiritual significance for Sarah, and crops up everywhere in the house. She had a 12-branched chandelier altered to hold 13 candles, and even the sink drain covers have 13 holes. In tribute to her obsession, on every Friday the 13th a large bell is rung 13 times. ◆

▲ Portrait of Sarah Winchester. She believed spirits would not settle in a house that was not finished.

BODIE

CALIFORNIA, U.S.A.

The spirits of several 19th-century residents walk the dusty streets of this former gold-mining town.

IN 1859 WILLIAM S. BODEY discovered gold in an area that soon became known as Bodie Bluff. By the end of the century, opportunists, bounty hunters, miners, store owners, robbers, and prostitutes from all over the world filled the town of Bodie. At one time there were 65 saloons, including brothels, gambling halls, and opium dens. Bodie was a nest of all possible vices.

By the middle of the 20th century, Bodie was in steep decline. The few remaining inhabitants deserted its ramshackle buildings, and a reputation for hauntings gained hold. It was said that if thieves stole anything from the abandoned buildings bad luck or personal tragedy would dog them.

The stories of hauntings took many forms. One man visiting the town's cemetery noticed his daughter playing and giggling with an invisible playmate—rumored to

> Witnesses claim to hear the clatter of tiles as the ghostly maid plays mah-jongg with Mr. Cain.

be the spirit of the so-called Angel of Bodie, a child accidentally killed by a miner's pick in 1897.

Another tale centered on the house on the corner of Green and Park streets, built by a Mr. Cain. According to the story, Cain hired a Chinese maid and rumors spread that the pair were lovers. When Cain's wife promptly fired the maid, the girl was unable to find work and so, penniless and desolate, she took her own life. The maid is reputed to haunt the site to this day. Witnesses claim to have seen an apparition cleaning an upstairs bedroom, caught the sound of mysterious music drifting through the rooms, and heard the clatter of mah-jongg tiles as the ghostly maid plays the game with Mr. Cain. ◆

▼ Once California's gold rush was over, the miners moved on, leaving many ghost towns across the state.

5 HAUNTED HOT SPOTS IN HOLLYWOOD

All kinds of glamorous ghosts are said to inhabit Hollywood's film studios, cemeteries, and hotels to the stars. Revisiting their favorite haunts, they yearn to rekindle their days of fame and glory.

1 ROOSEVELT HOTEL: Montgomery Clift stayed here while rehearsing his role in the 1953 movie *From Here to Eternity*. His ghost is said to play the trumpet and pace the hallway as he learns his lines in room 928 on the ninth floor. Others claim to have seen the image of a weeping Marilyn Monroe (left) materialize in a full-length mirror next to the elevator. The mirror was formerly located in her poolside suite.

2 CULVER STUDIOS: Thomas Ince's famous studio produced many movies, including *Gone with the Wind*. Ince (left) died in mysterious circumstances aboard the yacht of the publisher William Randolph Hearst. There were rumors that Hearst shot Ince. According to legend, Ince haunts the studio, walking through walls and creating poltergeist activity whenever there is a change of management.

▼ Hollywood Forever Cemetery, the silent resting place of many Hollywood stars

3 **HOLLYWOOD FOREVER CEMETERY:** In this cemetery to the stars, actor Clifton Webb (right) is rumored to haunt the Abbey of the Psalms mausoleum, where strange orbs, drafts of cold air, and the smell of eau de cologne lurk. A woman seen kneeling beside Rudolph Valentino's tomb is believed to be the spirit of a devoted fan named Ditra Flame. She leaves one red rose before disappearing into thin air.

4 **PANTAGES THEATRE:** Late at night, people claim to hear the spirit of a female fan of musicals who died during a screening here in 1932 sing in the empty theater. During a live performance of a musical in 1994, the woman's voice was allegedly picked up on a microphone. Some say Howard Hughes (right), who bought the theater in 1949, haunts the second-floor offices.

5 **PARAMOUNT STUDIOS:** It is said that silent cinema's heartthrob Rudolph Valentino (right) leaves his tomb in neighboring Forever Cemetery to visit Paramount's costume department. He is dressed in his robes from *The Sheikh*. The ghost of Heather O'Rourke, who starred in the film *Poltergeist* and died tragically at the age of 12, is said to run along the catwalks where she played between takes.

ISLAND OF DOLLS MEXICO

Severed heads and limbless torsos create a macabre atmosphere on this mysterious island.

ON THE ISLAND OF DOLLS, a swampy islet in the Xochimilco canals south of Mexico City, spooky-looking dolls hang on the branches of every tree. Severed limbs, decapitated heads, and mutilated torsos in varying degrees of decay swing in the light breeze; wherever you go on the island, hundreds of blank eyes follow.

The dolls began to appear about 50 years ago, when a lonely widower named Don Julian Santana set up home on the island. Tormented by the ghost of a little girl who had drowned in one of the canals, he hung an old doll on the branch of a tree to placate the dead girl's spirit. One doll in a tree, however, was not enough to calm his troubled mind. Still plagued by the girl's ghostly presence, he became convinced that the more dolls he gave the dead girl, the

> Be sure to offer the dolls a gift when you leave the island—or else ...

happier she would be and the more likely to leave him in peace. He fished dolls out of the canal whenever he saw them, scavenged dolls from trash heaps around the city, and eventually traded homegrown vegetables to create his doll shrine.

In 2001, Santana was found dead by his nephew in the same canal where the young girl had drowned. Rumors spread that the dolls were inhabited by tortured spirits and had conspired to murder the old man. Visitors to the island describe an eerie atmosphere and sometimes say they hear the dolls whispering their name behind their backs. Be sure to offer the dolls a gift when you leave the island, or else ... ◆

▲ Decayed by the weather, insects, and mold, the dolls look like demonic children in a horror movie.

LA SEGUA CARTAGO, COSTA RICA

An avenging she-devil preys on unfaithful men as they make their way home from Cartago's brothels.

A SEDUCTIVE GHOST WHO changes shape from a beautiful woman to a terrifying mare is reputed to haunt the streets of Cartago, Costa Rica's colonial capital.

According to legend, in the late 17th century a woman of mixed Spanish and Indian blood fell in love with a handsome Spanish officer in the town.

The officer found her beautiful white skin, dark hair, and jet-black eyes irresistible and promised to marry her if they became lovers. Unknown to her Catholic family, and against her usual strict moral code, she agreed to his request. However, it was not long before the Spanish officer left the city and disappeared back to Spain.

Heartbroken and overcome by guilt over the betrayal of her family honor, the woman wasted away and died. Now her spirit, known in Central America as La Segua—

> The men are bewitched, powerless to resist her seductive voice and beautiful face.

a female demon that attacks men—is said to haunt Cartago's streets, seeking out unfaithful men and luring them to their death.

Typically, La Segua waits for her victims on badly lit crossroads late at night, as they make their way home from taverns and brothels. When she asks for a lift home, the men are bewitched, powerless to resist her beautiful voice and face. As they ride home, or walk into the darker streets, La Segua asks for a cigarette. Turning obligingly toward her, the men come face to face with a terrifying monster—a horse's blood-filled skull with fiery red eyes. The shock of the ghastly apparition either kills the men or persuades them to give up their dissolute ways. ◆

▼ The deathly grimace of a horse's skull greets the men of Cartago as they turn to face the beautiful she-devil.

CHASE VAULTS BARBADOS

The souls of murdered children are thought to be behind the poltergeist activity in this mausoleum.

A FAMILY VAULT in Oistin's Christ Church Cemetery has been the focus of supernatural phenomena in Barbados since the early 1800s.

The stories began with a series of child burials. Ann Maria Chase was interred in 1808, followed by her younger sister Dorcas in 1812. When the vault was reopened for the burial of their brother Thomas, it was clear that the caskets of the girls had moved. The sexton discovered similar disturbances in 1816 and 1819. Rumors began to circulate that Colonel Chase, the children's father, had murdered the girls and the vault was cursed.

The island's governor ordered an investigation. Workmen sealed it and sprinkled sand on the floor to reveal the footprints of any intruders. It remained sealed for eight months, during which islanders reported hearing strange sounds and screams from within. When the vault was reopened, the coffins were found flung about the tomb yet no one had broken the seal. Detailed drawings of the scene were made.

Upset by the episode, the Chase family reburied the coffins elsewhere, but the children's spirits are still said to haunt the vault. If you visit the mausoleum, sprinkle salt near the entrance: The spirits are doomed to count the grains, and cannot harm you. ◆

▲ An eerie energy emanates from the tomb's dark and crumbling entrance.

DETERRING POLTERGEISTS Noisy spirits, or "poltergeists," like to make their presence felt. Sprinkling salt in corners of the room or on window ledges is a traditional way of sending the unwanted ghosts back to their spiritual home. Burning a bunch of dried sage is also thought to be an effective method of eliminating these restless spirits.

SALIMGARH FORT NEW DELHI, INDIA

The songs of a ghostly female poet soothe the spirits of tortured soldiers in this ancient bastion.

DURING THE TURBULENT BATTLES between rival dynasties that wracked northern India in the 16th and 17th centuries, many prisoners were executed at Salimgarh Fort on the Yamuna River. The footprint of their agony still seems to haunt the place. There are regular reports of apparitions and unexplained cries of pain, as well as a tangible sense of menace within its walls.

One of the most notorious episodes in Salimgarh's history occurred during the reign of Aurangzeb I (1666–1707), who used the fortress as a torture house. Guards washed the stone walls with the victims' blood to remind the other prisoners of their certain fate.

A ghostly lady dressed in white is reputed to move across the battlements, mostly at night but sometimes in the early morning mist. She is said to be Zebunissa, Aurangzeb's daughter, a gentle and well-educated woman who composed the most beautiful poetry in India. When her brother Akbar conspired against their father, she wrote letters to her brother, denouncing their father's tyranny. On discovering his daughter's treachery Aurangzeb imprisoned her in Salimgarh, where she died in 1701.

Zebunissa's phantom is said to sing her lyrical poems, enchanting the unhappy spirits of the tortured dead.

During World War II, until Indian independence in 1947, the British imprisoned some members of the Indian National Army in Salimgarh. Wanting to drive the British out of India, these independence fighters collaborated with the Japanese and were subsequently tried for treason and tortured. Their unearthly wails are said to echo through the cells at night. ◆

> **The guards washed the stone walls with the victims' blood.**

▼ A 19th-century watercolor of the Salimgarh Fort (left), where the prisoners of the tyrannical Aurangzeb were tortured

HIMEJI CASTLE

HYOGO PREFECTURE, JAPAN

Horrific suicide victims and a tortured beauty stalk the mazelike paths of this sprawling castle.

STANDING HIGH ABOVE THE town of Himeji, 30 miles (50 km) west of Kobe, this 14th-century castle and its later additions spread out across the hilltop. Its mazelike defensive system is famous. Even today, visitors easily lose themselves among its lonely and labyrinthine pathways. Sometimes they describe sensing unseen but menacing presences on its steps and in its gateways.

Locals attribute these supernatural experiences to the castle's bloody history. During the reign of the Shoguns, who ruled Japan from 1192 to 1867, the means of execution was suicide by ritual disembowelment. At the foot of the tower, known as the Donjon—next to Suicide Gate—stands the castle well, which was used to wash away the blood.

The well is known as Okiku's Well after the tragic legend of the Shogun's favorite and most devoted servant. The Shogun was elderly and frail, and his son and heir, seeking to show his love for the old man, presented him with ten gold plates. Every day the servant Okiku cleaned and polished the treasured gift. When she overheard Tetsuzan, one of the Shogun's chief retainers, plotting to usurp him, she revealed the plot to her master.

Tetsuzan escaped, but he vowed to take his revenge on Okiku and stole one of the precious plates. When Okiku admitted there were now only nine, the Shogun suspected her

> Visitors report seeing a ghostly form leaping from the battlements.

▼ Himeji is known as the White Heron Castle: It spreads out like a heron in flight.

JAPANESE GHOST CULTURE Ghosts are taken seriously in Japanese society. When a person dies a traumatic death, or if their final rites are not performed correctly, their soul becomes a *yurei*—a spirit that lives in limbo, eternally longing for peace in the afterlife. If the yurei has a strong attachment to the physical world, it will return as a ghost. Among the many different types of ghosts are the *onryo*—female ghosts who, in life, were abused or neglected by their lovers and wish to avenge them. Worse still are the *goryo*—vengeful destructive spirits of once powerful people who died stripped of their authority. These dangerous spirits destroy crops and conjure up natural disasters.

of theft. She was tried and found guilty, and Tetsuzan was given the task of carrying out her death sentence. He raped her beside the well and then stabbed her to death, throwing her body into the well.

Okiku's spirit could not rest until she had taken revenge. In the early hours of every morning her disembodied voice would wake the Shogun from his sleep, and every night she counted the precious plates from one to nine, screaming and wailing because she could not find the tenth. This nightly torture was too much for the Shogun, and he was on the verge of insanity when he discovered Okiku's innocence. It is said that Okiku's ghost continues to rise out of the well at night, but if you shout out the number ten she will be at peace with you and disappear.

Another legend tells of a master carpenter who helped build the castle keep. According to the story, Sakurai was dissatisfied with his work, feeling that the keep leaned in an unlucky direction. He became so distraught that he climbed to the top of the keep and jumped to his death with a chisel in his mouth. Many visitors to the castle have reported seeing a spectral form leaping from the battlements, and the sound of wood chiseling as night falls. ◆

▲ Demons feature strongly in Japanese culture. This Hannya theatrical mask represents a female demon tormented by jealousy.

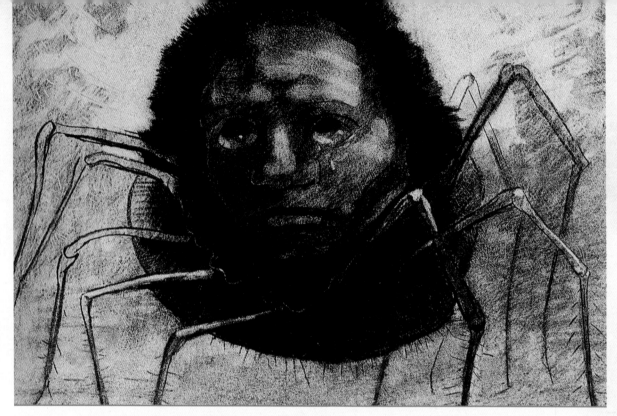

KOH LIPE ISLAND THAILAND

This tiny island teems with mischievous entities that play tricks on its lonely pathways.

▲ A spirit in the form of a spider with a human head was seen near Koh Lipe island's cemetery.

WHEN TO VISIT

Reports of ghostly activity peak in high season (December to February).

ACCORDING TO LEGEND, a mysterious force haunts a certain spot on the main path that bisects Koh Lipe island. Locals recount cases of the phantom force at work: for example, pushing a newcomer to the island to the ground as he walked along the path at dusk; lifting a woman off her bike and setting her down on her feet while a nearby scooter crashed into the jungle. Some people have described being gripped by invisible hands or unable to move.

A coconut tree is said to be the source of the strange energy, and the force itself a tree ghost—known as a *ha-too* in Thai. The tree was eventually cut down and used to build the nearby Banana Tree Restaurant, and now both restaurant and path seem to emanate a supernatural energy. Two young girls witnessed a group of pirate phantoms walk off the path into the restaurant's kitchen and then vanish, while tourists have reported seeing pirate specters dining in the restaurant. Many locals refuse to walk the path after dark.

Strange phenomena occur elsewhere on the island too. In tourist bungalows backing onto the Chao-le cemetery on the northeast point of the island, a guest claimed she saw a ghostly spider with a human head. Two Buddhist monks exorcized the spirit and banished it to neighboring Rawi Island, an uninhabited wilderness where gremlin-like phantoms named *waytan* are said to inhabit the trees and beaches. The ghosts of Koh Lipe are thought to be harmless, but those of Rawi are feared. Reported to be the spirits of unforgiven criminals, they seek to take revenge. ◆

MIRYANG

GYEONGSANGNAM-DO, SOUTH KOREA

The ghost of a woman murdered by a stranger wanders the streets of this quiet mountain town.

ABOVE THE CITY OF MIRYANG, in the foothills of the Yeongnam Alps, two shrines stand above the river—the Yeongnamnu Pavilion, with its famous stone-carved calligraphy, and the Aranggak pavilion, built to appease the spirit of a young woman who was murdered in Miryang in the 16th century.

According to legend, Arang was the daughter of Miryang's governor, a wealthy man who trusted an old nursemaid to chaperone his daughter. One day, a stranger in town watched Arang combing her hair in a window. He immediately desired her and bribed the old lady to leave the girl alone on their evening walk.

As soon as he got the chance, the stranger jumped on Arang and attempted to rape her. When she fought back he killed her, burying her body in the forest. The old nursemaid was convinced Arang had left town with a

> A new governor who believed in ghosts was able to communicate with Arang.

young man, and her father, overcome with grief, gave up his position and left the region too.

Arang wanted to avenge her death and ensure her father realized what had really happened. So, whenever a new governor was appointed she would appear in spirit in the hope of showing him where her body lay, but each time the governor would leave, terrified of the ghostly encounters. Finally, a governor unafraid of ghosts communicated with Arang and learned the location of her body. He promised to give her a proper burial and build a shrine for her. Today, a new shrine stands on the site of the original building, but Arang's story has not been forgotten. Every year a ceremony honors her liberated spirit. ◆

▼ The small shrine of Arang nestles in the forest where the murdered girl was buried.

FORBIDDEN CITY BEIJING, CHINA

China's most exquisite palace is cursed by the ghouls and ghosts of massacred courtesans.

FOR 600 YEARS THE FORBIDDEN CITY housed China's imperial family. Closed to outsiders, it bred scandals and intrigues, featuring scheming courtiers and treacherous servants, and witnessed appalling atrocities. On one horrific night in 1421, Emperor Yongle, one of the most feared rulers in Chinese imperial history, ordered the palace soldiers to massacre nearly 3,000 people connected to the emperor's harem. At the time, Beijing was full of foreign dignitaries invited to the unveiling ceremony of the largest palace in the world. By exterminating all signs of his scandalous harem, Yongle hoped to keep it a secret for eternity.

> The palace closes well before nightfall, when the hauntings are said to begin.

Girls as young as 12 or 13 were ripped apart by swords and left dying on the polished marble floors. The eunuchs and servants who watched over the concubines also lay in pools of blood, some decapitated, others hacked to bits. A few women—Yongle's favorite concubines—were spared. Among them was Lady Cui, through whose diary the true story of life in the emperor's harem eventually came to light. Born in Korea, the daughter of a government official, Lady Cui was brought to the Forbidden City as a 14-year-old virgin by Yongle's chief eunuch. Like hundreds of other girls, she was first sent to the palace in Nanjing to be taught the art of lovemaking. Favorite concubines such as Lady Cui became women of wealth, who were given special honors, beautiful clothes, and jewelry.

Even though Lady Cui outlived the emperor, a clause in her contract made sure she could never give herself to another man. On the day of Yongle's funeral she was executed, according to his wishes,

▼ The Forbidden City's bloody history has given rise to numerous ghost stories.

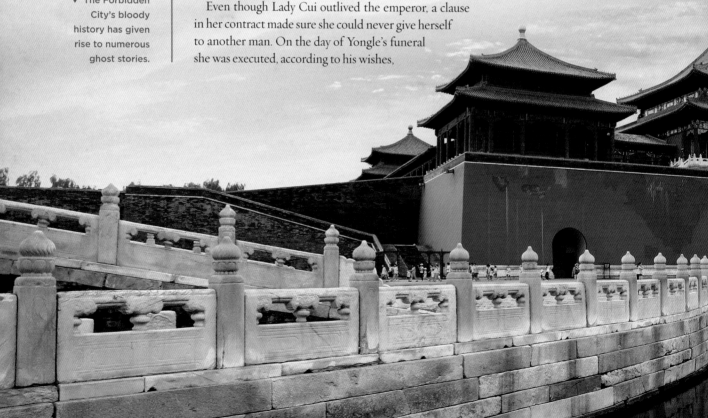

HIDDEN ENERGIES The Forbidden City was laid out according to the principles of feng shui, an ancient art designed to create harmony in the landscape, home, or workplace by balancing the energy in the environment. *Feng* means "wind" and *shui* means "water." Chinese ancients believed the flow of universal energy, the *chi*, connected everything in the universe. Wind was dynamic, active energy known as yang, and water was passive, receptive energy called yin. These days, Chinese enterprises and corporations use feng shui in the orientation and internal arrangement of tower blocks and other office buildings to promote success and prosperity.

along with 15 other favorite courtesans. Each woman was hung from a noose of white silk in one of the halls of the Forbidden City. Lady Cui was only 30 years old. After Yongle's death, his son, Emperor Hongxi, planned to move the court back to Nanjing, but he died a year later without having achieved this aim, causing many to belive the Forbidden Palace was cursed.

Today, the palace closes early, well before nightfall, when the haunting is said to begin. Even during the day, there is a sense of loss and sadness throughout the palace. Visitors have reported seeing a white lady with black hair streaming out behind her running across the hallway, pursued by a samurai soldier. Others have heard screaming, weeping, and the clash of swords, or seen phantom bodies heaped on polished floors. Some have seem orbs, pools of blood, and white silk floating through the air. ◆

▲ In feng shui, statues of animals are thought to help repel evil spirits. Pairs of protective lions guard important entrances, counteracting negative energy and promoting financial strength.

WITCH OF THE HEX RIVER VALLEY
WESTERN CAPE, SOUTH AFRICA

A lonely wraith searches for her lost lover among the vineyards and mountains of this beautiful region.

A HEARTBROKEN farmer's daughter who sent her lover to his death is believed to haunt Hex River Valley, a remote and beautiful area in South Africa's Western Cape. It is said you can hardly see her, for her ghost is pale and hesitant, and you can scarcely hear her voice, which is soft.

The apparition is reputed to be the spirit of a young woman named Eliza, who is searching for her lover, Frans. According to legend, many would-be suitors tried to win the beautiful Eliza's hand before the young teacher Frans finally succeeded. To prove his love, Eliza sent him to find a rare red flower growing on a cliff face in the mountains. Tragically, as Frans reached out for the flower, he slipped and plunged to his death.

Distraught with grief, Eliza went insane. One night she climbed the mountain, searching for Frans and collapsed on a ledge. As dawn rose, the rocks crumbled beneath her and she also fell to her death.

It is said you will know Eliza is present when you hear her bare feet tiptoeing through the grass behind you. And if you see a bunch of grapes left beside a road with only one grape eaten you'll know that she has passed. ◆

▲ When Eliza sent her lover on a quest for a rare red flower, tragedy ensued.

KIMBERLEY LIBRARY
SOUTH AFRICA

A suicidal librarian haunts his former workplace, where he knew both happiness and unbearable shame.

P EOPLE REGULARLY REPORT witnessing supernatural activity in the old Kimberley Library, now known as Kimberley Africana Library. The footsteps of a man pacing around the library have been heard by some while others report the book they are reaching for falls off the shelf, no matter how securely it was wedged in. Many people claim to have seen a man in period dress walking the corridors.

The library houses a large collection of antiquarian books. In the late 19th century, its diligent librarian, Bertrand

Dyer, began the painstaking task of restoring the most valuable volumes. However, he also fiddled the accounts. When this was discovered, he was unable to bear the shame and swallowed arsenic. It took three days for him to die.

The present librarians are convinced that Dyer's soul haunts the place he loved most. In 2012, in an attempt to pacify his soul, they tracked down his unmarked grave, held a proper funeral for him, and erected a tombstone. ◆

◄ Hand-colored postcard of the haunted library

L'AGULHAS
WESTERN CAPE, SOUTH AFRICA

This village at the tip of South Africa is the setting for the chilling legend of the *Flying Dutchman*.

A PHANTOM SHIP with bloodred sails and ghostly rigging is doomed to sail for eternity in the waters off L'Agulhas at the southern tip of Africa. According to the legend of the *Flying Dutchman*, in the 17th century, the captain of this ship—Van der Decken—determined to round the Cape of Storms, as the Cape of Good Hope was then called, at whatever price. Lashing himself to the ship's wheel, oblivious to the howling gale and ignoring the pleas of his crew, he raised his fist heavenward and cursed God, shouting that he had made a pact with the devil. Suddenly a shaft of light shot through the black clouds, lighting up the deck. The terrified crew trembled as the Holy Ghost pointed a glowing finger at the captain. For defying God he would sail on the stormy seas forever, never to land, never to die, but only to bring misfortune to those who saw his ship. Many seamen claim to have seen the *Dutchman*.

> Those who sail in these parts only look for the *Flying Dutchman* in the reflection of a mirror.

Those who look for it only do so in the protective reflection of a mirror.

There have been 250 known shipwrecks off the coastline of L'Agulhas in the past 200 years. Locals call it the "Graveyard of Ships." Ghostly encounters with the spirits of drowned sailors are often reported, and there are many stories of unfortunate castaways. It is said that a female survivor who died alone in a cave can sometimes be heard singing like an angel and calling for her loved ones.

On misty nights in recent years, there have been sightings of a headless man who walks the road at the entrance to L'Agulhas. Locals believe him to be a drowned sailor, whose head had been devoured by specters of the deep. ◆

▼ Countless sailors have perished in the treacherous waters off the tip of South Africa.

MONTE CRISTO HOMESTEAD NEW SOUTH WALES, AUSTRALIA

Myriad tragic incidents have led to a gallery of ghosts in this Victorian villa in New South Wales.

▲ Mrs. Crawley is often seen in the house, carrying a silver cross.

WHEN TO VISIT

Go just before closing time and shiver as the chilly aura of Mrs. Crawley passes by.

APPARITIONS, STRANGE ORBS, POLTERGEISTS, and phantom noises are attributed to the tragic history of this isolated house on a hill overlooking the town of Junees. Built by farm owner Christopher Crawley in 1884, the house passed to his wife, Elizabeth Crawley, on his death in 1910. Unable to get over her husband's death, Elizabeth spent the rest of her life as a recluse. She converted the upstairs box room to a chapel and immersed herself in the Bible, allegedly leaving the house only twice before her death from a ruptured appendix. Mrs. Crawley's ghost is said to haunt her former home—the sensation of ice-cold air falling like snow reportedly indicates her presence.

A chain of violent events in the house have triggered other supernatural incidents. A maid once plummeted to her death from the upstairs balcony, and the figure of a woman in period dress has been seen walking along the veranda to the blood-stained steps where she fell. A stable boy who burned to death in his bed at the hands of his master is thought to haunt the coach house, while the ghost of a mentally disabled man named Harold wanders the grounds. Kept chained in the caretaker's cottage for 40 years, Harold was found curled up at the feet of his mother's dead body. He died shortly after being sent to a home for the insane. The sound of clanking chains is said to warn of his approach. ◆

PRINCESS THEATRE MELBOURNE, AUSTRALIA

A ghostly baritone who died while performing *Faust* is reputed to haunt this Victorian theater.

In THE PRINCESS THEATRE, a Victorian edifice on Melbourne's Spring Street, a man in 19th-century costume is sometimes seen standing alone on stage. Bowing to an empty auditorium, as if reliving a moment in his past, he is thought to be the ghost of a well-known baritone named Frederick Baker, popularly known as Federici.

In 1888 Federici was performing the role of the satanic Mephistopheles in Charles Gounod's opera *Faust* at the theater. Toward the end of the opera, as Mephistopheles returned to hell with his prize, Dr. Faustus, a trapdoor opened and Federici was mechanically lowered to his descent into hell. Federici duly vanished from the audience's view, but on the way down the opera singer suffered a massive heart attack and died.

> It is auspicious for the play if his ghost—in full evening dress—appears.

The opera ended and the cast, unaware of events off stage, bowed to the usual applause. When they left the stage and were told Federici had passed away, they were astounded—he had, they said, just been with them, taking his bows.

For many years, there has been a tradition on opening nights of leaving one seat in the dress circle empty for Federici, and it is considered auspicious for a play if his ghost—in full evening dress—appears. Performers and makeup artists also claim to have seen the singer's ghost in the dressing room. They have spotted him in more than one outfit and seen him staring at the stage as if he is preparing to perform. ◆

▼ A painting of a performance of Charles Gounod's diabolical opera *Faust* by the French artist Jean Seignemartin

▲ Vicious vampire bats attack at night.

VAMPIRE

HAUNTS

HIGHGATE CEMETERY LONDON, ENGLAND

This Victorian necropolis has a sinister and unsettling energy, even on a sunlit morning.

At NIGHT, HIGHGATE CEMETERY is one of the creepiest places in London. Passersby sometimes describe being blown by a chill and sudden wind. By day, the dappled light reveals paths lined by family crypts overgrown with weeds, broken angels, and crumbling, ivy-clad gravestones. Among the dark shapes lurking in the tangled undergrowth lies a grave said by some to belong to a vampire.

In 1970 two young vampire hunters named David Farrant and Sean Manchester became convinced of vampire activity in the cemetery. Farrant claimed the vampire was a Romanian nobleman and practitioner of the black arts, brought to England in a coffin and buried on the hillside at Highgate in the 18th century. According to Farrant's theory, after the cemetery opened in the 19th century the vampire occupied one of the vaults.

Manchester claimed that modern-day satanists had stirred the beast, and that it was imperative to find its

> Vampire hunters converged on the cemetery and swarmed over the gates.

body, and then stake, behead, and burn it. He declared an official vampire hunt on Friday, March 13, 1970. On the evening of the hunt, vampire hunters from all over London converged on the cemetery and swarmed over the locked gates. But they found nothing.

Meanwhile, Farrant, under the guidance of a psychic, claimed to learn the location of the vampire's grave. One night, he entered an undisclosed family vault and lifted the massive lid off one of the coffins. He was about to drive a stake through the body when his companion persuaded him to stop. Reluctantly, Farrant shut the coffin, and left garlic in the vault. No one knows for sure which crypt this is, but if you walk through the cemetery at dusk, just before closing time, they say you may see a menacing figure lingering near the family vault of Sir James Tyler. ◆

▼ Highgate Cemetery is a city of the dead, with winding paths lined by vast family vaults.

CROGLIN GRANGE CUMBRIA, ENGLAND

A classic vampire tale began with a tap on the window of this spooky mansion in northern England.

HIGH AMONG THE windswept fells of Cumbria lies the ancient village of Croglin. The icy north wind whistles across low stone walls, sheep huddle close, and farmers shake the snow from their boots, quickly locking their cottage door before night falls.

The source of their fear is Croglin's vampire, described in Augustine Hare's 1875 tale of Croglin Grange. According to the story, Croglin's sinister reputation began when the owners of the hall, the Fisher family, moved away from the area and rented out their property. Their departure coincided with reports of an unseen presence in the village.

During the winter the house lay empty, but in spring two brothers and their sister, Amelia Cranswell, moved in. One night, Amelia saw a creature with flaming eyes tapping at her window. She sat bolt upright, unable to move, as the window opened and the figure entered. Coming closer, it pulled back her head and sank its fangs into her throat. Hearing Amelia scream, her brothers raced into her room and chased the vampire to the churchyard, where it disappeared into the crypt.

After Amelia's recovery in Switzerland, the brothers returned to Croglin to hunt down the vampire. Inside the crypt, all but one of the coffins had been opened and the bodies ripped out. Opening the one sealed coffin, they found the shriveled vampire. They dragged the coffin into the churchyard and burned it to ashes. ◆

◀ Croglin Grange, now known as Croglin Low Hall

CAIRNGORMS SCOTTISH HIGHLANDS

Among these craggy mountains, blood-lusting she-devils lead heedless travelers in a dance of death.

NEVER WANDER THROUGH the pine-clad slopes of the Cairngorms at night, for an ancient vampire called the *baobhan sitlh* is said to haunt them. Known as the White Woman of the Highlands, she lives on the lower slopes, but wails from the highest mountaintops in deep winter snow.

According to legend, baobhan sitlhs rise from the dead and hunt in packs. They lure young men to dance with them, then at the first kiss sink their fingernails into their necks and drain their blood.

One legend tells of a group of 18th-century travelers who camped for the night in a small glade. As they warmed their hands by the fire, four women emerged from the darkness and invited them to dance. As the women prepared to strike, one man escaped and ran toward the horses. Safe from attack thanks to the iron horseshoes—a metal said to be feared by vampires—the man survived, and by dawn the vampires had gone.

According to Scottish legend, the only way to stop baobhan sitlhs is to build a mound of stones, or cairn, over their graves. Disturbingly, there are many cairns throughout the Highlands. Remove them at your peril. ◆

▲ The voluptuous baobhan sitlh strikes at night.

BRAN CASTLE
TRANSYLVANIA, ROMANIA

A grisly medieval tyrant who impaled his victims on iron stakes stalks this Transylvanian castle.

WITH ITS GOTHIC TOWERS piercing the stormy Transylvanian sky, Bran Castle lives up to its reputation as a place of terror. Once inhabited by Vlad the Impaler, a descendant of the House of Dracul, it was the real-life inspiration for Bram Stoker's Gothic horror novel *Dracula*.

The medieval ruler of the ancient region of Wallachia, Vlad used the castle as a base in his war against the encroaching Ottoman Empire. A tyrannical ruler, he was allegedly responsible for the torture and horrifying deaths of more than 80,000 men, women, and children. His favorite method of execution was to drop prisoners from the castle's turrets, impaling them on a row of stakes below. It is said that the Turkish army fled when they encountered a forest of rotting corpses impaled on stakes beside the Danube.

Vlad impaled everyone he considered to be an enemy, whether a thief, a nobleman suspected of treachery, or a corrupt priest. It is said he liked to dine with his men among the impaled corpses, close to the castle walls. Some say he drank the blood of the dying and the dead.

The castle is currently used as a museum to display the paintings and furniture of Queen Marie of Romania, but something menacing lurks in the labyrinth of passages and in the extensive grounds. The ghostly chapel is an ideal hiding place for vampires, waiting for nightfall and the chance to feed on innocent visitors lost in the maze of rooms. Walk up the "Secret Stairs" of Bran Castle if you dare. ◆

▲ A 16th-century portrait of the terrifying Vlad the Impaler in his finery

▼ Deep in Transylvania's forest, the ghostly outline of Bran Castle emerges from the mist.

SNAGOV LAKE ILFOV COUNTY, ROMANIA

As night falls on this foggy lake, Vlad the Impaler rises from his grave in search of blood-filled prey.

ON A TINY ISLAND in the middle of Snagov Lake in Romania, Snagov Monastery was once only accessible by boat. A bridge now connects it to the mainland, but it still maintains an eerie atmosphere and a sense of isolation. Early in the morning, as the mist rises from the water, they say the bell tolls twice and the monastery door slams shut, but no one knows who causes this. When dawn breaks it is said a solitary vampire returns to his lonely tomb.

Here, surrounded by frescoes and religious paintings, is the burial place of Vlad the Impaler (see p. 58). Vlad was butchered, then decapitated by treacherous nobles in the forests near here in 1476 during the war against the Turks. They sent his head, preserved in honey, to Istanbul, where the Ottoman sultan displayed it on a stake to prove the Impaler was dead.

> The monastery bell tolls twice but nobody knows who rings it.

An excavation of the tomb in 1931 reportedly found an empty grave, though some accounts tell of the exhumation of a richly dressed decapitated body. Whatever the truth, as you gaze at the simple stone tomb, you may well wonder if a vampire rises from the grave at night to cross the bridge in search of prey. ◆

▲ Many of the frescoes in Romania's monasteries depict demonic scenes.

VAMPIRE CLASSIC The novel *Dracula*, written by Irish author Bram Stoker in 1897, has inspired movies, stories, plays, and art the world over. It tells the story of vampire Count Dracula's move from Transylvania to England and his battle with Professor Van Helsing, a doctor and vampire hunter. Helsing seeks to save the count's chief prey, the sweet and beautiful Lucy Westenra, and destroy the count.

KADAŇ

A vampire in this remote village struck eight times in eight nights, and pulled a stake from his own heart.

In 1337, in the village of Blow, not far from the Czech town of Kadaň, villagers claimed they were being targeted by a vampire shepherd. A book of 1687 recounts how the deceased shepherd left his grave and for eight nights drained the blood of eight villagers, all of whom died within eight days.

According to the story, the panic-stricken villagers dug up the grave and pinned the shepherd to the earth with a stake. But the vampire refused to be destroyed so easily. Taunting the villagers, it thanked them for providing a stick to keep the dogs away, ripped it from his corpse, and continued with its nightly feasting.

In despair, the villagers called in the local executioner, who loaded the corpse onto a wagon and took it to be burned. As the horse and cart rushed out of the village, the corpse sprang to life, screaming wildly and flapping its feet and hands. As soon as they reached a dark copse, the villagers staked the vampire over and over again until its blood gushed like a fountain over the cart. The villagers then burned the vampire and the cart, and from then on, it is said, the village of Kadaň was left in peace. ◆

◀ In most vampire stories, the corpses steal upon their victims while they sleep.

KRINGA ISTRIA, CROATIA

In the 17th century, a grinning vampire preyed on families in this town, ridiculing their efforts to stop him.

In 1656 the people of Kringa, on the Istrian peninsula, reported deadly encounters with a farm worker named Jure Grando who had recently died. Each night, they claimed, his corpse visited a different family in the town, and each time, a member of that family died. Jure also appeared to his terrified widow, who described how his smiling corpse sexually assaulted her while biting her neck.

The local priest, Father Giorgio, vowed to track down the vampire and eventually found and confronted it with a crucifix. But the vampire merely shed a few tears, revealed its terrible fangs, and vanished into the mist.

One night, nine people went to the graveyard, carrying lamps, a hawthorn stake, and a crucifix. When they opened Jure's coffin they found a perfectly preserved, smiling corpse. They tried to pierce its heart but the stake would not penetrate the flesh, so they decapitated the head with a saw. With this, the vampire screamed, the grave filled with blood, and the corpse shriveled and was gone. ◆

◀ Jure Grando ravished his own widow, draining the blood from her neck.

ČACHTICE CASTLE TRENČÍN, SLOVAKIA

In this ruined castle, a murderous countess butchered hundreds of virgins and bathed in their blood.

THESE HAUNTED RUINS were once the home of the notorious Countess Elizabeth Báthory (1560–1614), popularly known as the Blood Countess. Between 1585 and 1610, the countess murdered more than 600 girls in her quest for eternal youth.

The killing spree is said to have started when a maid pricked her finger while dressing the countess. When the blood spurted onto Elizabeth's cheek, she looked in the mirror and thought her skin seemed younger. A horrifying urge to bathe in the blood came over the countess, and with the help of her other servants she slit the maid's throat, hung her upside down, and drained the blood into a vat.

Believing she would stay young forever if she bathed in blood every day, Elizabeth followed a murderous pattern, luring young girls to the castle by offering them jobs as servants. Some were tortured to extract their blood, others were killed. As the new maids reached inside a cabinet to take out their mistress's jewelry, knives shot out and impaled them to the cupboard. The girls were said to suffer a slow and painful death, as their blood dripped into a channel that was connected to a bathtub in the next room.

Elizabeth's horrifying acts were eventually discovered. Bodies were found in the castle crypt and in the fields. As punishment, she was imprisoned in the castle walls, with only one small slit in the door for the delivery of food. Elizabeth died there four years later. Some say her body was taken to the family crypt in Ecsed, Hungary, but others say she was buried in the crypt, from where she rises each night to search for blood. Either way, the stories concerning the countess are so awful and powerful that the locals will not go near the castle. ◆

▲ Elizabeth Báthory, a notorious serial killer

▼ The creepy castle served as a setting for the 1922 movie *Nosferatu*, based on Bram Stoker's novel *Dracula*.

KISILJEVO BRANIČEVO DISTRICT, SERBIA

A series of deadly throttlings in a remote village led to an official investigation into vampirism.

NOT ALL BALKAN VAMPIRES are thought to be bloodsuckers. Some are believed to throttle their victims by sitting on their chests while they sleep. In the village of Kisiljevo, in modern-day Serbia, one case gained credence after the death of Petar Plogojowitz in 1725 led to another nine deaths within just eight days. On their deathbeds, the victims claimed Plogojowitz's corpse had throttled them during the night. The wife of the deceased attested that he had also visited her, asking for his shoes. Terrified, she fled the village. In another version of the story, Plogojowitz returned to his house, demanding food from his son. When the son refused, Plogojowitz murdered him.

The villagers became hysterical and the authorities sent a delegation of priests and officials to Kisiljevo to investigate. They exhumed Plogojowitz's corpse and examined it for what they thought were the signs of vampirism—sprouting hair, long nails, and blood in the mouth. The inspectors allegedly found no sign of decomposition, even though the burial had taken place 40 days previously. Plogojowitz's beard and nails were still growing, and there appeared to be fresh tissue under the decaying skin.

> The nails were still growing and there was fresh tissue under the decaying skin.

Without hesitation, it was agreed by all to stake the corpse. As they plunged a blackthorn stake into its heart, fresh blood was said to rush through the ears and mouth of the body. According to the mythology that now surrounds the case, the vampire gave a final blood-curdling scream and began to disintegrate, the fresh skin turning black. Kisiljevo's vampire was thus destroyed forever. ◆

▼ The belief that the recently dead can leave their grave to prey on the living survives in many Eastern European countries to this day.

PIRANI

PODRIMA, SERBIA

Roma legends about vampire pumpkins are common among the inhabitants of this farming region.

▲ Among the Roma people there are many oral superstitions linking the dead to rotting fruit.

WHEN TO VISIT

Go to Pirani between October and December, when the pumpkins start to rot.

O N THE FERTILE PLAINS of the Podrima region of northern Serbia, the Roma people have long believed that anything left outside the house on the night of a full moon will turn into a vampire. Watermelons and pumpkins, with their headlike shapes, are considered particularly prone to such transformation, with the blemishes that are common on their outer skin said to be drops of blood.

According to some legends, if pumpkins are kept for more than ten days they will start to vibrate and move around the house at night while making an unearthly growling sound. In Roma folklore, the pumpkins do not suck blood, unlike other forms of vampires, but engorge themselves with human excreta, lost hairs, flakes of skin, nail clippings, and other human substances. It is said that they even bleed themselves, and then soak up their own blood through their shriveling skins.

Variations on such tales are common in other areas of Podrima. Villagers in Pirani, for example, maintain that fresh pumpkins kept until after Christmas will turn into vampires, a proverb that probably originated in Roma superstitions that link the dead to rotten fruit. They say that the best way to destroy vampire pumpkins and melons is to plunge them into boiling water. Afterward, the liquid should be discarded, the fruit scrubbed with a broom and thrown away, and the broom burned. ◆

CHÂTEAU DE CHAMBORD **LOIR-ET-CHER, FRANCE**

Spy, alchemist, or vampire? Conjecture surrounds the 18th-century hedonist Comte de St. Germain.

TAKE CARE AS YOU WANDER the elegant salons and corridors of Chambord, for a vampiric count may lie in wait for you behind every door and secret staircase.

The Comte de St. Germain, a lover of women, jewels, and, some say, blood, was a mysterious figure even in his own lifetime. He stepped into the French court of Louis XV in the middle of the 18th century, ostensibly with no past and no name, though he later claimed to be son of Francis Rákóczy II, Prince of Transylvania. He reputedly introduced the king's mistress, Madame de Pompadour, to the elixir of life—possibly blood—then disappeared into thin air. He reappeared and vanished repeatedly. Rumors circulated that he was a spy, an alchemist, or a vampire.

At Chambord, St. Germain claimed he was many centuries old, and cultivated eccentric habits. He conjured diamonds from his pockets and never ate in public. He rarely left his room in the daytime, but at night liked to show off his musical talents to friends. Several of his associates died of a wasting disease. Even Madame de Pompadour and her only daughter, Alexandrine, died young of mysterious causes.

> Several of the count's many associates died of a mysterious wasting disease.

St. Germain was close to the rulers of Austria, who ascribed to a vampiric cult known as Nephilim. The French writer Voltaire said the count was "a man who knows everything and who never dies." In the 20th century, American writer Chelsea Quinn Yarbro immortalized the count in her novel *Hotel Transylvania*. Like the real count, Yarbro's vampire is elegant, deceptive, and devoted to pleasure. ◆

▲ Château de Chambord, the seat of the mesmerizing Comte de St. Germain in the 18th century

LAZZARETTO NUOVO
VENETIAN LAGOON, ITALY

Archaeologists have discovered a vampire's skeleton on this desolate death-island near Venice.

VISITORS TO LAZZARETTO NUOVO, an island nature reserve across the lagoon from Venice, do not visit to see the scrubby undergrowth and silent wildlife. Rather, they come to see where archaeologists unearthed the skeleton of a suspected vampire in a mass grave in 2005. The shocking skeleton of an elderly woman was found with a brick pushed between its jaws—an old method of thwarting shroud-eating vampires.

The island has a dark and grisly history. In the late 15th century, when the Black Death was sweeping through Europe, thousands died of plague here. It was thought that trade ships carried plague from the East, so the crews and passengers of all ships entering the harbor were quarantined on islands in the lagoon, including Lazzaretto Nuovo. As the number of plague victims mounted, the islands became mass graveyards. Even today, the soil of these islands mainly consists of human remains.

Some people thought vampires were the cause of plague, while others believed that the rotting corpses attracted vampires eager to feed on the dead. These beliefs were supported by the experiences of grave diggers, who often reopened the plague pits to discover the decomposing bodies seemingly coming to life—little being known about the decomposition of the human body at the time. They would find purging fluids from the bloated stomach flowing out of the corpse's mouth, just as blood might escape from a blood-gorged vampire, and the shroud covering the face in tatters, rotted by bacteria. It was widely believed that stones, bricks, or large coils of rope inserted into the mouths of alleged vampires would stop them from eating through their shrouds and leaving their graves. ◆

▲ The skull of Lazzaretto Nuovo's "vampire" skeleton, found in 2005 with a brick jammed in its mouth

▼ Plague ravaged Europe from the Middle Ages onward, decimating populations.

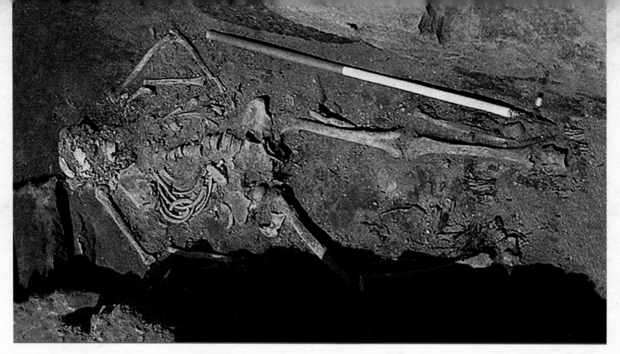

MYTILENE LESBOS, GREECE

A skeleton found nailed to its coffin inside a wall remains a mystery on this Aegean island of love.

▲ Archaeologists found the "vampire of Mytilene" staked through the neck, pelvis, and ankles in a stone-lined crypt set in the city walls.

THE BEAUTIFUL GREEK ISLAND of Lesbos, known for its rich mythology, gently lapping seas, and dense pine forests, harbors a ghastly grave. In the late 20th century, archaeologists working on the remains of an old Turkish cemetery near the main town of Mytilene made a horrific discovery near the North Harbor: a skeleton in a stone-lined grave hollowed out of an ancient city wall.

As in most 19th-century Muslim burial grounds, the majority of the skeletons in the cemetery were neatly aligned with their heads facing Mecca, and buried about 3 feet (1 m) deep in the earth. But this particular skeleton, of a middle-aged man, had been nailed to its coffin, with 8-inch (20 cm) iron stakes through his neck, pelvis, and ankles. While earlier 19th-century travelers to the island had reported the local custom of nailing suspected vampires to their caskets to prevent them from rising, for a Muslim to be buried apart from the other graves, in the wall itself, was unknown.

The skeleton was believed to be a suspected *vrykolakas*, which in Greek folklore usually takes the form of a werewolf. If killed, it shape-shifts into a vampire, retaining the canine fangs of the wolf. The vrykolakas is said to drink the blood of wild animals, throw people out of their beds and drive them insane, and tear its victims apart. It devours all flesh.

In Lesbos, a suspected vrykolakas was usually exhumed and reburied on a small offshore island, as a vrykolakas was thought to be incapable of crossing salt water. Burning the body was unthinkable as it risked inviting a new curse (and during Ottoman times cremation was punishable by a large fine). As the skeleton found in the cemetery on Mytilene reveals, the last resort was to nail the corpse to the coffin. ◆

WHEN TO VISIT

For a spooky experience, climb up to Mytilene's old city walls at sunset.

VOURVOULAKAS CAPE MYKONOS, GREECE

In a remote corner of this popular holiday destination a deadly *vrykolakas* met its end.

FAR FROM THE TOURIST SITES of Mykonos is a beach that is little known or visited. Even locals stay away from Vourvoulakas Cape, for it was here, in 1701, that villagers took part in the cremation of a reputed vampire. A French traveler and writer named Joseph Pitton de Tournefort recorded the horrifying event.

Mass hysteria led up to the burning. Following the death of a tyrannical local farmer, families on the island reported nocturnal visits from a ghastly and foul-smelling corpse. Within days of such an experience, some of the victims died, leading people to believe the farmer had become a vampire.

Under the protective prayers of the priest, the islanders exhumed the body and the local butcher cut out its heart. But the nocturnal menace reputedly worsened and panic spread through the island. A mob of villagers converged on the grave to exhume the body again. While the priest poured holy water into the vampire's mouth, the villagers rammed their swords and daggers into the grave, in the belief that metal prevented vampires from rising.

However, the islanders continued to be hounded. As a last resort, they agreed to cremate the vampire. A fire was lit on the isolated beach and all objects that had touched the corpse—sticks, spades, swords, and the wagon that had carried it there—were set alight, and the vampire at last destroyed. Or was it? A cursed place, this windswept beach between Agios Stefanos beach and Agios Sostis monastery is only for the courageous. Visit if you dare. ◆

▲ Joseph Pitton de Tournefort, witness to the burning

▼ Only by burning the corpse and everything that had touched it could the vampire be slain.

BAPTIST CHURCH

EXETER, RHODE ISLAND, U.S.A.

A grief-stricken father ripped out his dead daughter's heart and burned her body to save his dying son.

WHEN THE BODY of Mercy Brown was exhumed in a Rhode Island churchyard one day in 1892, witnesses gasped in horror. Fresh blood appeared to ooze from the corpse's mouth.

The girl had died of tuberculosis, a deadly disease that had become a global epidemic by the end of the 19th century. George Brown's family had quickly succumbed to the illness. His wife, eldest daughter, and daughter Mercy had died between 1890 and 1892, and his son Edwin had become sick.

Friends and neighbors of Brown convinced him that the cause of Edwin's illness was vampirism, and they persuaded him to have the bodies of his wife and daughters exhumed. When the coffins were opened, witnesses found that his wife and eldest daughter had undergone significant decomposition, but the more recently buried body of Mercy was relatively unchanged, suggesting vampirism, though in reality it had more to do with the freezing New England weather. Mercy's heart was removed from her body and burned on a flat stone not far from her grave. The ashes were then mixed with water for her sick brother to drink. But the gruesome mixture failed to cure the boy and within two months he was also dead.

The small church, known as Chestnut Hill Baptist Church, and the stone where Mercy's heart was burned still stand. Some say that if you hide a little way from her grave, you may witness Mercy taking a ghostly stroll through the graveyard. According to others, if you knock three times on her gravestone and ask, "Mercy Brown, are you a vampire?" her spirit will speak to you or appear. ◆

> If you knock on her grave and ask, "Mercy Brown, are you a vampire?" she will appear.

▼ Persecuted after death, Mercy Brown's spirit is said to appear to those who search for her.

THE COURTHOUSE MANCHESTER, VERMONT, U.S.A.

The site of a ritual sacrifice to a demon vampire lies beneath this quaint New England courthouse.

SOMEWHERE BENEATH Manchester's courthouse lies a hidden graveyard that once formed part of the old village green. It was here, in 1793, that the body of a young woman was exhumed, in order that her vital organs could be burned in a ritual sacrifice to a vampire.

The woman, Rachel, had been the wife of Captain Isaac Burton, but had died of consumption within a year of the marriage. Soon after, he remarried, but his new wife, Hulda, also became ill. While she was in the last stages of illness, the family became convinced that Rachel's corpse had been possessed by a vampire that was preying on Hulda. They believed that if Rachel's vital organs were burned in a charcoal fire, Hulda would be cured.

More than 500 people joined the procession from the cemetery to the blacksmith's forge, where Rachel's liver, heart, and lungs were removed by a doctor and burned to ashes. Tragically, this did not save Hulda, who died from consumption a few weeks after the sacrifice.

After the burning, Rachel's body was reinterred. Many years later, the Burton family graves were relocated to Dellwood Cemetery, but not Rachel's. Lost, forgotten, and cursed, Rachel's grave lies somewhere beneath the courthouse. Her ghost is said to wander the grounds searching for her heart. ◆

▲ The courthouse beneath which Rachel's grave lies

VAMPIRE REPELLENTS There are many ways thought to repel vampires. Hang garlic in your windows, or sprinkle mustard seeds along your window ledges and doorstep. Stop vampires in their tracks with a sacred item, such as a crucifix or rosary, or place a mirror outward on a door—vampires, they say, cannot bear seeing they have no soul.

HOLLYWOOD CEMETERY VIRGINIA, U.S.A.

Was the bloody figure that slipped into a vault in this sprawling Gothic cemetery a vampire?

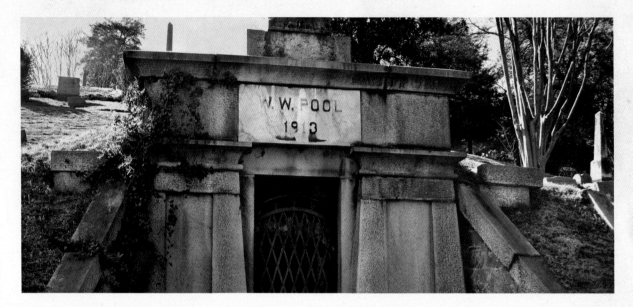

O N A WET, WINDY DAY in 1925, locomotive No. 231 creaked to a halt in Church Hill tunnel, Richmond, to await a load of excavated earth, before slowly moving on toward the western portal. But as it passed beneath 20th Street, bricks fell from the roof, destroying the lighting system and plunging the 4,000-foot (1,200 m) tunnel into darkness. As workmen fled through the eastern entrance, the tunnel collapsed, crushing the locomotive.

A few minutes later, a group of men saw a creature with jagged teeth, a bloody mouth, and burning flesh racing toward the James River. They pursued it to Hollywood Cemetery where, they claimed, it slipped into a crypt belonging to W. W. Pool, a bookkeeper who had died in 1913.

Some believe the monster who ran from the tunnel was 28-year-old railroad fireman Benjamin F. Mosby, who later died in hospital from his terrible injuries. But after searches of the wreckage failed to find one of the tunnel laborers, a theory emerged that the gruesome creature had been a vampire, who had snatched the missing laborer. The vampire, they reasoned, had no choice but to run for the crypt before the rescuers discovered him and the daylight penetrated his skin.

According to the local legend, the vampire still lurks in the cemetery, awaiting his next victim. ◆

▲ The monstrous figure ran to this crypt in Hollywood Cemetery.

GHOSTLY GUARDIAN Among the many statues in Hollywood Cemetery, a cast-iron dog stands next to the grave of a little girl named Bernadine Rees, who used to pet the statue when it stood outside a store in Richmond. When the girl died of scarlet fever in 1862, the dog was moved to the cemetery to watch over her grave. It is said that the dog comes alive and chases anyone who gets too close.

LAFAYETTE CEMETERY COLORADO, U.S.A.

Among the dark cedar trees in old Lafayette Cemetery, an invisible presence prowls among the graves.

IN 1918 A DEADLY FLU PANDEMIC swept through the small mining town of Lafayette, Colorado, striking many of its workers, who were mainly European immigrants supporting families back home. The authorities quarantined the town, and, as the deaths mounted, created a paupers' grave in Lafayette Cemetery. Many miners and poor people were buried here.

Curiously, a Transylvanian immigrant named Todor Glava bought a plot in the same cemetery on his arrival in the United States. Soon afterward, he was struck down by the flu as he was leaving the mine entrance. He died within hours and was buried alongside a fellow Romanian. Their names are still carved on their joint tombstone.

> An ancient cedar marks the spot where the stake plunged through Todor's heart.

Over time, a story arose that Todor was a vampire who roamed through the immigrants' section of the cemetery and terrorized the town. According to this tale, frightened townsfolk rammed a stake through Todor's heart, a spot now marked by an ancient cedar tree growing from the center of the grave. The story also claims that Todor's fingernails transformed into the thorny rose bushes that grow around the graves.

Todor's tombstone attracts many curious visitors. According to local superstition, if they dare stand on the grave, they will hear Todor's screams as the stake delivers its fatal blow. ◆

▲ In many cultures, the death of a vampire can only be achieved by ramming a stake through its heart.

5 KEY VAMPIRE HAUNTS IN THE CARIBBEAN

The countries of the Caribbean claim some of the most feared vampires in the world—voodoo demons that have bred with European revenants to produce fetus-eating fiends and blood-drinking fireballs.

① PARACLETE, GRENADA: In Caribbean folklore, an old woman called a *loogaroo*, in a pact with the devil, changes into a werewolf to tear out human entrails and drink blood. One story tells how a loogaroo in the guise of a beautiful woman fell in love with a doctor. As morning came, she turned to sink her nails into the doctor's stomach, but the light came too quickly and she shriveled into a heap of dust.

② AUX CAYES, HAITI: In the 1920s, a self-confessed loogaroo, Anastasie Dieudonne, admitted to draining blood from her nine-year-old niece. She was discovered when the girl's family, believing she was suffering from a wasting disease, called in a voodoo doctor to examine her. He pointed to a tiny unhealed incision hidden on the middle of her great toe which Anastasie had been sucking.

3 BAHORUCO MOUNTAINS, DOMINICAN REPUBLIC: This mountain range is said to be haunted by *biembiens*—18th-century slaves who ran away from their captors and turned into vampires. Short, deformed, and ugly, they walk backward, eating the entrails of their victims and using the blood for sacrifices to their gods. Listen for low growls and gurgling; it could be a biembien on the prowl.

4 PARAMIN, TRINIDAD: In northern Trinidad, a demon brought to the island on slave ships is said to trade voodoo spells for human blood. Each night, he sends a female vampire called a *soucouyant* to search for new victims. Transforming herself into a fireball, she enters homes through keyholes and sucks the blood from sleeping women. She then delivers it to her demon lord in return for evil powers.

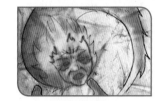

5 CASTARA, TOBAGO: Here, *churile*, the grieving and vengeful spirits of women who died in childbirth, or committed suicide during pregnancy, prey on pregnant women. Dressed in white and carrying a fetus, they wail through the night as their unborn child cries for milk. It is said that a churile possesses her victims and then causes them to miscarry, so that she can drink the fetus's blood.

▼ Offerings to voodoo spirits at a voodoo shrine in Port-au-Prince, Haiti

MOCA PUERTO RICO

An unknown creature bled Moca's pets and livestock dry, then went on a continent-wide blood-fest.

IN THE 1970S, the Puerto Rican town of Moca, named after its pink flowering trees, was plagued by a mysterious creature that killed livestock without devouring any of the carcasses. At first, the town's authorities blamed a satanic cult for the killings, but as more attacks came to light, locals became increasingly alarmed by the common cause of death—a circular incision through which the animals had been bled dry.

In the following years, similar animal deaths were reported in many South American countries, from Argentina to Mexico, and vampirism was suspected. The killings slowly died down, as did the hysteria, but in March 1995, again in Puerto Rico, eight sheep were discovered completely drained of blood with puncture wounds in their chests. By August of the same year, around 150 farm animals and pets were mysteriously killed in the town of Canovanas. Scientists eventually agreed that the culprits were coyotes with a bad case of mange, but not before the beast had been dubbed the *chupacabra*—the goat sucker.

The chupacabra appears in many forms in Central and South American legends. Some cultures describe it is a bear-like creature, while others say it resembles a spiny lizard, and some that it is a grotesque hybrid of man and beast. Eyewitnesses claim sightings as far north as Maine, in the United States, and as far south as Chile, and as far afield as Russia and the Philippines. Most reports have been disregarded as uncorroborated, but strangely, while the mysterious beast still strikes, nobody has yet caught one. ◆

> Sheep were discovered drained of blood with puncture marks in the chest.

▲ Was the so-called goat sucker a coyote with mange, or something much more sinister?

VILLARRICA LAKE ARAUCANÍA, CHILE

Above the plains of Chile, a giant serpent flies through the skies, snatching everything in its path.

In the legends of the Mapuche people of southern Chile, a vampiric serpent known as the *peuchen* is said to stalk the dusty plains. The monstrous creature whirls through the skies in tightening circles, whistling like a tornado as it descends on its prey. Paralyzing it with its gaze, it then coils around the body before sinking its fangs into the throat and sucking up the blood. The victim has no chance of escape.

Only Chile's female shamans (traditional healers) known as *machi* are said to have the power to destroy the peuchen or prevent it from attacking humans. Able to influence the weather and cure disease, the machi

can also ward off evil spirits. According to legend, a machi will draw on her own magical powers to fly faster than the snake. She tears across the skies, never looking back, until she reaches the deepest part of Villarrica Lake, where she plunges into the still, dark waters. In hot pursuit, the peuchen also hurtles toward the water, desperate to catch the machi and tear her enemy apart. But just before impact the peuchen catches sight of its hideous reflection in the surface of the water and is instantly transformed into a harmless puff of smoke. ◆

◀ The sinuous peuchen paralyzes its victim with its transfixing gaze before coiling itself around the body.

TEMPLO MAYOR MEXICO CITY, MEXICO

Beware the shriveled revenants who stalk unsuspecting travelers in the Aztec's main temple.

Since the bloodthirsty days of the Aztec, Mexicans have held a strong belief in revenants—zombie-like monsters that return from the dead. Such creatures are said to lurk at crossroads, in dark alleyways, and in the Templo Mayor in Mexico City. One of the Aztec's main temples, Templo Mayor was a major center of human sacrifice.

The Aztec believed their moon gods transformed noble women who had died in childbirth into horrific vampires, which were

known as *civatateo*. Seductive and hypnotic, they would shape-shift into beautiful women to mate with men, who then mysteriously died. The dreaded civatateo gave birth to vampire children, and murdered human babies to feed their lust for blood.

Modern Mexicans leave maize cakes at crossroad shrines to placate these evil entities. They say that you will recognize a civatateo by her shriveled body, chalky skin, and her shroud-like robes trimmed with crossbones. ◆

◀ If you see a civatateo, turn away. Her look might kill you.

TEFE AMAZONAS, BRAZIL

The venom of a demonic, bloodsucking snake induces insanity in the steaming Amazonian jungle.

AMONG THE MANY supernatural creatures feared by the Amazonian Indians is the *jaracaca*, a snake-like creature that feeds on human blood and milk. It is known by its spine-chilling cries. Some believe jaracaca are the spirits of ancient blood-drinking gods and others that they are the spirits of evil humans doomed to live in the outer reaches of the jungle for eternity.

The jaracaca specializes in drinking enough blood to weaken its victims without killing them. It is said that it will also transform itself into a great snake that slinks silently up to nursing mothers to drain the breast of milk without their knowledge. To prevent the baby from alerting the mother, it places its tail into the baby's mouth like a pacifier. As the milk-drinking vampire feeds, the baby weakens and eventually dies of starvation.

> It slinks up silently to nursing mothers to drain the breast-milk without their knowledge.

When milk is not available, the vampire coils itself around the upper arms of sleeping men and sucks their blood instead. During the night it exudes venom, which seeps into the man's skin, turning him into a raving madman by morning.

Another vampire from Brazilian folklore is the *lobisomem*, reputed to feed on the blood of young women. Only 2 inches (5 cm) high and resembling a furry monkey with a wizened face, it sneaks through the night on soft padded paws. But far from being a cuddly toy, it preys on sleeping virgins, making tiny wounds in their necks and then sucking up their blood. ◆

▼ The thick jungles of Brazil are full of strange and venomous creatures that have inspired a rich stock of supernatural tales and superstitions.

PONTIANAK WEST KALIMANTAN, INDONESIA

In Indonesian mythology, a bloodsucking vampire tears off men's genitals and feasts on their innards.

IN WEST KALIMANTAN, never leave your clothes outside at night. If you do, it is said, a bloodsucking woman will sniff you out and disembowel you. Known as a *pontianak*, the dreaded creature is believed to be the spirit of a pregnant woman. According to legend, the first sultan of Pontianak named the city after the vampiric stalker in an attempt to placate her.

The ghostly white pontianak lives in banana trees by day, but at night turns into a beautiful woman, dressed in white, who beguiles any man who comes near. If you hear a dog howling, the pontianak is said to be far away, while a dog whining means she is close. Sinking her long,

sharp fingernails into her victim's stomach, she rips out the organs and devours them, then tears off the genitals. Should her victim have his eyes open, she will suck them out of his head. The only way to fend off a pontianak is to plunge a nail into the nape of her neck: She will be tamed until the nail is removed.

The *kuntilanak* is related to the pontianak, but usually appears in the shape of a bird and sucks the blood of virgins and young women. Among the other female demons in Indonesia, the *lang suir* (see panel) is also chiefly associated with pregnancy. ◆

▲ Beware the frightening pontianak.

PREGNANT DEMON The much feared lang suir lives on the shores of rivers and oceans in Indonesia. Forty days after the death of a pregnant woman, her spirit is said to transform into a lang suir with red eyes and long talons. She is reputed to prey on other pregnant women, murdering them and drinking their blood, or causing them to miscarry.

CEBU ISLAND PHILIPPINES

Evil spirits are reputed to feast on pregnant women and their unborn children on this island paradise.

ON THE TROPICAL ISLAND of Cebu in the Philippines, legend tells of an evil spirit at large. More feared than the typhoons and storms that batter the island, the powers of the deadly *aswang* fasten on ordinary islanders going about their daily lives.

The aswang is said to appear on calm and balmy evenings between December and February, when the beaches are lit by glow worms and the islanders are off guard. Descending from the mountain volcanoes of the Philippines, they slip into social gatherings disguised as ordinary folk—shy, undemanding, and polite. At night, however, the interlopers shape-shift. Turning into horrific versions of cats, pigs, or bats, they eat unborn fetuses and devour the livers and hearts of babies and small children. Using their long proboscis, or some say barbed tongue, they suck or lick the fetuses out of the womb. They are quick, silent, and so thin they can hide behind a bamboo cane.

Deception is the secret of the aswang's success. An aswang known as the *tik-tik* is said to confuse its victims by making a loud ticking noise when it is far away and a quiet, barely perceptible noise when it is close at hand. Another kind of aswang, the *bubuu*, steals corpses from funeral wakes and creates replicas of them, sending them back to their families as zombies. The zombies then feed on members of their former family, creating more corpses for the bubuu's unquenchable thirst for blood. ◆

> They are quick and silent, and so thin they can hide behind a bamboo cane.

▼ The aswang specialize in attacking their victims when they least expect it—such as on calm and balmy evenings.

RAWANG SELANGOR, MALAYSIA

Not far from Kuala Lumpur, a vampiric woman with trailing viscera seeks out pregnant women.

AMONG MANY dark myths in Malaysia is the grisly tale of Penanggalan. According to the story, a beautiful woman taking a ritual bath in a mixture of honey and vinegar was startled by a strange man appearing by her side. In her fright, the woman swiveled her head so suddenly that it detached from her body, spilling entrails across the room. Enraged by the intruder, she flew after him, her decapitated head trailing viscera and dripping blood, while her twitching corpse slumped in the bathtub.

It is said that Penanggalan seeks out pregnant women or mothers with young babies. By night, she flies quickly like a bat, swooping through rain forests, plummeting down cliff faces, or traveling over the sea, her entrails dangling.

By day, she changes into a beautiful woman, but cursed by the smell of vinegar she is forced to live alone.

Penanggalan is believed to appear at birth rather than death. She perches on the roofs of houses where women are in labor, screeching when the child is born. Squeezing through cracks in the floorboards and walls, she laps up the afterbirth and scoops up newborns with her tongue. If she touches a mother or older child, they soon contract a fatal wasting disease, while anyone who is brushed by the entrails suffers open sores that will only heal with a shaman's magic. ◆

▲ Penanggalan attacks a baby trapped in her dangling entrails.

CAMBODIA'S SEVERED HEADS In Cambodia, the *ab*, similar to Penanggalan, is either a young or an old woman who sends her head into houses at night, looking for the lungs, hearts, and blood of dead or living animals. Abs are considered to be afraid of humans but will run after them if they show fear. According to legend, abs follow a fixed path, like a river, which they remember very carefully.

5 GRUESOME INDIAN BLOOD-FEST SITES

Hindu legends are filled with violent and evil creatures intent on attacking unwary innocents. In fact, wherever you go in India, there may be a bloodthirsty creature not far behind.

❶ KOLKATA, WEST BENGAL: The Kalighat Kali and Dakshineswar Kali temples are dedicated to Kali, goddess of time and death, depicted with terrifying fangs and wearing a garland of human skulls. In legend, Kali and the goddess Durga battle the demon Raktabija, who reproduces himself from every drop of blood spilled. Kali wins the battle, and forever after takes the blood of anyone she chooses.

❷ VETAL TEMPLE, MUMBAI: Flesh-eaters and blood-drinkers, resemble skeletons with large tattered wings. Malevolent spirits of the dead, trapped between life and the afterlife, they know the past, present, and future. They drug young babies, virgins, and pregnant women, then carry them back to their bloody lair. There they slowly rip apart the stomach, extract the bowels, and gorge on the flesh.

③ PATNA, BIHAR: According to Patna legend, *bhoots* are the evil spirits of a people who have not had a proper burial, or have committed suicide or been executed. Their feet face backward and they float about 3 feet (1 m) off the ground, casting no shadows. Bhoots like human milk best, but they will shape-shift into beautiful women to drain the blood of men.

④ RAVANA TEMPLE, KANPUR, UTTAR PRADESH: This temple is dedicated to Ravana, the king of the *Rakshasas*—a ferocious being with red eyes and flaming hair who drinks blood from human skulls. Evil spirits with long fangs that sniff out innocent women and children, Rakshasas live in the city's cemeteries, disrupting prayers, rituals, and funeral rites.

⑤ JAIPUR, RAJASTHAN: In Jaipur legend, bloody intestines wreathe the head of the vampiric *Brahmaparusha*. Making a small incision in its victim's neck or arm, it sucks the blood, which it then regurgitates into the skull of its previous victim. Drinking the blood from the skull, it then tears open the body to devour the liver and heart before wrapping itself in the intestines and performing a ritual dance.

▼ Kolkata's Dakshineswar Temple contains an idol of Kali, the Hindu goddess of time and death.

KAKUM NATIONAL PARK GHANA, WEST AFRICA

A grisly ghoul with hooked feet is reputed to pounce on careless travelers in Ghana's rain forests.

AMONG GHANA'S ASHANTI PEOPLE, the mythical asanbosam hangs from the rain forest's tallest trees. Hairy, with bloodshot eyes and dangling legs ending in iron hooks, it pounces on unwary hunters, clamping its legs around their necks and then driving in the hooks. It hauls its unfortunate victims into the trees to consume them, spitting out the bones: If these are impregnated with enough venom, the victims will rise again—as asanbosam.

Asanbosam are generally said to be people who have died by committing suicide or by doing wrong. They leave their graves via a narrow tunnel leading to an exit hole, emerging as a bat, a fireball, or a cloud of mist.

Some say they have heard the asanbosam while taking the Canopy Walk through the treetops of Kakum National Park. They report the ominous metallic sound of the creature sharpening its iron hooks.

The Ashanti also believe in a vampire known as the obayifo that feasts on the blood of children. It takes on human form by day, and at night transforms into orbs that dart quickly through the darkness. It is said that you can tell if someone is an obayifo by their fast-moving eyes and huge appetites. ◆

▲ Halfway along the Kakum Canopy Walk listen for the asanbosam sharpening its iron hooks.

BLOODSUCKING BEETLE Among the Ewe people of Togo and Ghana, the adze is a demon that shape-shifts into a firefly to steal beneath closed doors at night and suck blood from sleeping children. It can possess humans and turn them into witches. If it is captured, or cannot return to the wild, it changes into human form, inducing paranoia in others and stirring up vendettas.

VICTORIA FALLS ZIMBABWE, SOUTHERN AFRICA

An immortal bird of prey that cruises the skies of Africa is prized by witches and sorcerers.

▼ The impundulu uses its claws and talons to strike lightning and stir up violent storms.

WHEN TO VISIT

The lightning bird is most active during the stormy season from March through April.

IN THE FOLKLORE of the Zulu, Pondo, and Xhosa peoples of southern Africa, the fearsome lightning bird, or *impundulu,* craves human blood. Preying on young virgins, babies, children, and pregnant women, it takes the form of a human-size bird that can conjure violent thunder and lightning with its wings and talons.

According to myth, the impundulu can shape-shift into a seductive young woman, who lures young men into sheer ravines and sends them tumbling into the Victoria Falls. Turning back into a bird, she then flies away, returning later to lap up the blood. The huge winged bird is usually depicted as black and white but is sometimes shown with peacock-blue feathers and red legs, head, and tail. It lays its eggs wherever it strikes lightning; these are said to be prized in both black and white magic.

It is said that witch doctors, shamans (traditional healers), and sorcerers try to capture and tame the impundulu, for they treasure it above all other birds. According to legend, witches in possession of an impundulu can pass it on to the next generation. It will remain faithful to each of its owners as long as it is supplied with unlimited human blood or is able to fly by night, shape-shift, and seek out its own victims. According to the myth, the bird is immortal and can only be destroyed by fire. ◆

▲ Macbeth and the Three Witches in an engraving from 1805

WITCH

AND THE DARK ARTS
CRAFT

MOTHER SHIPTON'S CAVE
KNARESBOROUGH, ENGLAND

This Yorkshire cave is cited as the birthplace of a reputed witch who foretold the Great Fire of London.

ON A SUMMER'S NIGHT in 1488, as the full moon rose behind an outcrop of rocks, a young girl gave birth alone in a cave beside the River Nidd in the town of Knaresborough. The girl, it is said, died in childbirth, but the child survived and was fostered by a woman living on the outskirts of the town.

The baby was reputed to be hideously ugly and to possess supernatural forces from the start. One day, it is said, the child disappeared from her crib. When neighbors arrived to help find her, a poltergeist threw them around the room, furniture moved, plates flew off tables, and baby Ursula and her crib were found halfway up the chimney.

In spite of her crooked nose and goggle eyes, the child grew up to marry a local carpenter, Toby Shipton, and became known as Mother Shipton, one of the most celebrated soothsayers of the 16th century. She predicted the fates of several kings, the defeat of the Spanish Armada in 1588, the Great Fire of London of 1666, and the invention of iron ships. Dukes, lords, and pretenders to the throne consulted Mother Shipton. She was asked to put curses on rival families, send demons to torment murderers, and help reunite lovers.

No one knows how Mother Shipton died. Some visitors to Knaresborough claim to have seen her face peering from the waters of the "petrifying well," next to the cave associated with her birth. Others throw love letters, amulets, and, more recently, teddy bears into the calcifying waters to be turned to stone and blessed by Mother Shipton's supernatural powers. ◆

▲ An early 19th-century engraving of Mother Shipton with a pet demon at her side

▼ Items left by visitors turn to stone in the "petrifying well," next to Mother Shipton's Cave.

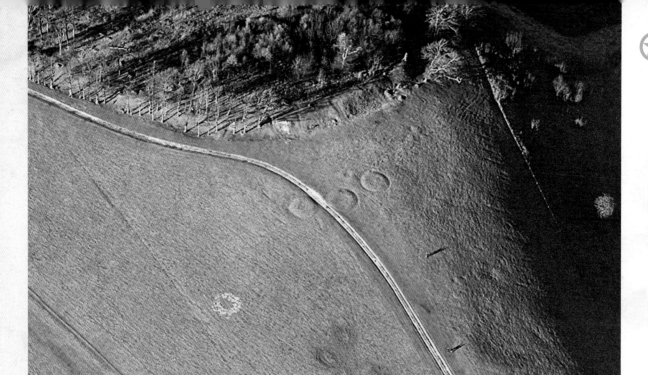

CHANCTONBURY RING SUSSEX, ENGLAND

An ancient earthwork in southern England is said to be a vortex of evil energy created by the devil.

IN 1987 A DEVASTATING HURRICANE hit southern England, leaving destruction in its wake. On the South Downs, in the county of West Sussex, it ripped out a circle of towering beech trees planted on the base of an Iron Age fort known as Chanctonbury Ring, which is also the site of two pagan temples.

Mysterious and silent—they say that no bird dares sing here—Chanctonbury Ring has a powerful and sinister atmosphere. Some believe that the many ley lines (alignments of ancient mystical sites) that cross this part of the South Downs produce a vortex of malevolent energy, attracting paranormal activity, satanists, and even the devil himself.

According to legend, the ring was created by the devil during the early Christian era. Appalled by the number of pagans converting to the new religion, the devil hatched a plan to drown them. During a wild, windy, and moonless night, he began digging a deep trench between a point near the modern-day village of Poynings and the sea. As he clawed out the earth, the soil piled up beside the trench, creating a series of earth mounds. However, an old white witch was determined to foil the devil's plan. Placing a sieve in front of a lighted candle in her window, she fooled a rooster into mistaking the diffused light for sunrise. As the rooster crowed, the world woke up, and the devil fled.

It is said that if, on a moonless night, you walk backward in a counterclockwise direction around the ring seven times without stopping, the devil will appear and offer you a bowl of porridge. If you accept, he will either grant you your dearest wish or take your soul to hell. ◆

> The devil will either grant you your dearest wish, or take your soul to hell.

▲ Chanctonbury's mystical atmosphere is reinforced by the many ancient burial mounds that surround the ring.

HELLFIRE TUNNELS WEST WYCOMBE, ENGLAND

In the 18th century, this underground labyrinth gained a reputation for orgies and black magic.

IN THE GREEN FOLDS of the Chiltern Hills in southern England, the mock facade of a Gothic church fronts a network of winding tunnels and secret chambers extending deep into the hillside. In the 18th century, this spooky labyrinth hosted the Hellfire Club, founded by notorious libertine Sir Francis Dashwood. The club, then called the Order of St. Francis of Wycombe, celebrated Venus and Bacchus—the Roman gods of love and wine. Its motto was *Fait ce que tu voudrais* (Do what thou wilt).

The club attracted writers, artists, and politicians. Famous guests included Benjamin Franklin, who has a chamber named after him. The hedonism turned to scandal when rumors of orgies and black magic began to circulate. By this time phallic symbols decorated the inner temples, while succubi and incubi (sexual demons) adorned the walls. Below the chapel, Dashwood created an imitation of River Styx—the river in Greek mythology that souls must cross in order to reach the underworld.

After the club's downfall, the tunnels were abandoned until they were opened to the public in 1951. Today's visitors can take guided tours. ◆

▲ Inside the Hellfire Tunnels

TASTE FOR THE OCCULT Among a number of occult orders that became fashionable in the late 19th century was the Hermetic Order of the Golden Dawn, founded by three English Freemasons. The second of its Three Orders taught alchemy and was represented by a symbolic seal (right). Members included the creators of the ever popular illustrated Waite-Smith tarot deck.

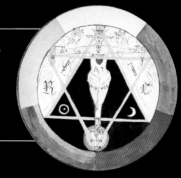

BENNAN HEAD SCOTLAND

From their base in a remote Scottish cave, a cannibalistic coven preyed on lone locals and travelers.

IN THE 17TH CENTURY, King James VI of Scotland is said to have led 400 men and a pack of bloodhounds in a hunt for Sawney Bean, the head of an incestuous clan of corpse eaters. Guided to a rugged stretch of Ayrshire's coast by the only victim to have escaped Bean's clutches, the king's party combed the caves in the cliffs for several hours before finding the secret hideout.

For more than 25 years Bean and his 46-strong clan are said to have murdered travelers and locals, and then pickled and salted their flesh for consumption. Hundreds of people went missing over the years, and discarded limbs were often found washed up on nearby beaches. It is said that an attack on a couple in broad daylight during a midsummer fair finally prompted the king to take action. The husband bravely fought to save his wife's life, but then watched helplessly as the clan ripped out his wife's entrails and feasted on her blood. The appearance of a large group of revelers from the fair caused the clan to flee, saving the man from the same fate.

> They found human body parts hanging from the roof and pickled limbs floating in barrels of vinegar.

When the king and his men stormed the cave, they found human body parts hanging from the roof, pickled limbs floating in barrels of vinegar, and the clothes, jewelry, and money of the dead strewn over the sandy floor. The clan had no chance to escape. The king's men took them to Edinburgh in chains, and from there to Leith for execution. The authorities were merciless: The men bled to death after their hands and legs were cut off, while the women were forced to watch the men's terrible torture and then burned alive. ◆

▼ Cannibals feast on roasted human body parts.

ST. PATRICK'S PURGATORY

LOUGH DERG, COUNTY DONEGAL, IRELAND

On a windswept island in the middle of Ireland's misty Lough Derg is a mysterious portal to hell.

ACCORDING TO Celtic mythology, Donegal's Lough Derg is the home of the terrifying Corra, a monstrous manifestation of a Celtic warrior goddess. The tranquil waters have other, equally hellish, associations from early Christian times. In the fifth century A.D., a revelation from Christ led St. Patrick to a tiny island in the middle of the lake. There, he was told, he would find a cave that was the entrance to hell, and therefore know that heaven and hell exist.

It is said that as St. Patrick paddled slowly across Lough Derg's misty waters at dawn, the great Corra rose from the shallows, opened her jaws, and swallowed him. It took St. Patrick two nights and days to cut his way free. As the monster floundered in her death throes, the lake ran red with her blood, giving it the name Lough Derg (Red Lake), and the monster's body turned to two large

stones—the two islands in the lake today. Finding the cave on one of the islands, St. Patrick descended into the darkness as a door closed behind him. Here, in Purgatory, he stayed for a day and a night and experienced a vision of hell.

Pilgrims have traveled to St. Patrick's Purgatory for many centuries, and tales of supernatural encounters abound. Legend tells of a wicked knight who wished to repent his sins. In the darkness of the Purgatory, he was thrown into a pit of fire, beaten by tormented souls, and forced to cross a narrow bridge across a sea of flames. The knight survived by calling out Jesus' name. On his return, the door was opened and the knight knew that all his sins had been forgiven. Pilgrims who did not make their way back to the Purgatory were never mentioned again. ◆

▲ St. Patrick opens the door to the Purgatory.

▼ Pilgrims have flocked to the mysterious site of St. Patrick's Purgatory for nearly 1,500 years.

PLACE DE GRÈVE PARIS, FRANCE

On a frosty winter's night, you may catch the smell of burning flesh on this atmospheric Parisian square.

▲ During a Black Mass, a woman would lie like a human altar on a table or floor, with a bowl placed on her stomach to catch the blood of a sacrificial infant.

WHEN TO VISIT

Cross the square in the dead of night, when the spirits of the executed rise in revenge.

A REPUTED SORCERESS and noted fortune teller in 17th-century Paris, Catherine Monvoisin exerted considerable influence at the court of King Louis XIV. A skilled apothecary, she concocted love powders and deadly poisons, using everything from moles' teeth and toads' bones to human blood and the dust of human remains. Known as La Voisin, she presided over a vicious ring of fortune tellers and poisoners at the court and personally befriended the king's official mistress, Madame de Montespan, who bought her aphrodisiacs and protective amulets. La Voisin also conducted Black Masses in which she called upon the devil to make Montespan's wishes come true. It was believed that the obsessively jealous Madame de Montespan herself participated in the Black Masses when her efforts to retain the king's attention eventually failed.

Montespan was enraged when the king found a new mistress, and in 1679 she persuaded La Voisin to concoct a poison to kill the pair. However, by then royal spies had infiltrated La Voisin's circle of occultists and the conspiracy was exposed. Louis XIV ordered the execution of any courtiers involved in supernatural activities at the court, regardless of their rank, gender, or age. La Voisin was arrested and imprisoned at Vincennes, where she was convicted of witchcraft. Along with her fellow conspirators, she was burned at the stake in the center of Place de Grève (now known as Place de l'Hôtel-de-Ville) in February 1680. It is said that the smell of burning flesh and the press of the frenzied crowds can sometimes be sensed on the square, especially on a clear winter's night. ◆

5 SATANIC HOT SPOTS IN FRANCE

France has a long history in the dark arts. Its medieval towns, châteaus, monasteries, and convents are richly embellished with tales of demonic possession, satanic worship, mass murder, and witchcraft.

① CHÂTEAU DE TIFFAUGES, VENDÉE: In the 15th century, Gilles de Rais, a Breton knight, hired a sorcerer to help him become the wealthiest man in France. Instructed by the sorcerer to sacrifice a child's heart, eyes, and sex organs, de Rais embarked on a killing spree, becoming one of France's most notorious serial killers. It was not until he kidnapped an important priest that he was arrested and hanged.

② PONT VALENTRÉ, CAHORS: According to local legend, the builder of this 14th-century bridge traded his soul for the devil's help in its construction. Just before the last stones were laid, the cunning builder realized there was one thing the devil would never be able to do—fetch water for the workmen's last mix of mortar in a sieve. Satan returned empty-handed, and the pact was broken.

3 AIX-EN-PROVENCE: In 1607 a young girl called Madeleine accused a priest in the town, Father Louis Gaufridi, of lurid sexual acts. Sent to a convent, she began to see demons, a claim that soon spread to other nuns. Found guilty of demonic activities, Gaufridi was burned at the stake. After his execution, Madeleine was cured, but in 1642 she herself was accused of witchcraft and sentenced to life in prison.

4 LOUDUN: Father Grandier, a Jesuit priest, loved to seduce women. In 1617 the Bishop of Poitiers conspired with Sister Jeanne de Ange to accuse Grandier of immorality and colluding with the devil. Soon after Grandier was found guilty and burned at the stake. Protesting his innocence, he told his inquisitors that within 30 days they too would see God. Many of them died soon afterward.

5 SÈVRES, NEAR PARIS: An abandoned church in Avenue de la Division Leclerc is thought to be where the Catholic priest Abbé Boullan practiced black magic and infant sacrifice in the mid-19th century. On January 8, 1860, Boullan reportedly sacrificed one of his own illegitimate children. He collapsed and died of a heart attack in 1893, reputedly cursed by a rival satanist.

▼ Château de Tiffauges, the seat of the serial killer Gilles de Rais

WÜRZBURG

NORTHERN BAVARIA, GERMANY

In the 17th century, mass hysteria gripped this pretty town, leading to witch trials and mass executions.

ONE OF THE cruelest figures in 17th-century Germany was Philipp Adolf von Ehrenberg, Prince-Bishop of Würzburg. In one of the longest witch trials in European history, he sent more than 900 people to the stake. They included his own nephew, 19 Catholic priests, and many children between the ages of 4 and 14, accused of having sexual intercourse with demons.

The trials took place between 1626 and 1631. Mass hysteria spiraled out of control as families accused others of devil worship and witchcraft. The most prominent clergy were the first to be executed, along with many of the most attractive women and girls, some of whom were accused of sorcery merely for smiling at a stranger. Many people, including vagrants, were burned at the stake simply for not being able to say where they were on a certain night:

If they could not remember, they were accused of fornicating with the devil.

As accusations spread through the surrounding region and into the wealthiest estates, people from all strata of society were drawn into the net, from church-goers and merchants to women living alone. One God-fearing man who witnessed the horrific execution of many children purported that the devil and 8,000 of his followers had held a Black Mass at a place he named Fraw-Rengberg. He claimed that the devil appeared in an explosion of flames and smoke and then vomited turnip rinds over the adoring mass, who scrabbled on the ground to taste the evil eucharist. ◆

▲ Philipp Adolf von Ehrenberg, the prince-bishop who resided over one of Europe's worst witch hunts.

▼ The witch trials shattered Würzburg's veneer of respectability.

HOUSKA CASTLE · BLATCE, CZECH REPUBLIC

Under the floor of this mysterious Czech castle a "hole to hell" is said to channel evil entities.

▲ The feared horrors of hell are captured in this 16th-century painting of the Portuguese School.

PERCHED ON A LIMESTONE CLIFF, about 30 miles (47 km) north of Prague, is Houska Castle, an imposing Gothic edifice with mysterious origins. According to legend, the castle straddles a bottomless crack in its limestone plinth, through which half-animal and half-human creatures rise at night to slaughter local livestock. Traditionally, local villagers would do anything to avoid passing the hellish portal after dark: If they came too close, it was said, they would turn into the most terrifying demons.

The site has no natural fortifications or water source, and there is no record of anyone actually living in the castle when it was first built. Some say the mysterious castle was built to trap the evil within its walls. The "hole to hell" lies under the thick stone floor of the chapel.

Later in the castle's history, it is said that a powerful duke set out to discover the truth behind the evil gateway. Striking a deal with a condemned prisoner, he offered the man a full pardon in exchange for going down the hole to investigate. Agreeing to the deal, the man was lowered into the opening by a rope. After a long silence the man suddenly began screaming from deep within the pit. When the duke's men hauled the prisoner back to the surface, his hair had turned white and he was completely mad. It is said he died soon afterward.

Some claim to have seen demonic entities in the chapel and courtyard, accompanied by strange moanings and screams. Sometimes, it is said, the devil himself appears near the castle on a charging black horse. ◆

WHEN TO VISIT

Houska is closed throughout winter, so go in midsummer when the days are long.

ZUGARRAMURDI CAVES NAVARRE, SPAIN

In the 17th century, a remote village in the Pyrenees became the center of a vicious witch trial.

NESTLED IN THE FOOTHILLS OF THE WESTERN PYRENEES, the sleepy village of Zugarramurdi looks like the very essence of a Basque village. However, its attractive red-roofed houses and sloping cobblestoned streets belie a dark and troubled history, involving witches, warlocks, and devil worship.

Zugarramurdi's association with the occult centers on a vast network of caves a quarter of a mile (400 m) west of the village, beside a gushing stream linked in legend to the underworld. Here, in the early 17th century, a coven of witches was reputed to practice black magic and hold devil banquets.

The activities came to light when a young woman called Maria Ximildegui moved to the village and became interested in the occult, at that time strong throughout the Pyrenees. When a man she liked rejected her, she took her revenge by telling the authorities about a witches' coven operating in the caves. Her action triggered one of the biggest witch trials that Spain has ever known.

As accusations mounted, the Inquisition (see panel) took action. Forty suspects were sent to be tried in the nearby town of Logroño: Twelve of them were burned at the stake, five died under torture, and one perished from fear. Accused witches who denied their guilt were stretched on a rack or hung upside down and dunked in a vat of scalding water until they confessed to their crimes. These included invoking satanic curses, fornicating with the devil, and attending witches' sabbaths in the caves.

> Those who denied their guilt were dunked in a vat of scalding water.

▼ On the summer solstice, El Día de la Bruja (Day of the Witch) is celebrated in the caves at Zugarramurdi.

THE SPANISH INQUISITION Established in 1478 by the Catholic Monarchs, Ferdinand and Isabella, the Spanish Inquisition was originally intended to convert religious groups, especially Muslims and Jews, to Roman Catholicism. After the mass expulsion of Jews from Spain in January 1492, the Inquisitors turned their attention to other so-called heretics. Thousands of innocent people were considered heretical in one way or another. The Inquisitors used torture to gain confessions from victims, then sent them to the stake to be burned alive. The Inquisition was eventually abolished in Spain in the early 19th century.

As in many towns in Europe at this time, mass hysteria broke out in Zugarramurdi and the surrounding villages. The young Inquisitor Frías, known as the Witches' Advocate, promised pardons to all those who admitted their crime and denounced their accomplices. Frías was not convinced by the stories of flying in the air, shape-shifting, and murder from afar, rationalizing that even the devil was incapable of such acts. Confessions from around 2,000 people, more than half of them children, implicated a further 5,000 people.

By the end of 1614, Frías's skepticism brought the authorities to their senses and the witch trials ended. This was the first step toward ending witch-burning in Spain, long before the rest of Europe. Near the entrance to the cave, a plaque commemorates the men, women, and children who died in the trials. The village's Witchcraft Museum highlights the terrifying tortures endured by the victims. ◆

▲ The Inquisition persecuted heretics, staged public executions, and employed many means of torture.

VALLADOLID SPAIN

A famous magician claimed he flew through the air with the devil and witnessed the sack of Rome.

EUGENIO DE TORRALBA was considered the most powerful magician in 16th-century Spain. He learned his trade in Rome, where the occult was fashionable, and his reputation soared when he claimed a spirit called Zequiel could help him foretell the future. Torralba predicted some of the most important political events in Europe, including the death of King Ferdinand of Spain in 1516.

According to Torralba, Zequiel appeared to him at each phase of the moon to transport him to distant places. On the evening of May 6, 1527, he claimed Zequiel appeared to him in the cloisters of Valladolid's old university and flew him to Rome, where he witnessed the sack of the holy city. Returning quickly to the Castilian court to report the event, Torralba gave Spain an advantage over other European powers.

Three years later, Torralba's reputation plummeted when a jealous friend accused him of witchcraft. The Inquisition tortured the sorcerer until he admitted that the spirit was the devil. In 1531 Torralba was released on condition that he did not contact Zequiel again. Torralba disappeared, and no records of his death exist. He does, however, appear in Cervantes's novel *Don Quixote*. ◆

▲ The cloisters of Colegio de San Gregorio, from where Torralba flew to Rome

THE RENAISSANCE AND THE OCCULT A fascination with magic sprang up during the Renaissance, helped by the Italian philosopher Marsilio Ficino. The work of two astrologers, Cornelius Agrippa and Dr. John Dee, who used spiritual objects such as crystal globes and special tables (right), attracted the patronage of scholars and the monarchy.

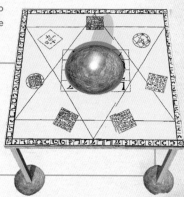

ENGOLASTERS ANDORRA, SPAIN

High in the Pyrenees, witches once danced by a sparkling lake and a knight buried a powerful charm.

According to one of many legends concerning the Pyrenees, the lake at Engolasters was created by God when a woman refused to give a piece of bread to a starving pilgrim. As a punishment, God sent a terrible flood to drown the local inhabitants. The stars in the sky,, entranced by the beauty of the deep, still lake that God had created, then fell into the water and were imprisoned for eternity.

In the Middle Ages, the lake was reputed to be a meeting place for witches' covens. Local villagers stayed well away, believing that anyone who saw the witches dancing naked on the shore would be turned to stone or into a dog.

A few miles from the lake, the 12th-century bell tower of Sant Miquel d'Engolasters, one of the jewels of Romanesque Andorra, is associated with another legend.

> Anyone seeing the witches would be turned to stone or into a dog.

The legend states that a beautiful witch, who desired a certain knight more than her own life, threw herself from the belfry after accusing him of demon worship in revenge for his taking another lover.

Hunted by the Inquisition, the knight hid in the tower, with only the local priest as a companion. One day, he found in his leather pouch a curious black stone with a talisman etched into the surface. Realizing it was a witch's spell, the knight buried the stone in the church's tiny graveyard to rid himself of her attentions forever. They say that this mysterious talisman is still in the churchyard and has the power to bring love to those who visit the church today. ◆

▼ It was believed that witches danced barely clothed or naked beside the lake.

ABBEY OF THELEMA CEFALÙ, SICILY

The self-proclaimed satanist Aleister Crowley created a dark utopia on this island paradise.

ALEISTER CROWLEY (1875–1947) was one of the most famous occultists of the 20th century. A British bisexual and libertarian, he founded a religion called Thelema, based on the philosophy of "Do what thou wilt."

He was dubbed the wickedest man in the world by sections of the British press, especially when his Sicilian villa, called the Abbey of Thelema, became a center for drug-taking, sexual rituals, and mystical practices. Crowley was also an intrepid explorer and mountaineer, and possibly a British secret agent.

Crowley borrowed the name of the villa from François Rabelais's novel *Gargantua,* about a lawless monastery where everyone lived according to their own free will. However, Crowley's hedonistic utopia did not last long. In 1923 a 23-year-old Oxford undergraduate called Raoul Loveday died at the villa and was later found to have been poisoned. The young man's wife, Betty, blamed the death on Crowley, who had forced the student to drink the blood of a sacrificial cat. When Betty sold her story to the British press, rumors about the villa's activities circulated in Italy. In 1923 Mussolini expelled Crowley from the country.

The Abbey of Thelema fell into disrepair but continued to be visited by satanists. The room known as the Chamber of Nightmares, where drug-induced sadomasochistic rites took place, was painted over by local people. In 1955 filmmaker Kenneth Anger uncovered many of the magic symbols and satanic images. They are still visible for those who dare to cross the threshold of this dilapidated place, curious to experience the energy of Crowley's potent black magic. ◆

▲ Crowley called himself the Great Beast 666.

▼ Satanic scenes and symbols cover the walls of the villa.

BENEVENTO CAMPANIA, ITALY

In this corner of southern Italy, the local dukes drew on supernatural powers before going into battle.

In the 15th century, the town of Benevento in southern Italy had a thriving community of witches, patronized and encouraged by the dukes of Longobard. Animal sacrifices and black magic rituals were daily events in the town, and the dukes sought the witches' help in war.

Before a major battle, the witches would meet under a walnut tree near the town. They would then slaughter an animal and hang its skin from the branches. At nightfall, by the light of burning torches, they ate the skin while riding their horses in circles. They were said to cover themselves in a magic oil to assist their flight.

There were also many other legends about the witches. After their frenzied sabbaths, they were said to fly across the countryside to copulate with men known to be rivals of the dukes of Longobard. While their victims slept, the witches stole their semen and mixed magical poisons for them to drink. Cursing the doomed men forever, they then disappeared in a gust of wind before dawn.

Local people still like to refer to the witches. They will often say, "You are a witch of Benevento" when commenting on a person's intuition or psychic powers. ◆

◄ The witches of Benevento held their sabbaths under a splendid walnut tree.

PIAZZA CASTELLO TURIN, ITALY

The city of Turin is said to be a meeting point for good and bad energy—be careful where you step.

Turin, together with London and San Francisco, is said to form a triangle of black magic, where negative energy aligns. It falls in the center of Piazza Castello, known as the black heart of the city. Eddies of dark energy are reputed to swirl from the west corner of the piazza, sending shivers through passersby even on a hot summer's day.

Yet, bizarrely, Turin is also a city of white magic. The magnificent green and gold gates of the nearby Palazzo Reale, Turin's royal palace, are said to stand on the "white heart" of the city—on one point of an international triangle of white magic, where positive energy aligns and feelings of relief, comfort, and happiness emanate. Prague and the French city of Lyon form the other points in this virtuous triangle.

In Roman times, it was believed that the west was the meeting point for light and dark and good and evil. As Piazza Castello was the most westerly point of Roman Turin, it was the designated place for executions and burials. The remains of a cemetery are said to lie deep beneath the square. Perhaps this is the source of Castello's dark energy. ◆

▲ Palazzo Reale is reputed to stand on one point of a triangle of white magic.

See Also: Würzburg, p. 94

SALEM MASSACHUSETTS, U.S.A.

In 1692 a ferocious witch hunt gripped this New England town, leading to mass hysteria and death.

WHEN REVEREND SAMUEL PARRIS AND HIS FAMILY arrived in Salem from Barbados with their slaves, John and Tituba, the exotic strangers immediately provoked suspicion and foreboding in the town. Matters were made worse when the young Betty Parris, who had listened to many tales of African witchcraft from Tituba, recounted the stories to her new friends. The bored young girls began to dabble in the occult, making talismans, casting spells, and drawing magic circles in the woods.

> She said she had ridden through the air on a pole and attended a witches' sabbath.

In January 1692, Betty and her friends began to have fits. According to Reverend Lawson, a former minister in the town, the girls screamed, threw things around the room, uttered strange noises, and crawled under furniture. When the authorities questioned the friends, the girls accused older members of the community, including Sarah Good, Sarah Osborne, and Tituba herself, of witchcraft.

During the interrogation of the accused women, the girls complained of being pricked with pins and pinched, and soon other young girls and women began to make similar claims. With investigations spreading across Massachusetts, Tituba confessed to being a witch, claiming that the devil's familiar, a huge black dog, had ordered her to hurt the girls. She told investigators she had ridden through the air on a pole with Good and Osborne, and attended a witches' sabbath. She gave the names of those who had signed the devil's book in blood.

> ▼ The witches were hung on Gallows Hill. One of the accused, ex-Salem minister George Burroughs, created consternation by reciting the Lord's Prayer before he died.

The town did not have the authority to try capital cases, but the three women were jailed and locked in irons. Osborne died while in captivity, but Tituba turned from accused to accuser. Hysteria and accusations mounted, and for six months nearly 150 people were imprisoned. Many were the victims of vengeful families or rivals in love. Everyone lived in fear of reprisal.

WITCH HUNTS ON STAGE AND SCREEN

Written by American playwright Arthur Miller and first performed on stage in 1953, *The Crucible* dramatized the Salem witch trials and the story of its main characters. Originally called *The Chronicles of Sarah Good*, it was later adapted by Jean-Paul Sartre for the 1958 movie *Les Sorcières de Salem*. Miller's screenplay for the 1996 movie adaptation, *The Crucible*, directed by Nicholas Hytner, earned him an Academy Award nomination.

In May 1692, a new governor, Sir William Phips, established a court of oyer and terminer (to hear and determine), in which suspected witches could be tried and found guilty. The first to be hung was Bridget Bishop in June of that year, followed by many others, including Sarah Good. Guilt was proved by the "touch" test (by which victims were immediately relieved of their symptoms on touching a witch) or the "falling from sight" test (when a victim collapsed or fainted when looking at the witch).

With prominent people soon under suspicion and accusations still flying, it was not long before the governor's wife was accused. Wisely, Phips dissolved the hearings and closed the court. The hysteria gradually died down. In 1711 Massachusetts Bay became one of the first governments to pardon and compensate the families of victims accused of witchcraft. A memorial to the dead is located at the Old Burying Point, a square with benches engraved with the victims' names. ◆

▲ The 1996 movie *The Crucible* told of the witch trials in Salem and starred Winona Ryder.

MANCHAC SWAMP
FRENIER, LOUISIANA, U.S.A.

A Creole witch is said to float through this steamy swamp, ready to snap up curious visitors.

▲ Mist rises through the Manchac Swamp, the final resting place of the witch Julie Brown.

WHEN TO VISIT

Take a guided boat tour to experience the silent terror of the eerie swamp.

JULIE BROWN WOULD OFTEN PADDLE HER BOAT through Manchac Swamp, along the trails of still black water, past mudflats, sunken tree stumps, and cypress logs draped in moss, through steamy air that was only slightly thinner than the water. The smell of mud and rotting vegetation would rise around her in the morning mist; a sudden whoosh indicated the presence of alligators.

Brown was well known in Frenier, where she was feared by her neighbors but also sought out for her voodoo spells, love potions, and magic charms. One morning in 1915 she wandered through the market singing about her imminent death. Those who could understand her were shocked to hear that when she died she planned to take the whole town with her.

Not long after this her prediction came true and Brown died of mysterious causes. On the day of her funeral, a violent hurricane roared through the town and the swamp, triggering a 30-foot (10 m) tidal wave that killed most of the townspeople, many of whom were attending Brown's funeral.

Fearing the lingering curse of the witch, the survivors buried the dead with Julie Brown in a mass grave that has since been reclaimed by the swamp. It is said that Brown seeks new victims among those who dare take a boat through the alligator-infested water in search of the hidden grave. You will know she is there, they say, if you hear singing. ◆

ST. LOUIS CEMETERY NEW ORLEANS, U.S.A.

Among the many grand mausoleums of this beautiful cemetery lies the queen of voodoo, Marie Laveau.

MARIE LAVEAU WAS BORN a free woman of color in 1794 and died an old woman in 1881. Respected and feared by all, she was a legend in her own lifetime and her supposed tomb in St. Louis Cemetery receives pilgrims to this day.

A devout Catholic, Marie attended Mass daily, but she also became the most famous and powerful voodoo priestess of New Orleans. A skilled herbalist, she was widely consulted on medical matters and would sit with dying patients or condemned prisoners in their final moments, serving them their last meal. Widely sought after by people from all levels of society, Marie helped clients get a lover, keep a lover, or get rid of a lover.

At the age of 25 Marie married Jacques Paris, who mysteriously disappeared six months later. She then lived as common-law wife to Christopher Glapion and went on to have 15 children. The youngest of these, also called Marie, followed in her mother's footsteps.

It is said that if you visit Marie's tomb to petition her, your wish can come true. She accepts money, cigars, white rum, and candy as offerings. Some people mark three crosses on the side of her tomb to activate the magic. In voodoo it is believed that when a priestess dies, her spirit reenters the river of life and moves to the next realm, adjacent to the earthly one. ◆

▲ Laveau (seated) as an old woman in the year before her death

▼ The tomb of the Laveau family in St. Louis Cemetery

See Also: Poveglia Island, p. 24

HELLAM YORK, PENNSYLVANIA, U.S.A.

Deep in the woods beside this small town, an old mental asylum stands on an ominous portal to hell.

IN THE 19TH CENTURY, an isolated mental asylum stood in the woods of Hellam, not far from Toad Road (now Trout Run Road). Mentally ill patients from all over Pennsylvania were sent here. They were bound in straitjackets and locked in cells. Sadistic doctors made the place a living hell. Over time gossip sprang up among the local community that satanic practices took place at the hospital.

When the building caught fire one day, local firefighters arrived too late to stop the inferno. Many of the patients burned to death on the upper floors of the hospital, while hundreds of others fled. Some of the dangerous inmates disappeared into the forest as the fire spread. When the fire was extinguished, officials hunted down the escaped inmates but, believing the escaped inmates were possessed by the devil, they butchered many of those they found.

After the tragedy the townspeople changed the name of the road and tried to put the matter behind them. Many say Trout Run Road and the woods are cursed. Seven barriers along the path to the asylum, erected to keep people out, are reputed to mark seven invisible gateways to hell. It is said that the sense of evil around the fifth gate is palpable, and that whoever manages to pass all seven gates will stand not only on the ruins of the mental hospital, but on the portal to hell itself. ◆

> It is said that whoever passes all seven gates will stand on the portal to hell.

▲ *The Madhouse* by Francisco Goya

TAR RIVER EDGECOMBE COUNTY, NORTH CAROLINA, U.S.A.

Known as the messenger of death, a banshee wails a legendary warning: "As I am, so shall you be."

DURING THE REVOLUTIONARY WAR a young grain merchant from England opened a mill on the side of the Tar River. Sympathetic to the cause of the colonists and the aspirations of the new nation, he provided the local militia with supplies of flour.

In 1781 British redcoats attacked the mill, which they knew to be in the hands of a rebel. Fearing for his life, the miller called upon his knowledge of a local legend about a banshee, a terrifying, vengeful spirit that was a harbinger of death. The miller cried out that the banshee would haunt and curse anyone who killed him. The soldiers laughed, and threw him in the river. As he sank to the bottom, a bloodcurdling scream echoed downstream.

The soldiers set up quarters in the mill, but remained fearful of the miller's curse. One night the banshee appeared in the room where the men slept. Hypnotized by her ghastly spell, all but one man followed her back to the river where they fell into the water and drowned. According to legend, if you hear the banshee's wail, death is imminent. ◆

◀ Beware the banshee on the banks of the Tar River.

DEVIL'S TRAMPING GROUND BENNETT, NORTH CAROLINA, U.S.A.

The devil is said to pace this barren circle, devising ways to destroy the world and bring down mankind.

IN THE WOODS near Harper's Crossroads, close to Bennett, a barren patch of land has long been the subject of conjecture. Nothing has grown within the 40-foot (12 m) circle of land for hundreds of years; objects disappear without a trace; dogs howl unaccountably; and there is a pervading sense of malevolence. It is said that any object placed on the path around the circle will be thrown out into the shrubs.

According to local legend, this is the spot where the devil himself rises from the underworld to pace in eternal circles, thinking up evil plans to destroy the world and cursing those in power on the earth. Few people have dared to spend the night on the devil's tramping ground, but in the 1960s two teenage boys decided to discover the truth about the spot by camping here. While they crouched inside their tent, the wind outside turned into a gale and then a spiraling typhoon. As it intensified, the tent was ripped from the ground. Convinced it was the work of the devil, the boys fled. ◆

▲ The devil is said to be at work in this peaceful corner of North Carolina.

TANTAUCO PARK CHILOÉ ARCHIPELAGO, CHILE

In the remote regions of the Chiloé Archipelago warlocks and their lackeys rule the forests.

▲ The imbunche
is an evil creature
that guards the
warlock's cave.

IN CHILOÉ LEGEND a sudden scream outside a house foreshadows a death within the family. The sound is said to be made by a *chón-chón*—a warlock (male witch) that has shape-shifted into an owl-like creature with gray feathers. If there is a sick person in the house, it is believed the chón-chón will attack their weakened spirit by sucking their blood until death takes hold.

Warlocks are reputed to create evil accomplices known as *imbunche* from newborn male babies stolen from human couples. To ensure the imbunche can never escape, the warlock deforms the baby by breaking one of its legs and twisting it over his head. A magic ointment is then applied to the child's back to produce a thick coat of black hair that will protect the creature from the freezing cold of deepest winter. Destined to guard the warlock's cave, the imbunche lets out bloodcurdling screams to scare off approaching strangers. It is said that anyone who sees an imbunche will be frozen to the spot forever.

Female witches—*brujas*—can transform into birds or animals. They can place people or creatures in a trance, cause illness, death, accidents, and murder, and even raise and lower the sea level. Apprentice brujas cleanse themselves of Christian rites and influences by standing beneath a waterfall for 40 days. They must then kill a loved one and make a pact signed in blood with the devil for the deliverance of their soul. Only then can a witch enter a coven and draw on the power of the devil himself. ◆

WHEN TO VISIT

Warlocks are
said to be the
most active
between
December
and March.

ROSE HALL MONTEGO BAY, JAMAICA

A former mistress schooled in voodoo is said to stalk the halls of this great plantation house.

ONE OF JAMAICA'S FINEST plantation houses, Rose Hall, is steeped in stories of witchcraft. They concern a woman called Annie Palmer, born in England but raised in Haiti by an old Creole nurse, who taught her witchcraft. On reaching adulthood, Annie moved to Jamaica and married John Palmer, the owner of Rose Hall Plantation.

Within months of the marriage, Annie started taking slaves to her bed. One day her husband caught her with a lover and beat her with a riding crop. In revenge Annie murdered him by poisoning his coffee. She then inherited Rose Hall and her reign of terror began.

It was said that Annie murdered any slaves, lovers, or suitors who displeased or bored her. Her cruel behavior, coupled with rumors that she dabbled in voodoo, earned her the name the "White Witch of Rose Hall."

> Annie murdered any slaves, lovers, or suitors who displeased or bored her.

But Annie's invincibility was not to last. She made the fatal mistake of placing a curse on Millicent, the granddaughter of a local witch doctor. At the time Annie was trying to win the love of an English bookkeeper named Robert Rutherford, who loved Millicent. Annie cursed Millicent with a withering disease. Supported by a mob of slaves, the witch doctor strangled Annie.

Annie and her possessions were buried on Rose Hall estate. According to the story, a voodoo ritual was carried out to "lay her ghost," but it was not completed according to strict protocol. Annie's demonic spirit is said to haunt Rose Hall to this day. Subsequent owners suffered early or tragic deaths, and the cursed house was left abandoned for more than 150 years. ◆

▼ Rose Hall before it was restored in the 1960s

5 KEY VOODOO HAUNTS IN THE CARIBBEAN

Vengeful gods, terrifying sorcerers, and death-dealing demons populate the legends and beliefs of the Caribbean, which derive from a potent blend of voodoo, Catholicism, and folklore.

1 PORT-AU-PRINCE, HAITI: In the home of voodoo, the god of death, Gede, is said to stand at the crossroads to the afterworld. Represented as an undertaker, his clothes are black and he wears dark glasses, while his followers are disguised as corpses. Some voodoo sorcerers own a magic stick called a *coco macaque* that walks by itself and is sent out to perform vengeful deeds.

2 VIEUX FORT, ST. LUCIA: Practitioners of obeah, a form of voodoo found on St. Lucia, can bestow authority and riches as well as pain and death. But their power can backfire. One legend tells of a sorcerer who, in the guise of a spirit, used magic dust to drug a man and make love to his wife. One night the dust failed to work, and the husband plunged a knife into the spirit, killing the sorcerer.

▼ A voodoo ceremony takes place around a holy tree.

❸ BRIDGETOWN, BARBADOS: In obeah and voodoo beliefs, a person has two souls—a good soul and an earthly one. In death, the good soul goes to heaven, while the earthly one stays in the coffin for three days. If the earthly soul escapes, it becomes a harmful entity known as a *duppy*. In Barbados, duppies are repelled by walking backward, or by hanging herbs or funeral clothes in a window.

❹ HAVANA, CUBA: When a man is seriously ill in Cuba, the god Icú appears to demand his body and soul. To fool the god, the obeah witch makes a life-size puppet of the dying man, which the man's wife dresses in her husband's clothes and then takes to the cemetery at midnight. Seeing the woman crying over the grave, Icú is convinced that the man is dead and already in the underworld.

❺ LAUDAT, DOMINICA: A devil woman known as La Diablesse lives alone in this village, plotting revenge on cheating husbands. She hides behind trees on lonely roads, waiting to catch them. Although she is beautiful, there is something that betrays her—her cloven hooves. If these are spotted, she must fly toward the safety of Titou Gorge before she turns into a hideous old hag.

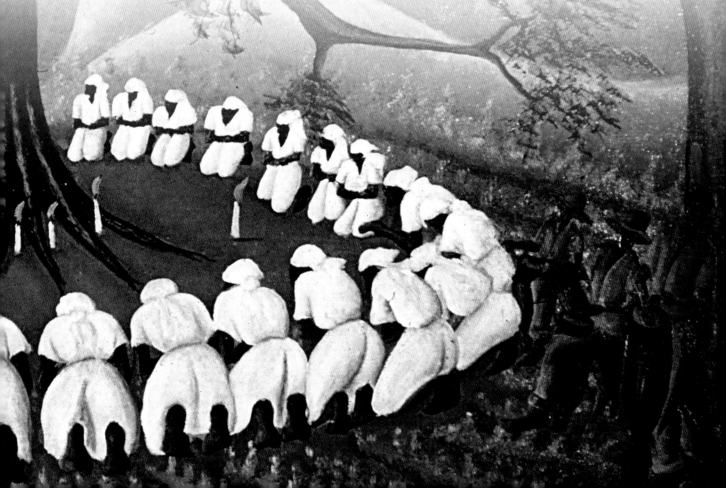

MAYONG ASSAM, INDIA

Known as the land of black magic, this region of India has been a center of witchcraft for centuries.

▲ An uncanny atmosphere pervades Mayong at dawn.

WHEN TO VISIT

Mayong's magic is said to be especially potent during the winter months.

A GOVERNMENT EMPLOYEE TRANSFERRED to Mayong was invited to a feast organized by a villager. He was served with a delicious banquet of steamed pork, fish, and other local delicacies. But one ingredient was missing: There were no chilis. The officer requested chilis from his host. Smiling graciously, the villager clapped his hands, and the chilis came hopping into the room across the floor.

Such tales of witchcraft have entranced the people of Assam for generations. It is said that just the gaze of a witch in Mayong can turn people into animals or subdue a wild tiger. There are countless stories of how magic spells saved the district from attack: Several Mughal texts reveal how the mystics of Mayong stopped a rival army of Emperor Aurangzeb in the mid-17th century. In the 18th century, during an invasion of tribes from nearby Myanmar, magicians cast a spell around Mayong, conjuring up a ring of fire that no enemy could penetrate. An earlier attempt at invasion in 1332 by Muhammad Shah resulted in the whole army perishing without trace in the land of witchcraft. It is said that even today conjurers and mystics come from far and wide to learn at the feet of Mayong's famous magicians. ◆

BHANGARH FORT
RAJASTHAN, INDIA

Tinkling bells and whispering phantoms haunt the ruins of Bhangarh, a site doomed by a double curse.

IN THE 17TH CENTURY, a powerful sorcerer called Balu Nath agreed to the construction of Bhangarh on one condition—that none of its shadows would fall upon his home. It is said that a later prince ignored this proviso and raised the palace to a height that plunged Balu Nath's house into darkness. In retribution, the sorcerer placed a curse on the town.

According to another 17th-century legend, Princess Ratnavati, known as the jewel of Rajasthan, began to receive offers of marriage from princes in far-off lands on her 18th birthday. A young sorcerer in Bhangarh, Singhia, was in love with the princess, and fearing she would leave Bhangarh, decided to cast a love spell over her. Spotting the princess and her maid buying perfumed oils in the market, he pulled out his magic sword and drew a symbol in the air, turning the oil into a love potion that would enchant the princess as soon as it touched her skin. But the princess poured the oil on the ground and walked away. When the oil struck the ground, it turned into a boulder that rolled across the square and crushed the sorcerer. As he lay dying, he cursed Bhangarh and all who lived there.

The following year the princess was butchered in a battle, and famine swept through Bhangarh. The town and its fort were abandoned.

Today, the fort is a beautiful ruin, closed to tourists between sunset and sunrise. According to many, the once illustrious Bhangarh is waiting for the princess to return and end the curse. ◆

▲ Singhia's sword could turn oil into a magic love potion.

▼ The haunting ruins of Bhangarh await the return of Princess Ratnavati.

AOKIGAHARA FOREST HONSHU, JAPAN

An inescapable sense of death and darkness pervades this forest at the foot of Mount Fuji.

KNOWN AS THE SEA OF TREES, the foreboding Aokigahara Forest spreads around the base of Mount Fuji, Japan's highest mountain. Dark and ominous and draped in giant creepers, the forest is eerily silent. The sheer density of trees means that the forest is windless. There is no wildlife here, and the ice caverns never melt. Compasses are said to malfunction in the forest.

In Japanese legend, Mount Fuji is believed to be a gateway to heaven where the fire goddess Fuji first descended to earth, her fiery tracks scouring deep channels of supernatural energy down the mountainside. Working like a magnet, this energy is said to prevent anyone who enters the forest from escaping.

Demon spirits called *yurei* are said to haunt the forest slopes. They are reputed to be the trapped souls of those

> There is no wildlife, the ice caverns never melt; compasses malfunction.

who did not atone for their sins before their death. According to Japanese mythology, one particular demon is the *tengu*, a destructive creature in bird form. One notorious 12th-century tengu was believed to be the specter of Emperor Sutoku. Forced by his father to abandon the throne and go into exile, the wandering Sutoku died in torment, swearing to haunt the nation as an evil monster. Using his long talons and eagle eyes, the tengu began to hunt young boys and priests, eating their genitalia to empower his half-human form. The boys were often returned to their homes castrated and weeping, but the priests would be tied upside down to the trees in Aokigahara Forest until they died or went mad. ◆

▲ Hokusai's woodblock print of Mount Fuji captures the mountain's grandeur.

JOREN FALLS
IZU, SHIZUOKA, JAPAN

A demonic spider weaves a web of death at this famous Japanese waterfall.

IN JAPANESE FOLKLORE a *jorogumo* is a spider that acquires magical powers upon becoming 400 years old. Transforming into a seductive female demon, the spider lures men to their death.

One legend tells of a man who suddenly found his feet trapped in a spider's web as he stopped to rest at the foot of the Joren Falls. He cut the threads and tied them to a tree stump, but the web pulled up the stump, forcing him backward into the water, where he drowned.

According to the legend, the villagers stopped going to the waterfall after this, for fear of the evil spider. However, one day, a woodsman from another village, chopping wood in the trees around the falls, saw a beautiful woman bathing naked. Overcome with desire, he visited the falls every day, seeking out the secret bather. But each time he went he grew weaker.

In an attempt to shake off the curse, the woodsman engaged a monk from a nearby temple to go with him to the waterfall and read out a Buddhist prayer. On hearing the chanting, the woman changed back into a spider and entangled the men in a silken web. Although the prayer proved powerful, and the men broke free and fled, the infatuated woodsman foolishly ran back to find the enchantress. Caught in the silk threads, he fell into the waterfall, never to surface again. ◆

▲ The dangerous jorogumo spider changes into an evil temptress, trapping men in her web.

▼ The beautiful Joren Falls are deceptively serene.

See Also: Rawang, p. 79

BANGKOK THAILAND

A disembodied head swoops through the villages and forests of Thailand, dripping blood and entrails.

▲ With hair and entrails flying, the krasue is a terrifying demon who preys on pregnant women.

WHEN TO VISIT

In the month of December you may spot the krasue flying low in the cooler air.

COMMON TO LEGENDS ACROSS SOUTHEAST ASIA is a demon that manifests as the disembodied head of a beautiful woman. Known in Thailand as the *krasue*, the head is evil in nature, with viscera hanging from its open neck.

According to Thai folklore, the krasue is the spirit of a Khmer princess who was promised in an arranged marriage to a powerful nobleman. Her true love, though, was a soldier. When the prince caught her with her lover, he sentenced her to be burned at the stake. Just before the execution the princess spoke to a sorceress, who cast a spell over her body to protect it from the flames. The spell was powerful, but too late, and only the princess's head and some of her viscera were saved. From then on, her remains were destined to haunt the land forever.

The krasue is sometimes thought to be the spirit of a dead woman cursed for aborting her child. The spirit takes revenge on others by using a proboscis-like tongue to scoop out the fetus or placenta in a woman's womb. To protect pregnant women, relatives place thorny branches around the house to stop the krasue from floating through the windows. After delivery, the woman's relatives may take the placenta far away for burial in order to hide it from the krasue. During the day, the krasue may disguise itself as an old woman, but if it fails to find a decapitated corpse before daybreak, it is said to die in terrible pain. ◆

BAHLA AD DAKHILIYAH, OMAN

At the foot of the Jebel Akhdar, djinn, or evil spirits, haunt the sandstone towers of a fortified town.

AN IMPORTANT TOWN on ancient trade routes, Bahla was reputed to be a center of black magic long before the arrival of Islam. There are many legends about its dark past, especially concerning people who vanish or change into animals.

Recent archaeological work to restore Bahla's fort, in keeping with its status as a UNESCO World Heritage site, have been frustrated by unseen forces. Work completed during one day is often reported vandalized by the next morning, in spite of the excellent security. It is widely believed that demon spirits are responsible.

More than 1,000 years ago, the villagers of Bahla are reputed to have stoned a man to death for practicing wizardry. The foundations of the fort were supposedly built over his grave to prevent his disciples from turning it into a shrine. According to local stories, the man's ghost began to appear in the back alleyways, and rumors circulated that he was teaching black magic from beyond the grave. With the completion of the huge fortress in the 13th century, the sorcerer turned his attention to tribal leaders, wreaking death and destruction among them.

A bewitched frankincense tree in the heart of Bahla's old souk was once believed to harbor the wizard's soul. It was reported that if anyone from outside Bahla touched the tree, great misfortune and an untimely death would befall them. When the tree was eventually cut down, it reputedly burst into flames when the ax struck the trunk, destroying all around it. It is said that the ancient wizard still haunts the labyrinth of mud-brick dwellings around the fort. ◆

▲ A bewitched frankincense tree was said to contain the soul of the evil wizard until it was cut down.

▼ Bahla's ancient fort rises above the town in the shadow of the Jebel Akhdar.

DURBAN KWA-ZULU NATAL, SOUTH AFRICA

Zulu legends are full of demons, but the *tokoloshe* is especially feared, even by modern city dwellers.

ACROSS THE DRY SAVANNAS, in remote mountain villages, and even in the heart of Durban city, modern South Africans regard Zulu folklore with respect and terror. A particularly potent story concerns the *tokoloshe*, a demon spirit that disguises itself as a human. Sorcerers employ tokoloshes to harm, curse, or frighten people.

Resembling zombies with gouged-out eyes, tokoloshes may simply scare robbers away, or cause serious illness and death to enemies. They are said to impregnate sleeping virgins, who then raise the demon children as their own, unaware of their true nature.

Only a witch doctor is said to be able to really banish the demon, although a common way to stop a tokoloshe from impregnating a virgin is to raise her bed on bricks so that the tokoloshe cannot reach her.

Belief in the tokoloshe remains strong to this day and newspapers often run stories on people who claim experience of its evil influence. During the 1970s, one Zulu witness described how a tokoloshe had possessed his wife. Fearful she would give birth to a terrible monster, the man consulted a witch doctor. After many spells and rituals, the woman gave birth, but the baby's legs were deformed, and the skin red and raw as if burned. The witch doctor cast a special spell to rid the child of the demon, and within a few months, the man said, the child's skin and legs were cured. ◆

◀ Witch doctors can cast out the tokoloshe.

ASABA DELTA STATE, NIGERIA

A long history of rivalry has led to a vigorous belief in witchcraft among the tribes of the Niger Delta.

IN THE SWEEPING DELTA of the Niger River, there is a belief among the Igbo people that their Yako neighbors enlist the help of witches in campaigns against them. These witches are said to kill their victims at night by sucking out their heart and blood until the body is drained of fluid. Witches may also crush the airways of the Igbo while they sleep, or sit on their rooftops, casting spells.

It is also believed that these Yako witches can control a victim's recently departed spirit to terrorize their grieving family. The witch is said to cut out the corpse's tongue, drive a peg into the brain to create a zombie, and then send it to hypnotize another victim in the dead of night.

It is believed the Yako witches may have been summoned in error by a shaman propitiating the spirits of the Igbo ancestors. Traditionally, if the souls of the ancestors did not respond, the shaman would elicit the help of unknown spiritual entities. It is said among the Igbo that a Yako witch usurped a good ancestral spirit, causing death and destruction among the innocent. ◆

▲ The witching hour on the Niger Delta, where belief in the supernatural is still strong

MOUNT KEIRA SCOUT CAMP

WOLLONGONG, NEW SOUTH WALES, AUSTRALIA

In the subtropical rain forests of Australia's eastern coast, a flesh-eating devil is waiting to pounce.

WITH ITS LIVID RED SKIN, oversize head, protruding veins, and fingers and toes like octopus suckers, the *yara-ma-yha-who* of Aboriginal mythology sits monkey-like in the foliage of fig trees. It likes nothing better, they say, than the towering Moreton Bay fig in Mount Keira Scout Camp, near the town of Wollongong. The creature's toothless mouth can open wide enough to engulf a whole human being.

The yara-ma-yha-who spends its days lying in wait for an unsuspecting man or woman to sit down and rest at the base of the tree. Once the victim is sound asleep, the gruesome creature clambers down the trunk, clamps its suckers to their skin, and syphons off the blood until the very brink of death. Too weak to escape, the victim must lie immobile until the yara-ma-yha-who returns to swallow them whole. After washing down its meal at the nearest river, the yara-ma-yha-who takes to the fig tree to digest and sleep. The next day it regurgitates its victim whole and unharmed, as though the attack never happened.

According to aboriginal myth, a yara-ma-yha-who hunts only by day. It never misses an opportunity to attack the same person twice, or even multiple times. On each occasion the grotesque creature leaves the victim a little smaller and paler, and a little keener to taste blood for himself. The Aboriginals say that anyone foolish enough to sleep more than a few nights under a Moreton Bay fig tree will turn into a yara-ma-yha-who before the day is out. ◆

▲ Red and naked like a fetus, the yara-ma-yha-who fixes its prey with its sucker-tipped fingers and toes.

▼ The yara-ma-yha-who likes to sit in the branches of this large Moreton Bay fig tree.

▲ A 19th-century engraving of the entrance to the temple of Abu Simbel

SACRED

PLACES

STONEHENGE WILTSHIRE, ENGLAND

On a windswept plain in southern England stands one of the world's most evocative ancient sites.

THOUSANDS OF PEOPLE GATHER AT STONEHENGE for the summer solstice on June 21, when the main axis of the stones aligns almost perfectly with the sunrise. Among them are many modern-day Druids, upholders of ancient Britain's "old religion." The 17th-century English historian John Aubrey believed megalithic sites such as Stonehenge were places of worship for ancient Druids (see panel).

Radiocarbon and bluestone analysis date Stonehenge to between 3000 and 2000 B.C., with several phases of construction, beginning with a circular ditch and bank dug with antler horns. The stones were raised from around 2600 B.C., with the smaller bluestones hauled here from southwest Wales, 156 miles (250 km) away—a considerable feat for Neolithic man.

Many theories and legends are attached to the site. In 1136 the monk Geoffrey of Monmouth wrote a purported history of the kings of Britain in which he claimed the wizard Merlin transported the stone circle from Ireland at the behest of Ambrosius Aurelianus, King of the Britons. According to Monmouth, Ambrosius wished to build a memorial to the Britons who had been tricked and murdered by the invading Saxons on Salisbury Plain.

Monmouth states that Ambrosius was buried at Stonehenge, and he makes the same claim for Uther Pendragon, the father of King Arthur. Monmouth also claims that Merlin tutored King Arthur here, marking the beginning of Arthur's association with the site.

> Monmouth claimed Merlin transported the stones by magic from Ireland.

▼ The stark and haunting outline of Stonehenge on Salisbury Plain

DRUID MAGIC Although there is no doubt that Druids were important in ancient British society, there is no clear evidence of their exact function. According to Julius Caesar, Suetonius, and Cicero, among others, Druids practiced sorcery and performed human sacrifices. Modern commentators, however, have questioned the idea that even primitive people should have venerated murderous magicians, and suggested that these early historians were merely recording gossip that blackened the reputation of Rome's enemies. In the absence of reliable data, it seems more likely that the Druids were respected elders who dispensed advice and justice to their fellow men and women.

Outside the main entrance to Stonehenge stands the so-called Heel Stone or Friar's Heel, a rough, tapered stone, 16 feet (5 m) high, that leans inward toward the stone circle. At the time of the summer solstice, anyone standing within the stone circle and looking northeast, through the entrance to the site, will see the sun rise above the Heel Stone. According to one legend, this stone was thrown into place by the devil, who had bought all the standing stones from a woman in Ireland, then wrapped them in a cloth and carried them to Salisbury Plain. When the devil triumphantly shouted out that no one would know how these mysterious stones came to be here, a passing friar laughed at the arrogant remark. Furious that he had been overheard by someone, the devil threw one of the stones at the priest, striking him hard on the heel. The stone then sank deep into the ground and became known forevermore as the Heel Stone or Friar's Heel. ◆

▲ A Druid holding a ceremonial sickle and sword to cut mistletoe. According to the Roman writer Pliny the Elder, Druids used mistletoe to cure infertility.

LUD'S CHURCH
STAFFORDSHIRE, ENGLAND

Swirling mist and mossy banks create an elemental atmosphere in this deep natural chasm.

HIGH ABOVE THE hamlet of Gradbach a deep cleft in the rock, created by a landslip millions of years ago, encompasses a primeval microworld. Sun penetrates the secret chasm only once a year, on midsummer's day. Known as Lud's Church, it is named after a Celtic river god associated with mythical fertility figures, such as the Green Man and the Fisher King. It has been a refuge for runaways and renegades for centuries.

In the 15th century, a group of religious dissidents known as the Lollards met in the forested area around the site. Led by John Wycliffe, the Lollards were persecuted for their religious beliefs. Some Lollards claim the name of the chasm refers to Walter de Ludank, who was captured here one night as he attended a secret meeting.

A ship's figurehead, nicknamed Lady Lud, said to commemorate the death of the daughter of one of the Lollard preachers, once stood in a high niche above the chasm, placed there by a forest landowner in 1862.

The magical silence, mossy hollows, and dewy ferns of this secret spot create a mysterious and elemental atmosphere in which pagan gods and goddesses can easily be imagined. It is said that a ghostly huntsman, covered from head to toe in moss and leaves, like the Green Man of English folklore, roams through the woodland around the site. According to a local story, his horse stopped suddenly on the edge of the chasm and threw him into the rocky cleft. ◆

▲ The legendary King Lud flanked by his sons, Androgeus (left) and Theomantius

▼ The moss-covered rocks and gnarled trees around Lud's Church lend it a primordial atmosphere.

NEWGRANGE COUNTY MEATH, IRELAND

For millennia people have witnessed the winter solstice in the inner chamber of this Neolithic temple.

AROUND 5,000 YEARS AGO, priests and rulers squeezed through the passageway of Newgrange annually to mark the winter solstice—the day when the sun is at its lowest in the sky. They waited until the precise moment when a narrow beam of light penetrated the roofbox, an opening above the entrance of the temple, and then fell upon the floor. The event marked the start of the new year.

People still go to witness the winter solstice at Newgrange, though entry to the sanctuary is now controlled by lottery. As the sun rises on December 21, the beam widens and fills the whole room with light—a phenomenon that begins around 9 a.m. and lasts for 17 minutes. Newgrange is constructed from quartz crystal, a stone known for its luminosity, and which was thought by some to link earth and sky, thus symbolizing the life force or spirit.

> As the sun rises higher, the beam widens and fills the whole room with light.

In pre-Christian Celtic mythology, the significance of Newgrange (known in Irish as Brú na Bóinne) arises from the story of the warrior god Dagda and the water nymph Boann, who loved each other but had to keep their affair secret because they were both married to other deities.

Dagda therefore made the sun stand still for nine months so that Boann could conceive and give birth in only 24 hours, before anyone noticed she was pregnant.

Their child was Angus, the god of youth and poetry. When Angus grew up, he fell in love with Caer Ibormeith, a goddess who took the form of a swan. The only way he could win her was by becoming a swan himself. Having changed his shape, he flew off with his sweetheart to his birthplace, which thereafter became a shrine where he was worshipped. ◆

▲ Intricately engraved stones form part of the monument.

CARNAC STONES   BRITTANY, FRANCE

Mysterious megaliths in southern Brittany share the same alignment as Pythagoras's theorem.

APPROXIMATELY 4,000 MEGALITHS cover fields around Carnac on the south coast of Brittany—a mesmerizing army of silent knights erected by pre-Celtic people in about 4000 B.C. According to legend they are Roman soldiers petrified by God for persecuting St. Cornelius, a local saint. They form three distinct groups, known as Ménec, Kermario, and Kerlescan.

Many theories attempt to explain the forest of stones. Some hold that they mark out a pathway to an ancient temple that has long disappeared; others refer to the stones' alignment with the sunlight at the winter and summer solstices, positing that they were part of an ancient astronomical observatory.

The most widely accepted theory is that the stones form a huge necropolis in which the graves and bones

Did an extraterrestrial civilization worship its own galaxy from here?

have eroded away completely while the granite stones remain standing. The larger megaliths found in the area are generally considered to have been tombs, while the tumuli (earth mounds) have yielded grave goods, such as stone chests, beads, and ax heads.

Some have observed that the stones align to the mathematical geometry of Pythagoras's theorem, an observation that raises more questions than answers. However, Pythagoras was born ca 570 B.C.—long after these stones were erected. Could it be that a highly intelligent, extraterrestrial civilization used this corner of southern Brittany to communicate with its own distant galaxy? ◆

▼ The Ménec alignment is formed of 11 converging rows of different-size stones.

LASCAUX CAVES DORDOGNE, FRANCE

Did the four teenagers who discovered these Paleolithic caves stumble upon an astronomical map?

ONE HOT SUMMER IN 1940, Marcel Ravidat and three friends, Jacques Marsal, Georges Agnel, and Simon Coencas, entered a cave that they had stumbled upon near the village of Montignac. With a small flashlight, they gazed in wonder at what they saw—extraordinary depictions of animals all over the walls.

The Lascaux cave paintings are estimated to be 17,300 years old. About 900 of the images have been identified as animals, including equines, stags, cattle, bison, felines, and even a bear and a rhinoceros. One of the larger caves, the Great Hall of the Bulls, includes a 17-foot-long (5 m) bull, one of the biggest individual figures in cave art.

However, that may not be all. Some believe the figurative images in the Great Hall may together represent an astronomical map, with specific points on the major figures corresponding to constellations as they would have appeared during the Paleolithic period. Some researchers suggest the paintings may tell more mysterious stories, or have spiritual or symbolic significance. A bird-man lies on the ground with an erect phallus, one claw-like hand pointing to a bison, the other to a bird on the end of a stick. What does this symbolize? ◆

▲ The Great Hall of the Bulls

THE ALTAMIRA CAVES Sixty years before the Lascaux find, this subterranean complex in northern Spain was rediscovered by chance after having been hidden for 15,000 years behind a rockfall at the entrance. The Paleolithic wall paintings at Altamira (right) were executed using techniques that had previously been assumed to be Common Era developments.

See Also: Knossos, p. 222

CHARTRES LABYRINTH FRANCE

Chartres Cathedral contains one of the great labyrinths, once a feature of many Gothic cathedrals.

Set into the floor of Chartres Cathedral is an extraordinary 13th-century labyrinth. Measuring 42 feet (12.9 m) in diameter, it completely covers the width of the nave. Chairs usually obscure the view, but these are cleared away on Fridays between February and November so that visitors can follow the path of the labyrinth and experience the curious draw of its center.

In the Middle Ages, clergy used labyrinths to mark out their Easter dances. But labyrinths also symbolized the path taken by pilgrims to the cathedral, and represented the final stage of their journey. Later, the Christian church ordered labyrinths to be removed from cathedrals in Europe on account of their pagan origins. Somehow the labyrinth at Chartres escaped.

In ancient Greek mythology, Daedalus built a labyrinth to imprison the Minotaur beneath King Minos's palace at Knossos (see p. 222). The plaque at the center of the Chartres labyrinth was originally engraved with a scene of Theseus killing the Minotaur, and Ariadne holding the thread that enabled Theseus to find his way out of the maze. During the French Revolution, people ripped out the plaque and melted it down for cannon. ◆

▲ No one has yet cracked the symbolic significance of the labyrinth.

WINDOWS TO THE SOUL Chartres has three 13th-century rose windows. The western rose depicts the Last Judgment, with angels blowing trumpets to summon the dead from their tombs. The rose above the north transept is dedicated to the Virgin, and shows doves and adoring angels, while the rose window to the south is dedicated to Christ.

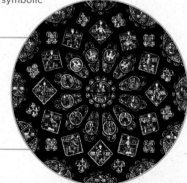

MONT SAINT-MICHEL
NORMANDY, FRANCE

This fairy-tale castle can be seen for miles around, the spire of its abbey church soaring heavenward.

AT SUNSET, THE SANDS and tidal pools of the Baie de Saint-Michel glow a deep red, throwing the monastery of Mont Saint-Michel in sharp relief against the skyline. The French writer Guy de Maupassant compared this ancient Christian isle at sunset to a "gigantic jewel, cut like a cameo and as dainty as lace." Others attribute the red glow of the sunset to the bloody ghosts of 2,000 Englishmen killed by the garrison here during the Hundred Years' War, when it withstood a long and bloody siege by the English.

The island was a Gallic-Roman stronghold in the fifth and sixth centuries, and was ransacked by the Franks in the eighth century. According to Christian legend, in A.D. 708, the archangel Michael appeared to St. Aubert, the Bishop of Avranches, and told him to build a church on the rocky islet. Aubert initially ignored the angel's instruction but quickly changed his mind when Michael reprimanded the bishop by burning a hole in his skull with his finger.

> The archangel Michael burned a hole in Aubert's skull with his finger.

Like Rome and Santiago de Compostela, Mont Saint-Michel was one of the spiritual and intellectual centers of the Middle Ages and has therefore become an important place of pilgrimage. For nearly 1,000 years, men, women, and children have journeyed to the mount, braving the perilous quicksands and tides. During the French Revolution (1789–1799), monasticism was abolished in France, and the abbey became a prison. Some 300 monks were incarcerated in the dungeons. The abbey was restored at the end of the 19th century. ◆

▲ Part of the mainland in prehistoric time, Mont Saint-Michel emerged as an island as the sea level rose.

EXTERNSTEINE

NEAR DETMOLD, GERMANY

Five sandstone pillars in Germany's Teutoburg Forest are said to have mystical significance.

WEATHERED INTO extraordinary shapes over millions of years, the rock pillars known as Externsteine rise abruptly out of the forest—they are primordial and totemic. Stone tools discovered in the vicinity suggest humankind has lived in the area since prehistoric times, while astronomical alignments with the pillars may indicate ancient cosmological or sacred significance.

Records show that Christian hermits lived in freezing caves at the base of the pillars where they sought to drive out the pagan power attributed to the rocks. Over time, the monks cut staircases into the pillars and carved sculptures in the walls, including a depiction of Christ's descent from the Cross. In the 12th century, Externsteine became a place of worship for knights returning from the Crusades. Later still local counts used the pillars as a fortress, a pleasure palace, and even a prison.

People ascribe supernatural properties to the five pillars. Some speculate that holes driven into the rock are entry points into the earth or channels for the release of powerful planetary energy. New Age mystics and Druids gather below the pillars for the summer and winter solstices, and on Walpurgis Night (the Night of the Witches on April 30).

The tallest pillar is topped by a roofless chapel accessed by a metal bridge. Its rock-cut altar lights up with the first rays of the sun at the summer solstice; the sunlight falls through a small round window cut into the rock above, as does the most northerly rising of the moon. ◆

▲ In the Middle Ages, monks inhabited the base of the pillars.

▼ Humankind has been fascinated by the pillars since prehistoric times.

BOLSHOI ZAYATSKY ISLAND RUSSIA

Who placed the stone labyrinths on this seemingly insignificant island, and for what purpose?

STREWN ACROSS A TINY, desolate island in Russia's White Sea is a unique collection of structures dating from around 3000 B.C. They include more than 30 stone labyrinths, stone barrows, and sanctuaries, hundreds of piles of stone, and a stone symbol resembling a spoked wheel that is believed to represent the sun.

The labyrinths, clustered on the western part of the island, are especially curious. Between 20 feet (6 m) and 80 feet (24 m) in diameter, they were formed with lines of boulders. The lines are twisted like spirals, and the entrance of each labyrinth is also its exit.

Archaeologists have long pondered the significance of the labyrinths. Could they symbolize a shrine or sanctuary where ancient people prepared for the afterlife, or do they represent the actual boundary between earth and the underworld, a final stopping place before death? Were the labyrinths a channel in which specific rituals helped ease the soul of the dead into the underworld?

In ancient Slavic myth, people worshipped the earth, sealed oaths by touching it, and confessed their sins into the earth before death. All rituals and prayers were performed in the open air, and every rock and stone was sacred. Was this tiny island considered to be a sacred repository of earth's energy? ◆

▲ Labyrinth on the western end of Bolshoi Zayatsky Island

SWEDEN'S STONE MAZES The Trojaborg labyrinth in Gotland dates from abound 1000 B.C. Comprising several hundred stones, it is one of more than 300 similar labyrinths in Sweden. According to local superstition, if you succeed in walking along the twisting path without moving any of the stones you will receive good luck and happiness.

GODDESS TEMPLES MALTA AND GOZO

The islands of Malta and Gozo are home to a vibrant goddess culture dating back 6,000 years.

GGANTIJA TEMPLES, GOZO

The Neolithic temples on the island of Gozo were built between 3600 B.C. and 2500 B.C., making them older than the Egyptian pyramids. Also erected to honor a fertility goddess, they stand in a green and fertile spot fed by springs. Some people have pointed out that the curvature of the Ggantija temples resembles the female form. The rounded thighs, arms, breasts, and head of a woman—similar to the voluptuous figurines of the mother goddess discovered in Malta's Temple of Hagar Qim—are seen most clearly in the South Temple. According to Gozo mythology, a giantess built the temples and ordered the islanders to worship her—hence the name Ggantija (Maltese for "giant").

The curvature of the temples resembles the female form.

MNAJDRA TEMPLE COMPLEX, MALTA

The discovery of bone fragments, shards of pottery, and signs of fire scorching have led archaeologists to deduce that human beings have lived on Malta since at least 5200 B.C. From around 4000 B.C., the islands were the center of a sophisticated goddess culture, with worship taking place in temples. Archaeologists know from astronomical alignments of the Mnajdra temple complex—their near-perfect alignment with the sun's rays has occurred only twice in the last 15,000 years—that it dates from about 3700 B.C. The lowest temple was probably used as an astronomical observatory or a calendrical site. At the time of the equinoxes, sunlight passes through its main doorway and lights up the major axis. On the solstices, sunlight illuminates the edges of megaliths to the left and right of the doorway.

▼ The Mnajdra Temple complex on Malta

WORSHIP OF THE MOTHER GODDESS Throughout the world, before patriarchal civilizations created their own band of potent male gods, primitive societies revered a mother goddess, often referred to simply as the goddess. Excessively voluptuous, she embodied fertility, motherhood, bounty, and the sacred power of earth itself. People paid homage to the goddess with offerings and sacrifices. Sometimes she was upheld as a symbol of peace. Many archaeological excavations throughout the Mediterranean and in the Middle East have unearthed fat lady statues. In Malta, archaeologists uncovered three figurines in the Temple of Hagar Qim.

TARXIEN TEMPLES, MALTA

The temple period on Malta reached its peak with these three connected temples dating from around 3100 B.C. Their intricate stonework includes carvings of domestic animals, and spiral designs decorate the altars and screens. A chamber set into the thickness of the wall between the South and Central temples contains a relief showing a bull and a sow. This chamber is believed to be an ancient site for ritual sacrifice in honor of the mother goddess. An underground ritual chamber known as the Hypogeum represents the goddess's regenerative womb.

The fortuitous rediscovery of this site by farmers plowing the fields in 1914 was of immense significance, not only archaeologically, but also to Malta's sense of nationhood. The completion of the excavation works after World War II confirmed to the Maltese that their culture was ancient, and helped to strengthen the political movement for independence from Britain, which was eventually achieved in 1964. ◆

▲ One of three "fat lady" figurines discovered in Malta's Temple of Hagar Qim

CATHEDRAL OF SANTIAGO DE COMPOSTELA GALICIA, SPAIN

The most popular pilgrimage route in Europe has its origins in the pagan "Route of the Stars."

▲ The apostles load the body of St. James onto a boat bound for Spain.

WHEN TO VISIT

Come early in the day in May or June, when the cathedral is most peaceful.

ACCORDING TO THE NEW TESTAMENT, after the Resurrection of Christ the apostles left the Holy Land to spread the Gospel across the Roman Empire. The apostle James, it is said, went to Spain. On his return to Palestine in A.D. 44, King Herod Agrippa arrested the apostle and sentenced him to death.

Following the execution, James's fellow disciples retrieved James's body, laid it in a marble sarcophagus, and placed it in a boat at Jaffa. From there, the current carried the body to Iria Flavia on the Spanish coast, where St. James (Santiago in Spanish) was secretly buried in a forest. Centuries later, celestial music and a guiding star led a hermit to the grave. The place became known as the "field of the star," or *compostela*, on which the Cathedral of Santiago de Compostela is now said to stand.

Over the centuries, a popular pilgrimage route grew up between northern Europe and the cathedral. Known as the Way of St. James, it is still used by thousands of pilgrims seeking forgiveness, penance, and miracles, as well as hikers on a more general journey of spiritual discovery inspired by the scenery. Yet the well-loved route has another, pre-Christian purpose that few of the pilgrims or hikers know about—it was an old Roman trade route that followed stars in the Milky Way, and was often referred to as the "Route of the Stars." ◆

SAN MINIATO BASILICA FLORENCE, ITALY

What mystical messages lie behind the enigmatic artworks in this beautiful Florentine church?

THE BASILICA DI SAN MINIATO is an artistic and theosophical puzzle, for its decoration and structure incorporate many pagan as well as Christian symbols. Especially intriguing are the carvings in the apse and the zodiac floor mosaic in the nave, both the work of a team of unknown stonemasons although one name—Ioseph (Joseph)—has been incorporated into the inscription of the zodiac. Some accounts suggest these masons may have belonged to a heretical organization that subscribed to ancient Jewish, Egyptian, and Greek mystical traditions and had knowledge of astrology and alchemy.

The inscription accompanying the zodiac—a poorly written hybrid of Greek and Latin—includes the names of the planets Venus, Mercury, and Saturn, as well as the sun and the moon. It also reveals the alignment of planets in the constellation of Taurus on the day the masons laid the zodiac stones. Some commentators believe the reference to this alignment indicates the masons' belief in the dawning of a new and brighter period in history.

In the early 13th century, Italian theologian Joachim di Fiore prophesied the coming of the Antichrist and the end of the world. Widespread belief in the prediction caused much social and psychological misery. Did the Taurus alignment in the heavens symbolize something very different for Ioseph and his fellow initiates—not the end of the world, but the beginning of something eternal that neither time nor mortality could erode? Could the secrets of this new cycle be contained in the marble floor of the basilica? ◆

> Joachim di Fiore prophesied the coming of the Antichrist and the end of the world.

▼ San Miniato is a Romanesque jewel box, incorporating both pagan and Christian symbols.

CUMAE ARCHAEOLOGICAL PARK POZZUOLI, NEAR NAPLES, ITALY

A womb-like cave at Cumae purports to be the seat of the sibyl consulted by the Trojan hero Aeneas.

ANCIENT CUMAE lies on the edge of the Phlegraean Fields, a volcanic area on the Bay of Naples, often compared to Hades, the underworld in ancient Greek mythology. Cumae was famous because of the Cumaean sibyl (prophetess). Aeneas consults the Cumaean sibyl before entering the underworld in Virgil's *Aeneid*.

The sibyls were known throughout ancient Greece and Rome for their ability to speak the oracles of Apollo. The Cumaean sibyl tried to sell nine volumes of her prophecies to King Tarquin, promising that they would protect Rome. To begin with Tarquin laughed at her, but when the sibyl began burning the volumes, he bought the remaining three volumes and placed them in the Temple of Jupiter, where the Senate consulted them on important occasions.

> The Senate consulted the prophecies on momentous occasions.

Two of the books were destroyed by fire in 83 B.C., and the last in A.D. 405. Some viewed the invasion of the Visigoths in A.D. 415 as the fulfillment of the sibyl's prophecy.

Modern visitors to Cumae can enter a womb-like cave that purports to be the sanctuary of the sibyl. The approach is via a long tunnel that is often likened to the birth canal.

▲ The tunnel leading to the sibyl's cave, where people seeking an audience with the sibyl would wait their turn

TEMPLE OF OLYMPIAN ZEUS ATHENS, GREECE

The imperious strength of the father of the gods is embodied in this temple to Zeus in central Athens.

IN GREEK MYTH, ZEUS was the ruler of Mount Olympus, the home of the gods. The master of many guises, he was portrayed as both a benefactor and a tyrant, revered and feared in equal measure. Wildly irresponsible, he was also an infamous womanizer, who ravaged nymphs and fathered hundreds of children.

Zeus's most unfortunate lover was the priestess Semele. When she became pregnant with his child, she made Zeus promise he would prove his divinity. Forced to fulfill his vow, he came to Semele as a bolt of lightning, and incinerated her. Zeus saved the unborn fetus and sewed it into his thigh, where it later emerged as Dionysus. When the child grew up, he rescued his mother from the underworld and took her to Olympus.

The Temple of Zeus was intended to be the greatest temple in the world when work began in the sixth century B.C. However, it was not completed for another 600 years, and its glory was brief. By the third century A.D. it was in ruins. Nowadays, the modern city of Athens spreads around the temple, but the imposing columns still hint at the power of the god who inspired it. ◆

▲ The Temple of Olympian Zeus in Athens

THE TWELVE OLYMPIANS The major deities in Greek mythology, often portrayed on pottery (right), resided on Mount Olympus. Chief among them were Zeus and his wife, Hera; Poseidon, the god of the oceans; Demeter, the fertility goddess; Athena, the goddess of wisdom; and Apollo, the sun god. The others were Artemis, Aphrodite, Hermes, Hestia, Ares, and Dionysus.

See Also: Externsteine, p. 130

GÖREME OPEN AIR MUSEUM CAPPADOCIA, TURKEY

In a landscape sculpted by erosion, the Göreme Open Air Museum brings early Christianity to life.

O VER THE MILLENNIA, WIND AND RAIN WORKED THEIR MAGIC on the soft rock of the Cappadocia region, carving out a spectacular landscape of dramatic gorges, phallus-shaped cones, and soaring pinnacles known as fairy chimneys.

In the fourth century A.D., Christian monks began to inhabit these natural structures, turning them into cave churches, chapels, and monasteries, which they decorated with spectacular frescoes. The monks followed the teachings of the Bishop of Kayseri, who believed the only way to gain a place in heaven was to live in austere conditions on earth. By denying themselves all material goods, and living a simple life, the monks believed they drew closer to God. Later on, they defended themselves against Arab invasions by creating troglodyte villages and even small subterranean towns, such as Derinkuya. Three miles (5 km) outside Göreme, at the highest point in Cappadocia, there is a rock-cut castle.

The Göreme Open Air Museum is a vast complex of monasteries in the heart of the region, each with its own fantastic church. They range from the Nunnery, a seven-story warren of rooms and passages with stone doors to seal off areas in time of danger, to the Snake Church, with two chambers elaborately decorated in ocher-colored frescoes.

A ghostly Christ carrying a book stands between Constantine and St. Helena.

▼ The weird and wonderful landscape of Göreme Open Air Museum

SHOWCASE FOR AN ICON One of Turkey's most beautiful rock churches is Sumela Monastery, perched on a cliff face in the Trabzon province of the Black Sea region. It was founded in A.D. 386, reputedly by two priests who carved it out of the rock with their bare hands after discovering a miraculous icon of the Virgin Mary in a cave. According to legend, St. Luke made the icon and angels carried it to Trabzon from Athens. They placed it in the cave for the monks to find. Before long, pilgrims were flocking to the site to see the icon.

A ghostly Christ carries a book between Emperor Constantine and St. Helena while next to it St. Theodore and St. George kill the beast (the snake that gives the church its name). Such figurative work dates from the 11th or 12th centuries, while the red-painted crosses and simple abstract ornamentation visible in some of the churches date from the iconoclastic period of the eighth century. Under the Byzantine emperor Constantine V (A.D. 718–755) the representation of living creatures was considered to be the devil's attempt to reintroduce paganism. Paintings of Christ and the saints were banned.

Constantine VI (A.D. 771—ca 804) reintroduced figurative work. Some of Göreme's finest examples decorate the 12th-century Dark Church, reached via a winding tunnel. Vivid scenes from the life of Christ cover the walls, and three graves lie near the western entrance. ◆

▲ Many layers of frescoes decorate Sumela Monastery. The oldest flank the courtyard.

SERPENT MOUND OHIO, U.S.A.

Did Halley's comet or a supernova inspire this curious earthwork, or was it an offering to the gods?

THIS HUMAN-MADE earthwork in Ohio is in the shape of an uncoiling serpent nearly a quarter of a mile (0.4 km) long. The head is aligned with the setting sun, and it appears as though the snake is about to swallow an egg. The winter solstice and the equinox sunrise align with the serpent's coils.

The purpose of this impressive effigy is unknown. Some have speculated that the earthwork was an offering to the gods—a serpent's tail being a symbol of sacred earth forces throughout the ancient world. Others say it is the hub of a powerful network of ley lines connecting sacred sites.

Scholars currently think the Fort Ancient Culture (A.D. 100–1650) built Serpent Mound in about A.D. 1070. Its construction may have been at least partly inspired by two great astronomical events that were visible from Earth. One was the appearance in A.D. 1054 of a bright supernova in the Crab Nebula, which was observed at the same time by astronomers in China. The other was the passage across the sky in A.D. 1066 of Halley's comet, the long fiery tail of which, some people believe, may have given the early Americans the idea of a snake. ◆

▲ The sinuous lines of the Serpent Mound earthwork

BIGHORN MEDICINE WHEEL WYOMING, U.S.A.

Cairns known as medicine wheels dot the Great Plains and none is more famous than the one at Bighorn.

WHEN CROW INDIAN hunters came upon the medicine wheel at Bighorn 300 years ago they immediately feared this sacred site. Created hundreds of years previously by their Native American forebears, the wheel-shaped circle of stones is 80 feet (24 m) in diameter, containing 28 "spokes." News of the discovery quickly spread to other Native American tribes.

According to Crow belief, the medicine wheel at Bighorn was built by a boy called Burnt Face, who had fallen into a fire when a baby. When Burnt Face reached 13, he went into the mountains on a

vision quest—a spiritual retreat undertaken by young men—during which he fasted and built the medicine wheel. He placed a large stone cairn at the center of the wheel to mark the exact point of a passageway to the underworld from which it is said the first people on earth rose as spirits.

While in the mountains, Burnt Face purportedly helped drive away a wild animal that was attacking baby eaglets. In return, it is said, an eagle carried off the boy and made his face smooth again. ◆

▲ View over the medicine wheel at Bighorn

MOUNT SHASTA CALIFORNIA, U.S.A.

Heaven and earth meet on Mount Shasta, the home of the Great Spirit of Native American legends.

TWO NATIVE AMERICAN tribes share very similar myths about Mount Shasta. The Modoc people believe that the Great Spirit and his family moved to Mount Shasta from the sky. One night, they say, the daughter of the Great Spirit fell from the mountain and was found by grizzly bears, who raised her as their own. The Great Spirit's daughter went on to marry the eldest male cub, and their offspring became the first humans. However, the Great Spirit could not endure the loss of his daughter. In his grief, he condemned bears to walk on four legs and scattered their children all over the world.

According to the Shasta people, the Great Spirit created the mountain by pushing ice and snow through a hole in heaven. He then used the mountain as a step to reach the earth. The Great Spirit created trees and asked the sun to melt the snow to provide rivers and streams. Breathing on the trees, he brought the birds in the branches to life, and broke up small twigs to create fish, while longer branches became animals.

> Breathing on the trees, the Great Spirit brought the birds in the branches to life.

Mount Shasta is sacred to many groups of people. The Wintu tribe of North American Indians invoke its spirit with ritual dances to ensure the flow of its sacred springs. It also attracts a variety of alternative sects, who come in search of peace and harmony or to spot UFOs. Some mystics even see the mountain as an entry point to another world or as a source of magic. ◆

▼ A sacred site for many, snow-covered Mount Shasta glitters in the setting sun.

CRATER LAKE CASCADE MOUNTAINS, OREGON, U.S.A.

Startlingly blue and eerily still, Crater Lake has long been a setting for Native American spirit quests.

CREATED IN THE COLLAPSED cone of Mount Mazama, a volcano that erupted more than 7,000 years ago, Crater Lake is a deep blue circle of crystal-clear water. In places, it is nearly 2,000 feet (600 m) deep and more than 6 miles (10 km) across. Wizard Island—a volcanic cinder cone shaped like a pointed hat—appears to float on the top.

The Native American Klamath tribe reveres but also fears this geological phenomenon. They have an ancient myth that tells of two chiefs, Llao of the Underworld and Skell of the World Above, pitted against one another in a fierce battle that ends in the destruction of Llao's home, Mount Mazama.

Traditionally the Klamath people sent their young men to Crater Lake on vision quests—spiritual retreats during which they interacted with a spiritual guardian. These quests included physical challenges, such as swimming across the deepest part of the lake or undertaking dangerous climbs along the rim of the volcano. Some men ran down the wall of the crater to the lake itself. Anyone who reached the lake without falling acquired spiritual kudos. Sometimes young men built stone cairns on the highest peaks and ridges to prove their endurance and spiritual powers.

Crater Lake was not discovered by non-Native Americans until 1853, when three gold prospectors stumbled upon it. They named it the Deep Blue Lake. Today the lake's haunting beauty draws hikers, campers, and assorted New Age followers in search of pristine nature. It is still a sacred place for Native Americans. ◆

> Young men sought spiritual power by running down the wall of the crater to the lake itself.

▼ Wizard Island's volcanic rock rises from Crater Lake.

OCMULGEE MACON, GEORGIA, U.S.A.

Could this 11th-century earth lodge by the Ocmulgee River have been an astronomical observatory?

ONE THOUSAND YEARS AGO Creek Indians heaved baskets of soil from the floodplain of the Ocmulgee River to a rocky outcrop high above the water. Using stone hoes and riverine shells as scoops, they built the Great Temple Mound there, a ceremonial center for ritual activities, such as those connected with death.

Just across from the mound they built an earth lodge, a subterranean structure dating from about A.D. 1015, where male members of the tribe purified their bodies through fasting. Ringed by seats for 50 men, it centered

on a fire pit, with a hole in the roof for the smoke to escape. Opposite the door, an altar in the shape of an eagle with an eye like a two-tailed comet was positioned, ostensibly to catch the sunrise as it streamed through the door on a particular day. However, this happens on October 22—not the summer solstice or vernal equinox but the date in the 11th century when the Taurid meteor shower created by the comet Encke peaked. It would seem that the Creek Indians were keeping a wary eye on the heavens. ◆

◀ The inside of the Ocmulgee earth lodge

COLUMBIA HILLS PETROGLYPHS WASHINGTON, U.S.A.

Sacred rock art rescued from the Dalles Dam has been given a home in Columbia Hills State Park.

FOR HUNDREDS OF YEARS the Wishram tribes lived alongside the Columbia River, hunting game and fishing for salmon. During the height of the salmon runs the valley filled with tribes from farther afield, who came to trade, harvest the abundant salmon and huckleberries, and to socialize. They also carved petroglyphs in the rocks.

In 1957 the Dalles Dam flooded the valley. The authorities saved many of the ancient rock carvings, and later removed them to the Columbia Hills State Park.

The petroglyphs peep through the grassland, visible from a walkway. One of the most haunting images is the Tsagaglalal, or She Who Watches, a rock painting of a face with large staring eyes. According to Wishram legend, the figure was a female chief turned to stone by the trickster Coyote.

Prehistoric peoples worldwide painted and carved images on rocks and other surfaces. Anthropologists and archaeologists have long attempted to explain their similarity across cultures and continents. Theories range from sharing common ancestry to having similar experiences, such as eating hallucinogenic plants or witnessing astronomical phenomena. ◆

▲ Petroglyph of bighorn sheep and a buck

SUPERSTITION WILDERNESS ARIZONA, U.S.A.

A secret gold mine and a portal to another world are said to lie in this remote mountain paradise.

▲ The classic Wild West wilderness is crisscrossed by Apache trails.

WHEN TO VISIT

In late fall the heat is more bearable and gold may glisten in the ground.

A LAND OF JAGGED MOUNTAINS AND DEEP CANYONS, the Superstition Wilderness is both feared and worshipped by the Native American tribes of the area. There are numerous legends about the area. The Apache say the dust storms that blow up here emanate from a portal to the lower world, while the Prima people, who call Superstition Mountain Ka-Katak-Tami, or the "crooked top mountain," believe that mountain spirits will take revenge on anyone who tries to find its hidden gold.

European farmers arrived in nearby Salt River Valley in the early 19th century. Mountain legends and reports of hidden wealth began to circulate among the settlers, leading to the Superstition moniker. In the 1840s, the Peralta family from Mexico began mining gold in the area, desecrating the sacred mountain in the eyes of the tribes. As the family returned to Mexico laden with gold, Apache warriors attacked and killed all but two of the party. Thirty years later, a prospector called Jacob Waltz rediscovered the mine with the help of a Peralta descendant. It is said that Waltz shot two people who followed him to the mine, and died without revealing its location. People who continue to look for the lost gold mine risk incurring a local curse that may lead to their disappearance and untimely death. ◆

KANEANA CAVE OAHU, HAWAII, U.S.A.

On the west coast of Oahu, this lava tube cave has inspired some of Hawaii's most colorful legends.

ACCORDING TO HAWAIIAN LEGEND, Kaneana Cave is the source of life itself. It is the womb of the earth from which Kane, the god of creation, emerged. Long after Kane had filled the seas with fish and the land with people, it is said the shark-man Nanaue terrorized Hawaii from this cave. Born to a shark father and human mother, Nanaue had a slit in his back that changed into a shark's mouth as he grew older. His mother concealed his back under a cloak and kept him away from meat, but his true nature could not be suppressed. He was a predator who fed on humans.

Nanaue would assume human form to trick his victims, then drag them back to the cave for dinner. The large stone at the back of the cave is said to be where he laid out his victims before he ate them. According to the story, the Hawaiian people eventually caught and butchered Nanaue, then burned him in an oven.

It is also said that the lava tube cave was once the home of Kane's sister Pele (see p. 232), the goddess of fire and volcanoes. When angry with her lovers, she stirred up the island's volcanoes and poured lava down the mountains. Pele's rival was Poli'ahu, one of the four goddesses of snow, against whom she fought many battles. Poli'ahu eventually triumphed and turned Pele's lava to stone. ◆

> Nanaue's true nature could not be suppressed. He was a hungry predator.

▼ Associated with Hawaiian creation myths, Kaneana Cave is a place of pilgrimage, where offerings are sometimes laid.

TIKAL EL PETÉN, GUATEMALA

In Guatemala's rain forest, six huge pyramid temples are evidence of a Maya civilization at its zenith.

UNDER A STEAMING LAYER of cloud, the thick, warm air in Guatemala's rain forest is alive with the buzz of winged insects and the roar of howler monkeys. Large black vultures slowly circle overhead, much as they would have done when this Maya city was at its peak.

Originally a small village, Tikal had become an important ceremonial center by 300 B.C., featuring pyramids and temples. Most of the ruins visible today, including six towering pyramid temples, were built between A.D. 500 and 700 when Tikal's art, architecture, farming, writing, and city planning were at their height. For reasons that are unclear the city was eventually abandoned and the jungle swallowed up the ruins. Their rediscovery by Ambrosio Tut, a collector of *chiclero* (gum found in the sap of trees) in 1848 triggered a rush of explorers, archaeologists, and treasure hunters to the site.

Many of the monuments are funerary complexes. The king's tomb, found at the center of Pyramid I, contained jade, pearls, seashells, and the spines of stingrays (symbols of human sacrifice).

Tikal means "the place of spirit voices." If you listen carefully, you might hear the gentle whisperings of the spirit voices amid the animal noises of the jungle. ◆

▲ The Maya built their temples high in order to be closer to the gods.

ANIMAL MAGIC The Maya believed that every human soul was shared by an animal companion. Each Maya king was accompanied by a jaguar, a symbol of strength and power. By night, the jaguar god would rule the Maya underworld; by day, he would prowl across the sky, returning to the underworld at dusk.

TIWANAKU NEAR LAKE TITICACA, BOLIVIA

Aymara Indians celebrate the winter solstice at this abandoned capital, once the site of human sacrifice.

HIGH ON THE ANDEAN PLATEAU, on the southern shore of Lake Titicaca, stand the temples, pyramids, and palaces of ancient Tiwanaku. The center of an empire that covered half of Bolivia and parts of Peru, Agentina, and Chile, the city thrived from A.D. 300 until the end of the first millennium. It had paved roads, a sophisticated solar and lunar calendar, and many of its buildings were covered in gold.

As the seat of the emperor-god, Tiwanaku was an important religious and ceremonial center. In times of crisis the priests appeased the gods with human sacrifices—usually young men or women who were specially groomed for the honor. Public

> Dismemberment of the sacrificial victims took place on the top of the Akapana Pyramid.

dismemberment of the sacrificial victims took place on the top of the Akapana Pyramid.

In the 13th century, the Inca Empire emerged beyond the northern frontier of the Tiwanaku state. The Inca took over the abandoned city of Tiwanaku, believing it was built not by an earlier civilization, but by the creator god Viracocha.

Nowadays, on June 21, the winter solstice for the southern hemisphere, the Aymara people celebrate Machaj Mara (New Year) at Tiwanaku. Sunrise streams through the temple's eastern entrance, just as it would have done in Tiwanaku's heyday. ◆

▲ In times of crisis, human sacrifices would be made.

CHAPEL OF CHRIST OF THE TEARS
COCHABAMBA, BOLIVIA

A small statue in Cochabamba has supposedly wept tears of blood every Good Friday since 1995.

IN 1994 KATYA RIVAS, a resident of Cochabamba, in central Bolivia, went to visit a relative in nearby Conyers. Kneeling at the foot of a crucifix, she prayed to become a daughter of Christ and bear some of his suffering. At the moment of her prayer, she claims she felt a burning sensation in her ribs, feet, and palms.

When Katya returned to Cochabamba, believing she had been touched by Jesus, she prayed for the conversion of Silvia Arévalo, a relative who had abandoned her Catholic faith. Silvia duly regained her faith and one day bought herself a statue of Christ. She placed the statue on her mantelpiece, where it began to shed crystal-clear tears with a strong smell of roses.

As the tears rolled down the statue's face, they reportedly turned to blood. Soon hundreds of devout believers and curious locals were arriving at the Arévalo home.

The statue has cried on numerous occasions since then and is said to weep every Good Friday. Some claim that scientists have tested the tears in a laboratory and found them to contain human blood. They also say that skeptics have examined the statue for fraudulent mechanisms that could trigger the tears and found it to be hollow. The small wooden statue now has its own chapel and is a major tourist attraction in the town. ◆

▲ Blood is said to stream down the face and neck of the statue.

▼ The town of Cochabamba, home of the weeping Christ statue

MARKAWASI ANDES, PERU

Theories put forward to explain these gigantic stone figures include many with a supernatural basis.

▲ The Face of Humanity, so called because its various "faces" show different racial characteristics

WHEN TO VISIT

Visit in the spring months, when the sculptures are accentuated by the bright light.

HIGH ON A WINDSWEPT PLATEAU in the Peruvian Andes, Markawasi seems suspended between heaven and earth. Fantastical rock carvings—giant heads of animals from different continents and creatures from a prehistoric age—appear at every turn. Some dismiss these massive monoliths as simply rocks weathered by the elements over time into recognizable shapes or faces; others claim they are evidence of a lost civilization that crossed the oceans, or part of a divine landscape shaped by nature spirits.

An 80-foot (24 m) statue known as the Face of Humanity is the first to greet visitors at the northern entrance to the plateau. It reveals a number of different human faces, depending on the angle from which it is viewed. Just beyond the figure, across a ravine, is the stone monolith of a giant sea turtle cresting a wave.

Some people claim that the mysterious stone figures are former entrances to tunnels into the inner earth, where the Markawasi people retreated following a natural disaster. Inside, they say, is a large underground cavern and temple complex where the Markawasi performed rituals in the worship of Viracocha, the great Inca's creator god.

The plateau is said to have a mystical atmosphere that affects even hardened skeptics. Some visitors report paranormal experiences, such as UFO sightings, while almost everybody claims to experience heightened sensory perception. ◆

5 SACRED HOT SPOTS IN SOUTH AMERICA

The Inca held many places in South America sacred, especially Lake Titicaca, where their great civilization took root and many of their legends are set.

① LAKE TITICACA, PERU/BOLIVIA: According to Inca mythology, after a great flood the creator god Viracocha rose up from Lake Titicaca to make the sun, moon, and stars. According to some versions of the myth, Viracocha then went to Tiwanaku to create the first human beings, Manco Cápac and Mama Ocllo, out of stone. He commanded them to go out and populate the world.

② ISLAND OF THE SUN, BOLIVIA: This island on the Bolivian side of the lake was regarded as the home of the supreme Inca sun god, Inti. At the north end, on the road to Challapampa, are two indentations in the rock. Resembling footprints, they are said to have been created when Inti came down to earth. Nearby is the Chinaka, or labyrinth, a huge stone maze that may have been a training center for Inca priests.

3 ISLAND OF THE MOON, BOLIVIA: Twin to the Island of the Sun, the Island of the Moon is the legendary home of the Inca moon goddess, Mama Quila. During Inca times, the Isla de la Luna housed the Virgins of the Sun, women who lived a nun-like existence. Chosen for their beauty or rank from the age of eight, they wove garments from alpaca wool and performed ceremonies dedicated to the moon.

4 ARAMU MURU, PERU: This gateway that seemingly leads nowhere was carved out of the rock thousands of years ago. Some say that warriors passed through it to an immortal life, while others claim that an Inca priest fleeing from the conquistadores placed a sacred golden disk, like a key, in an indent beside the gate and disappeared inside. It is said that only those in harmony with the sun can enter.

5 HORCA DEL INCA, COPACABANA, BOLIVIA: The pre-Inca Chiripa people used the later-named Horca del Inca to observe the night skies in the 14th century B.C. Like many other ancient civilizations, the Chiripa performed rituals here at the time of the winter solstice. Thinking the structure was Inca, the Spanish later destroyed most of the site in a search for hidden gold, and gave it its name—Inca Gallows.

▼ Straddling the border between Peru and Bolivia, Lake Titicaca is the source of many legends.

See Also: Chalk Giant, p. 219

NAZCA LINES ICA, PERU

Were these mysterious desert carvings designed by priests flying in primitive hot-air balloons?

MANY THEORIES ATTEMPT to explain the Nazca Lines, enigmatic geoglyphs (carvings in the earth) in the desert in southern Peru. Some say they have an astrological or astronomical significance; others believe they were created by extraterrestrial beings.

The most likely explanation, perhaps, is that the Nazca people (100 B.C.–A.D. 800) made the carvings, some of which are 660 feet (200 m) across, as offerings to their gods. The Nazcas built Cahuachi, a sacred ceremonial site close to the city of Ventilla, which overlooks some of the lines. It was ruled by an elite band of priests who, as depicted on pottery, sported dreadlocks and used hallucinogens to produce visions. Some historians have theorized that the priests may have directed the creation of the geoglyphs by flying over the site in a primitive version of hot-air balloons.

Two natural disasters took place in the fourth century A.D. that led to the collapse of Cahuachi's religious power. First, a flood cut off the city's natural water supplies, then a massive earthquake split the temples apart. Believing that the mountains, sky, rivers, floods, and earthquakes were all created by the gods, the Nazca assumed they had caused these disasters by displeasing their deities. They abandoned the ceremonial center around A.D. 500. ◆

▲ Some patterns are geometric while others resemble animals.

TROPHY HEADS The Nazca continued an ancient tradition of presenting trophy heads to the gods. Decapitated during warfare, the heads were displayed as evidence of a warrior's prowess. Nazca pottery portrays people dressed in ritualistic finery, and holding a severed head in one hand and a club in the other.

MACHU PICCHU

CUSCO, PERU

One of the world's most iconic cultural sites, Machu Picchu's original purpose perplexes archaeologists.

SOME ARCHAEOLOGISTS believe Machu Picchu was a summer retreat for the court of Emperor Pachacuti (1438–1471). Others think it was primarily a religious site for the worship of Inti, the Inca sun god. Visitors to the site say being so perilously high in the mountains, with the ruins shrouded in cloud, is like standing among the gods themselves.

The Inca believed they were chosen to build a new civilization after a dark period of political division and warfare in the Andes. They called themselves the Children of the Sun and went on to build the largest pre-Columbian empire in South America.

High up in the ruins of Machu Picchu is the Intihuatana Stone, or Hitching Post of the Sun. This is astronomically aligned so that it points directly at the sun during the winter solstice on June 21. The Inca believed

> Touch your forehead on the Intihuatana Stone to see the spirit world.

the stone anchored the sun, keeping it on its annual track through the sky, and they performed rituals to keep the sun in place. If the Intihuatana Stone was ever destroyed, the Inca believed their gods would depart and the world would turn upside down. There is a legend that if you touch your forehead on the Intihuatana Stone, you will see the spirit world.

Atahualpa, the last Inca emperor, thought the Spanish conquistador Francisco Pizarro was Viracocha, the Inca creator god, who had come back to honor the Children of the Sun. By the time Atahualpa discovered his fatal error, it was too late, and the Inca Empire had succumbed to the Spanish conquest. Machu Picchu was the only Inca city that the Spanish never found. ◆

▼ Machu Picchu sits on a promontory looped by the sacred Urubamba River.

EASTER ISLAND OCEANIA

Approximately 800 stone monoliths guard one of the most isolated inhabited islands in the world.

▼ The statues stare
across the island,
their backs to the
sea. According
to one legend,
the island's king
charmed the
moai to come to
life and ordered
them to walk.

DUTCH EXPLORER JACOB ROGGEVEEN discovered this remote island, over 1,000 miles (1,600 km) off the coast of Chile, on Easter Sunday, 1722. He was the first outsider to see the *moai*—the 900 or so human-shaped monoliths that ring the island, most of them facing inland with their backs to the sea.

The island was first settled by the Polynesians around A.D. 400. It is believed that the Rapa Nui, descendants of those first settlers, erected the statues for which the island is famous from the tenth century. By then, agriculture and fishing, with canoes made from palm trees, supported a growing population.

Exactly why they erected the statues is not fully understood, although archaeologists believe them to be representations of deified ancestors charged with a magical essence called *mana* that endowed power and authority. The Rapa Nui hewed the figures out of a volcanic crater in the center of the island. Unfinished sculptures still dot the area around the quarry, including one that is about 70 feet (21 m) tall—twice the height of most of the moai. Fragments found around the base of the figures show that the carved eye sockets once held slabs of white coral and obsidian, a black volcanic glass.

THE BIRDMAN A competition was held annually on the island to harvest the first egg of the season. The winning tribe's chief was known as Tangata Manu—the Birdman. On receiving the egg from the winner, the chief became sacred, the representative on earth of Make Make, the creator god of fertility. For the next year, the Birdman lived in seclusion, apart from a single attendant who prepared his meals. During this time he grew his nails and wore a headdress of human hair. The Birdman remained magical even after his tenure had expired. When he died, a stone figure would be raised alongside those of his predecessors, so that he could watch over his tribe with his supernatural power.

For many years, uncertainty about the history and purpose of the moai created an information vacuum that was filled with theories, some of which were plausible, many of which were not. That the creation of the monoliths was abandoned, apparently suddenly, with statues left unfinished and tools lying on the ground, gave rise to speculation that Easter Island had suffered some geological or meteorological cataclysm. These notions were later convincingly debunked by modern science. The truth is that the unfinished statues were left for practical reasons, such as the discovery of unworkable fault lines in the rock from which they were being hewn. Other monoliths were evidently works in progress when the statue-building period ended in around 1540. The ancestor cult was then succeeded by the Birdman cult, known as *manutara*, at Orongo, a ceremonial center in the far southwest of the island. ◆

▲ Make Make was usually represented with a bird's head and a half-human body.

SUKHOTHAI HISTORICAL PARK THAILAND

The capital of the first Kingdom of Siam (Thailand), the old city of Sukhothai, radiates tranquillity.

EVERY STONE AND STATUE in this former capital of Thailand expresses the principles of Theravada Buddhism, an ancient spiritual pathway that seeks the "middle way" between asceticism and sensual indulgence. Wat Mahathat's Seated Buddha presides over an enormous lotus pond. The embodiment of calm, the Buddha's closed eyes and smiling face cast a spell over everyone who strolls the paths.

The Loi Krathong Festival encapsulates the spirituality of Old Sukhothai. On the night of the full moon in the 12th lunar month—usually November in the Western calendar—people launch tiny, handmade

> On the night of the full moon in the 12th lunar month, people launch tiny handmade rafts.

rafts filled with gardenia flowers, incense, coins, and candles, and watch them float away. Nang Nopphamat, the consort of the 14th-century King Loethai, was the first to launch a decorated raft here. This ancient tradition is to honor the water goddess Phra Naret, who is also the goddess of good fortune, prosperity, and beauty. Born of water, she overflows with fertility, abundance, and wealth. According to tradition, if the candle stays lit until the float passes out of sight, the wishes of the person who launched it will come true. ◆

▲ Enormous tree roots enclose the Buddha's head.

PURA TIRTA EMPUL BALI

Indra allegedly created this sacred spring to revive his poisoned army and thwart the evil Mayadenawa.

IN HINDU MYTHOLOGY, Mayadenawa was a cruel king who changed into a shape-shifting magician. Intoxicated by his powers, he turned to black magic. This infuriated the god Indra, who set out with his army to destroy the king.

Realizing what was afoot, the king tried to trick Indra. As his army slept, Mayadenawa crept into Indra's camp, walking on the sides of his feet so as not to leave any footprints. He then created an alluring but poisonous lake from which the army would drink when they woke the next morning.

In the morning Indra awoke to find many of his men already dead from drinking the water, and scores more sick or dying. With immense force, he pierced the ground with his staff, thereby creating a healing spring of holy water—the Pura Tirta Empul.

All around the sides of the spring are tilted palms, known as *tampak siring* (angled footsteps), which symbolize the way Mayadenawa infiltrated Indra's camp. An inscription dates the founding of a temple on the site to A.D. 926. Since then, the Balinese have come to the temple to pay homage to Indra. First they make an offering at the temple, then they bathe and pray. Many visitors take home bottles of the holy water. Nearby are two smaller pools fed by the spring, along with shrines to Shiva, Vishnu, Brahma, and Indra. ◆

▲ Indra seated on his white elephant, Airavata

▼ The sacred springs, purportedly conjured up by the great god Indra

ELEPHANTA CAVES NEAR MUMBAI, INDIA

Deep inside a hillside on an isolated island, a sumptuously decorated shrine celebrates the god Shiva.

FAR FROM THE BUSY CROWDS of Mumbai lies hilly Elephanta Island, famous for a network of caves in which statues, shrines, and even a whole temple to the Hindu god Shiva were sculpted out of the bare rock in the sixth century. Who created these extraordinary interiors is unknown, although legend claims the sculptors were not human.

There are seven caves altogether. The main northern entrance, surrounded by chattering monkeys, and tamarind and palm trees, leads into the highlight of the complex, the massive hall known as the Shiva Cave. An 18-foot-high (5.5 m) statue of Shiva in his three-headed aspect as Creator, Protector, and Destroyer dominates the space. Other sculptures and panels in the room celebrate Shiva's various manifestations and episodes in his life, such as bringing the Ganges River down to earth by letting it trickle through his matted hair, and his divine marriage to Parvati, attended by Brahma, Vishnu, Indra, and other Hindu deities. One panel shows Shiva and Parvati playing dice while the demon-king Ravana shakes their mountain home behind them. ◆

▲ The towering, three-headed bust of Shiva shows him as Creator, Protector, and Destroyer.

▼ The entrance to the caves, an underground world of Hindu deities

AJANTA CAVES MAHARASHTRA, INDIA

This underground labyrinth conceals astonishing frescoes depicting the life of the Buddha.

▲ Many of the frescoes have retained their superb colors.

WHEN TO VISIT

Go to Ajanta in March, when the weather is cooler and there are fewer tourists.

BUDDHIST MONKS CARVED the Ajanta Caves out of a horseshoe-shaped cliff along the Waghora River in the second century B.C. They used the caves as prayer halls and monasteries until around A.D. 650, after which they abandoned them for unknown reasons and the caves fell into obscurity. A British officer rediscovered the caves in 1819 while hunting in the area.

The caves are scooped out of the rock like huge ice-cream cones. Around 700 Buddhist monks lived, taught, prayed, and meditated here. In the fifth century, powerful aristocrats commissioned artists to decorate the rock-cut monastery, carving elaborate stupas (shrines) and covering the walls in frescoes. The evolved technique and style place the paintings among the major achievements of the Gupta Empire (A.D. 320–550), a period of artistic flowering.

The frescoes illustrate events in the life of Prince Siddhartha Gautama Buddha, the founder of Buddhism. In the monastery in Cave 17, celestial musicians and maidens dance on the ceiling, and spirits, guardians, goddesses, lotus petals, and scrolls adorn the doorway. One of the murals depicts the tale of Prince Sinhala overcoming the man-eating female monsters of Sri Lanka to become the Sri Lankan king. A panel above the doorway depicts the seven Manushi Buddhas. These are Buddhas in human form, seated under their respective Bodhi trees—cool, calm, and resplendent in their spiritual tranquillity. ◆

See Also: Bagan, p. 242

KONARK SUN TEMPLE ODISHA, INDIA

In the early 20th century, archaeologists found an unusual temple buried in sand on the Bay of Bengal.

BUILT IN THE SHAPE OF a gigantic chariot with elaborately carved stone wheels, pillars, and walls, the Konark Sun Temple represents the Hindu sun god, Surya, and his team of seven galloping horses. It was built in the 13th century under the direction of King Narasimhadeva I of Orissa.

Source of light and warmth, the sun god is linked to fertility in Hindu creation myths. In a myth that explains the solar eclipse, his wife, Sanina, unable to bear her husband's heat, flees to the dark forest where she turns herself into a mare. Disguising himself as a stallion, Surya finds her, and the pair are reunited. But to diminish Surya's brightness, the celestial engineer Vishwakarma removes a piece of Surya year by year.

> It was said that magnets in the tower allowed the throne to hover in midair.

According to legend, the Konark Sun Temple has two magnets built into the tower, allowing the king's throne to hover in midair. European sailors, who called the temple the Black Pagoda, believed shipwrecks were caused by the magnets' effect on the tides.

After an attack by the Muslim Yavana army in the 15th century, temple priests smuggled the central statue to Puri, but the rest of the building was destroyed. Over the centuries, the sea receded, sand engulfed the structure, and the salt-laden winds eroded the stone. It remained buried under a huge mound of sand until the early 20th century. ◆

▲ The temple represents the sun god's chariot as it is pulled across the heavens.

BODH GAYA BIHAR, INDIA

A Bodhi tree in Mahabodhi Temple is said to descend from one that shaded Buddha in the fifth century B.C.

IN SEARCH OF SPIRITUAL AWAKENING, Prince Siddhartha Gautama finally abandoned years of rigorous fasting and asceticism. After nearly starving himself to death by restricting his food to one leaf or nut per day, he collapsed in a river while bathing and almost drowned. It was then that Siddhartha began to reconsider his path. He remembered a moment in childhood when he'd been watching his father's first plow of the season. As he focused on the moment, he attained a state that was blissful and refreshing, so he sat down beneath a Bodhi tree and vowed not to move until he attained enlightenment. After days of concentrated meditation and battles with Mara, the demon of illusion, Siddhartha became the Buddha, or the Enlightened One.

In the third century B.C., Sanghamitta, the daughter of the Indian emperor Ashoka, took a branch of the Bodhi tree under which Siddhartha had achieved enlightenment to Sri Lanka and planted it in Anuradhapura, where it flourished. When, in India, the young wife of the emperor destroyed the original Bodhi tree in her jealousy of the time her husband spent meditating, a shoot from the Sri Lankan tree was brought to Bodh Gaya to replace it.

The path the Buddha walked after his enlightenment at Bodh Gaya is marked by Chankramanar, the "Jewel Walk," lined with 19 lotuses, on the north side of the Mahabodhi Temple. Pilgrims walk alongside it to follow in the Buddha's footsteps. ◆

▲ Statue of Buddha, the founder of Buddhism

▼ Buddhist monks in Mahabodhi Temple, where Buddha attained enlightenment

GANGES RIVER INDIA

The mighty and divine Ganges River flows through many Hindu creation myths.

FROM HIGH AMONG THE GLACIAL PEAKS of the Himalaya, the Ganges River meanders 1,560 miles (2,500 km) across India to the Bay of Bengal. Hindus consider it a holy, life-giving, and purifying source, and the personification of the Hindu goddess Ganga.

In many legends, Ganga is consort to three major deities of Hinduism: Brahma, Vishnu, and Shiva. In order to create the universe, the supreme god Vishnu extended his left foot to the end of the cosmos and pierced a hole through its edge with his big toenail. Through the hole, the pure water of the Divine Ocean poured into the universe as a sacred river. Washing over Vishnu's red saffron-colored feet, the river became a beautiful pink color and Ganga came into being.

> Ganga decided to destroy the earth as she descended from the heavens.

Many years later, it is said that a king named Sagara magically acquired 60,000 sons. On a mission to the underworld to save mankind, the sons came face to face with a terrifying sage who set fire to the 60,000 sons and burned them to ashes with just one glance. Their souls wandered as restless spirits because nobody had performed their final rites.

When one of the king's descendants, Bhagiratha, learned of their fate, he vowed to bring Ganga down to earth so that her waters could cleanse their souls and release them to heaven. The god Brahma agreed and told Ganga to help. But Ganga didn't like being ordered around by her husband and decided to destroy the earth as she fell from the heavens. Shiva heard the prayers of Bhagiratha, and trapped Ganga in his hair, only letting her out in trickles to cleanse the underworld and release the sons to paradise. One of the streams remained on earth to purify all human souls who deserved to go to heaven. This river—the Ganges—became the source of *moksha*, where the soul could find liberation from the cycle of death and rebirth.

A string of cities along the banks of the Ganges River are pilgrimage sites.

▼ The city of Varanasi (formerly Benares) is one of the holiest places on the Ganges. Many Hindus come here to be cremated.

KUMBH MELA Every third year a mass ritual bathing is held at one of the four main holy towns on the Ganges River—Allahabad, Haridwar, Ujjain, or Nashik. The festival is thought to be the world's largest religious festival, with an estimated 80 million people attending. It celebrates one of the stories about the Elixir of Immortality in which the Devas and Asuras, rival demigods, fight a 12-year battle for the pot of elixir. During the battle, Lord Vishnu flies away with the pot, spilling it in four places—thus creating the four holy sites.

Gangotri marks the source of the Ganges, while Allahabad, Haridwar, Ujjain, and Nashik are the four places where the drops of the Elixir of Immortality, or Amrit, fell. According to Hindu legend, Amrit was accidentally spilled from the bird god Garuda's pitcher as the primordial ocean churned the universe into being.

The Ganges is a place of life and death. Millions of Indians make their living on the river, and when they die, Hindus aspire to be cremated on the banks of the Ganges, from where the soul is said to ascend to heaven. If this is not possible, relatives will take their ashes to the Ganges for blessing. Without the purification of Ganga, the dead will exist only in a limbo of suffering and become spirits that torment those who are still alive. ◆

▲ At Kumbh Mela *sadhus* (holy men) wear garlands of flowers and smear their bodies in ash. They immerse themselves in the river at dawn, while facing east.

MOSQUE CITY OF BAGERHAT BANGLADESH

In the 1980s, archaeologists uncovered a magnificent Islamic city hidden in the jungles of Bangladesh.

ONE OF THE LOST CITIES of the world until its rediscovery in the 1980s, the mosque city of Bagerhat stands at the meeting point of the Ganges and Brahmaputra Rivers in southwest Bangladesh. Khan Jahan Ali, a pious local ruler, founded the city in the 15th century. He wished to create the ideal Islamic city in this inhospitable area of jungle and mangrove swamps. In just 45 years he built a magnificent and thriving city, with mosques, *madrassas* (religious schools), mausoleums, and tanks supplying salt-free water. According to legend, he built 360 mosques, 360 tanks, and had 360 disciples.

> According to legend, Khan Jahan Ali built 360 mosques, 360 tanks, and had 360 disciples.

After Jahan Ali's death in 1459, the city fell into disuse and the land reverted to jungle. When archaeologists and surveyors moved in to excavate the site in the 1980s, they were amazed by what they found; so far, more than 50 Islamic monuments have been restored.

Bagerhat centers on Shait Gumbad—the Sixty Dome Mosque, an impressive structure with tapering walls decorated with terra-cotta and red brick. The tomb of Khan Jahan Ali, a much-loved place of pilgrimage, lies on the northern bank of a crocodile pool inside the complex. ◆

▲ **The Sixty Dome Mosque, containing the tomb of Jahan Ali**

BOUDHANATH KATHMANDU, NEPAL

Influenced by Tibetan Buddhism, the stupa of Boudhanath is the highlight of the Kathmandu Valley.

ACCORDING TO NEPALI LEGEND, a grief-stricken prince commissioned the stupa of Boudhanath in memory of his father. During the reign of King Vrishadev a severe wind blew through the land. The king's astrologers told him to appease the rain gods by finding and sacrificing a man with 32 auspicious marks on his body. The king summoned his son, Prince Manadeva, and told him to wake at dawn and kill whoever he found sleeping in a particular place. Manadeva did as he was told, and rain started to fall. He was horrified to find that he had murdered his own father.

In his grief, the prince prayed to the goddess Vajrayogini for forgiveness. The goddess responded by setting free a white bird, and commanded him to build a temple where the bird landed. This is said to be the site of the Great Stupa at Kathmandu.

Four Buddhas mark the cardinal points of the compass, with the fifth, Vairocana, enshrined in the dome in the center. They personify the five elements identified by Buddhism—earth, water, fire, air, and ether. Symbolic numbers are also present in the stupa's nine levels, representing the mythical Mount Meru, the center of the cosmos. The 13 rings rising from the base to the pinnacle symbolize the path to enlightenment or "Bodhi" suggested by the stupa's name. ◆

▲ Figurine of Vairocana, the principal deity of the mandala (plan of the cosmos) represented by the stupa

▼ The layout of Boudhanath Stupa follows the mandala.

MOUNT TAI SHAN SHANDONG PROVINCE, CHINA

Mount Tai Shan is said to bestow longevity on all who visit its extraordinary peak.

THE EMPERORS OF ANCIENT CHINA regarded Mount Tai Shan as the son of the Emperor of Heaven. It was the mountain, they believed, that gave them their authority to rule. Seventy-two emperors are said to have climbed the mountain to pay homage to Son of Heaven since 219 B.C.

An enormous entourage of servants, merchants, soldiers, guards, farmers, and women would accompany the emperor on his regular pilgrimage up the mountain. Sometimes, the line of people would stretch from the bottom of the mountain to the top, a distance of more than 6 miles (10 km). Chinese artists and poets were also drawn to the holy peak. They posted poems and dedications praising the beauty, energy, and divine power of the mountain on the walls

lining the path. It is said that anyone who climbs to the top of the mountain will live until they are 100 years old.

Two important temples sit at the peak: the Temple of the Jade Emperor, the heavenly ruler of this world, and the Bixia, the Temple of the Princess of the Azure Clouds, the daughter of the Jade Emperor. The Temple of the Princess is perhaps the preeminent place of pilgrimage for Chinese women. Mothers whose daughters are unable to conceive come to pray for grandchildren. Two attendant goddesses stand beside the statue of the princess. These are miracle-working figures—one for curing eye ailments, the other for childhood diseases. ◆

◄ Inscriptions line the path leading to the top of Mount Tai Shan.

ISE JINGU HONSHU, JAPAN

Deep in a forest of Japanese cypress trees a magical shrine pays homage to the Shinto sun goddess.

BELIEVED TO BE THE HOME of the legendary Sacred Mirror, Ise Jingu is one of Shinto's holiest shrines, dedicated to the sun goddess Amaterasu Omikami. In Japanese mythology, the mirror and jewels of Amaterasu were hung from a tree to lure her out of a cave where she was hiding after a battle with her moon god brother. Because of the conflict, the sun no longer shone in heaven or on earth.

When Amaterasu peeped outside the cave and saw a woman more beautiful than herself, she did not realize it was her own reflection. Furious, she ran from the cave, intending to destroy the woman,

but was captured by the other gods, who forced her to stay in heaven.

Amaterasu's jewels and mirror were given to her descendants, and then to the emperor. Ever since, it is said, mirrors in Japan have represented truth, but are also regarded as a source of mystique, reverence, and magic.

Pilgrims to the shrine make offerings such as rice, abalone, sea bream, salt, miso, and earthenware, all of which must be prepared in the traditional way. ◆

▲ Visitors must keep to the sides of the path leading up to the shrine; the middle is reserved for the goddess.

MOUNT FUJI HONSHU, JAPAN

A shrine on the top of volcanic Mount Fuji honors one of the most venerated goddesses in Japan.

ON A CLEAR DAY, the highest mountain in Japan, Mount Fuji, can be seen from Tokyo, its volcanic cone often capped in snow. Sacred to the Shinto goddess Sengen-Sama, whose shrine is at the summit, it is the most revered of three holy mountains in Japan and considered by the Fujiko Shinto sect to be a divine being with a soul.

According to legend, when Sengen-Sama became pregnant by her husband Ninigi, the god of rice, suspiciously soon after their wedding, Ninigi became convinced his wife had been unfaithful. To prove her innocence, Sengen-Sama built a doorless hut in which to give birth and said she would set it alight when she was in labor. If the baby was not Ninigi's, she said, she and the child would die; if the baby was her husband's, they would survive. In the event, she had twins, both of whom survived.

Because of the mountain's beauty and spiritual associations, it has become a popular subject in Japanese art. Fuji's nickname Konohana-Sakuyahime means "causing the blossom to bloom brightly," referring to the pink cherry blossoms that frame the snowy mountain in the spring. It is said that to climb Mount Fuji is to reach the heights of one's soul. ◆

> It is said that to climb Mount Fuji is to reach the heights of one's soul.

▼ Katsushika Hokusai painted Mount Fuji numerous times.

MECCA SAUDI ARABIA

Each year millions of Muslims make the trip to Mecca, where the Kabbah contains a heavenly stone.

Mecca is the holiest city in Islam, and the destination of the hajj, the journey that all faithful Muslims are encouraged to undertake at least once in their lifetimes.

The religious focus of Mecca is the Kabbah (Cube), a building made from granite that extends vertically 43 feet (13 m) above a solid marble base. The structure is traditionally held to have been built by Ibrahim (Abraham in the Old Testament of the Judeo-Christian Bible) as the first place on earth for the worship of Allah (God).

Of all the artifacts and relics within the Kabbah, the most sacred is the Black Stone (al-Hajar al-Aswad), which is said to have fallen from heaven to show Adam and Eve where to build their first altar. Certainly, the Black Stone predates Islam, and was venerated by ancient Arabian pagans. It may have been brought to its present location by the Prophet Muhammad in A.D. 630.

The Black Stone is small, but accounts of its exact dimensions vary, partly because of the accidental damage that it has from time to time sustained, and partly as a result of its exposure every year to, on average, three million pilgrims, most of whom ritualistically touch or kiss it seven times, once for each of the circuits that they have completed counterclockwise around the surrounding square before entering the Kabbah. It is generally agreed that the Black Stone is currently approximately 30 inches long and 18 inches wide (72 x 36 cm). ◆

> The Black Stone predates Islam, and was venerated by Arabian pagans.

▼ A sea of pilgrims surrounds the Kabbah.

JERUSALEM ISRAEL / PALESTINE

High on a plateau in the Judean Mountains is one of the oldest and holiest cities in the world.

IMPORTANT TO Jews, Christians, and Muslims, Jerusalem is packed with sacred sites. The holiest Jewish site is the Western Wall, known as the Wailing Wall, a remnant of the Second Temple, built by Herod the Great, to replace the First Temple, believed to have been built by King Solomon. According to Jewish legend, the Second Temple took 11 years to construct, during which it only ever rained at night, allowing the builders to work without interruption. Jews have gathered here to lament the loss of the temple since its destruction by the Romans in A.D. 70.

The Muslim shrine known as the Dome of the Rock also stands on Temple Mount. It marks the spot where Muslims believe the Prophet Muhammad came on his miraculous night journey from Mecca, and from where he then ascended to heaven to speak with God.

The Church of the Holy Sepulchre stands on the purported site of Christ's crucifixion, and above the tomb where he was buried. During the course of Emperor Constantine's excavations of the site in the fourth century A.D., his mother, St. Helena, is said to have discovered three crosses near the tomb. According to legend, to prove which one was Christ's, a sick man touched each cross and the true cross miraculously healed him. ◆

▲ Temple Mount, with the golden Dome of the Rock and Jews praying at the Wailing Wall

THE CRUSADES For around 200 years, from the 11th to 13th century, the Catholic Church endeavored to recapture Palestine from the Muslims and conquer pagan areas. Thousands of Christians from all over Europe took part in the wars, but many never returned home. Their fights were frequently documented on parchment (right).

GIZA PYRAMIDS NEAR CAIRO, EGYPT

Archaeologists and scientists still strive to unlock the secrets of these miracles of ancient engineering.

O N THE DESERT PLATEAU WEST OF CAIRO, the Giza Pyramids loom in the distance, shimmering in the sunlit dust. Immutable, they are the last survivors of the Seven Wonders of the World listed by the ancient Greeks. Travelers have stood in awe before them for thousands of years.

Archaeologists know that the Giza Pyramids were built as burial chambers for pharaohs, and have dated them to around 2500 B.C. But the symbolic importance of the pyramids is not entirely understood. In 450 B.C., Egyptian priests told the Greek historian Herodotus that the pyramids at Giza were built for Khufu, a 4th dynasty king (2475–2465 B.C.). It has been estimated that the first of these monuments, the Pyramid of Khufu, known as the Great Pyramid, took 400,000 men 20 years to build, with 100,000 men at a time working in three-month shifts. It contains 2.3 million stone blocks and weighs around six million tons. Inside the pyramid is a mortuary temple, where the pharaoh's body was mummified, in addition to the valley temples, three small pyramids built for Khufu's wives, a series of flat-topped pyramids for the remains of his favorite children, and five pits for solar boats: full-size boats that were possibly intended for transporting the pharaoh's body across the heavens in the company of the sun god Ra. Khufu's son, Khafre, built the second pyramid at Giza around 2520 B.C. His necropolis also includes the Sphinx, a mysterious creature with the body of a lion and a pharaoh's head, which is connected to the pyramid by a causeway. A third large pyramid is Menkaure's, built around 2490 B.C.

The pyramids were packed with all the necessities for sustaining the pharaohs in the afterlife, including furniture, statues of servants to be set to work in the spiritual world, boats for travel, and mummified animals and pets.

> The Great Pyramid took around 400,000 men 20 years to build.

▼ The majestic Pyramids of Giza pose many questions.

THE VALLEY OF THE KINGS Between the 16th and
the 11th centuries B.C. this stretch of the west bank of the Nile
River near Luxor (ancient Thebes) was a burial place for pharaohs
and numerous prominent nobles of lesser rank. The Valley of the
Kings became world-famous after British archaeologists Howard
Carter and the Earl of Carnarvon found the tomb of Tutankhamun,
Pharaoh of the 18th dynasty, in 1922 in one of the most spectacular
archaeological discoveries of all time. Tutankhamun died around
1323 B.C. and was almost completely forgotten after his burial
place became hidden beneath piles of loose rocks.

But what of the pyramids' mystique? In the 1990s, a Belgian engineer, Robert Bauval, noticed that the arrangement of the Giza Pyramids is similar to that of three stars in the constellation known as Orion's Belt, named after the great hunter of Greek mythology. Orion's predecessor was the Egyptian god Osiris, believed to live on one of three stars of the belt alignment of the constellation. Inside the pyramids are four air shafts and Bauval calculated that in 2500 B.C. the southern vent in the King's Chamber would have pointed directly at Orion and the southern air-shaft in the Queen's Chamber would have pointed at the star Sirius, the planet sacred to Osiris's consort, Isis. Bauval believed that the vent was a channel to direct the pharaoh's soul directly to Orion, where he would become a god. Others maintain that the pyramids were constructed as channels for the gods to descend to earth.

The Great Pyramid is also perfectly aligned to true north, south, east, and west, leading to speculation about astrological significance and extraterrestrial activity. ◆

▲ The mask
of the boy king
Tutankhamun, who
some say placed a
curse on those who
disturbed his tomb

ARK OF THE COVENANT AXUM, ETHIOPIA

Does the lost Ark of the Covenant lie in a small church in Ethiopia, guarded by a single monk?

ACCORDING TO THE OLD TESTAMENT, the Ark of the Covenant contains the tablets of the Ten Commandments that God gave to Moses on Mount Sinai. The biblical account states that four guarding angels carried the Ark using two long bars of gold-plated wood. The Israelites took the shrine with them wherever they went. They believed its divine powers would prove fatal for anyone who tried to steal it. When King Solomon built the Temple of Jerusalem, he enshrined the Ark there.

At some point, however, the Ark disappeared. Theories about its whereabouts mention a tunnel in Jerusalem and the top of Mount Nebo in Jordan.

According to Ethiopia's royal chronicles, the Ark left Jerusalem in the days of King Solomon. Menelik, the son of Solomon and the Queen of Sheba, took it to Ethiopia, where it was kept for 800 years by a Judaic sect. The Knights Templar then seized the Ark, thinking it was the Holy Grail. It is said that the Knights then converted the sect to Christianity, and hid the Ark in a church. In the 1960s, the Ethiopians built the Old Church of St. Mary of Zion in Axum to house the reputed Ark—now said to be in the treasury building next door. ◆

▲ Painting in the church of St. Mary of Zion, said to be the home of the Ark

THE ROCK CHURCHES OF LALIBELA In northern Ethiopia's Amhara region, 11 medieval monolithic churches were carved out of rock, creating one of the country's holiest sites. It is said that the 12th-century king Lalibela had these spectacular rock churches constructed in an attempt to build a new Jerusalem after Muslim conquests halted Christian pilgrimages to the Holy Land.

BAKAU CROCODILE POOL GAMBIA

Many pilgrims flock to this sacred crocodile pool to search for a cure in its healing waters.

IN A WOODED GLADE near Bakau, Gambians from all over the country come to visit a muddy crocodile pool believed to have miraculous powers. It is said that a palm tree tapper discovered the sacred crocodile pool about 100 years ago, when he stopped to rest for the night. Fearing the crocodiles, he decided to climb into a tree and spend the night there. In the morning, he crept away, hoping the crocodiles would not see him. In fact, they merely blinked and slithered past him into the water—a sign, it was thought, that the pool was blessed.

Although there are healing pools in other parts of the country, the pool near Bakau is the only one with more than 100 crocodiles. The Bojang family, who tends the pool, is not permitted to exploit the site or make any financial profit from it, although it has become a popular tourist spot.

Infertile women travel great distances to bathe in the holy waters. The crocodiles are now so tame that they allow visitors to pet them. While the crocodiles lie sleeping, with their jaws firmly closed, Bojang pool attendants perform ritual washings for the women. After bathing and prayer, the women are given a bottle of water from the pool to pour over their body before going to bed. In return, visitors make a small donation and offer a kola nut. The money is shared among the village elders and the kola nut is thrown into the pool to appease the crocodiles and prolong the healing powers of the pool. ◆

> After bathing and prayer, the women are given water to pour over their bodies before going to bed.

▼ The crocodiles float on the surface of the pool.

GIITUNE SACRED FOREST KENYA

A beautiful forest rescued by the Meru people from the degradations of man-made changes.

THE ANCIENT AND SACRED FOREST of Giitune lies directly on the equator. Yet, among the dense undergrowth and the shadows of the towering trees the air is surprisingly cool. Among the lianas and fig trees the haunting call of the rare colobus monkey carries on the air.

The forest is slowly being restored to its natural wilderness state after many years of destruction caused by conflict and climate change. The Meru people have begun to reclaim their forest by replanting trees. They value the mystical properties it is said to embody.

Over the years, the Meru have developed many myths and taboos about the forest. For example, the Meru are only allowed to cut a tree or its branches with a blunt stone, for no man-made tools are permitted in the forest.

> Anyone who breaks a taboo must sacrifice a sheep and offer prayers to the Meru god, Murungu.

The collection of driftwood, fallen seeds, fruits, and berries is closely supervised by the elders. The killing of any animal is strictly prohibited, as are acts of violence in the forest itself. Anyone who breaks a taboo must sacrifice a sheep and offer prayers to the Meru god, Murungu.

Myths are passed down through oral tradition. It is said that trespassers will be followed and cursed by a gigantic serpent that lies coiled in the deepest undergrowths. There is also said to be a mystical lake in the middle of the forest where trespassers drown. In this serene, closely guarded place, the spirit of the forest is believed to animate every tree, rock, bird, and flower. ◆

▲ The sacred forest world of the Meru

MOUNT KILIMANJARO TANZANIA

Both feared and loved by the local people, magnificent Kilimanjaro has inspired a rich fund of legends.

COMPOSED OF THREE independent peaks—Kibo, Mawenzi, and Shira—Mount Kilimanjaro was shaped by volcanic activity more than 700,000 years ago. In a legend of the Chaga people, who farm the fertile lower slopes, Mawenzi was always pestering Kibo, his bigger and more capable neighbor, begging for food and fire when his coals went out. One day, when Kibo was away from home, Mawenzi went into Kibo's house and helped himself to food and coals. He piled them high and wheeled them out. Kibo, returning home, spotted the glowing coals from afar and realized what had happened. Losing his temper, he thundered across the plain, pulled himself up to his full height, and struck Mawenzi with a mighty blow, leaving a jagged wound across his top.

Kibo last eruped around 200 years ago (Mawenzi and Shira are extinct). The local tribes still fear it; some believe that the lack of snow in recent times is God's punishment for allowing too many foreigners to climb the mountain. According to the Chaga people, mountain spirits guard precious stones hidden in the center of the mountain. Anyone who tries to dig for them will perish. ◆

▲ Snowcapped Kilimanjaro rises from the savanna plain.

MASAI DEITIES Although the local Nilotic people are increasingly embracing Christianity, they traditionally worship Enkai, a deity with a dual nature: Enkai Narok (Black God) is merciful while Enkai Nanyokie (Red God) is retributive. The sacred mountain of the Masai is Ol Doinyo Lengai in northern Tanzania. The Masai use masks (right) for their religious rituals and as ornaments.

AYERS ROCK NORTHERN TERRITORIES, AUSTRALIA

The concept of Dreamtime is most palpable at the spectacular site of Uluru, known as Ayers Rock.

Marindi's blood streamed down the sides of the rock, turning it red in the sunset.

I N THE LATE AFTERNOON, as the sun sinks toward the horizon, Ayers Rock glows a deep red, its radiant hulk an extraordinary interruption to the otherwise featureless desert plain and sky. People travel hundreds of miles to see this geological phenomenon in the outback of the Northern Territories. It rises 1,142 feet (348 m) above ground, and is 5.8 miles (9.4 km) in circumference. For the Aboriginal Anangu people, who have lived here for more than 10,000 years, Uluru, as Ayers Rock is known to them, was created in Dreamtime (see panel opposite), when spirits journeyed across the featureless earth creating or becoming rivers, gorges, mountains, caves, grass, and boulders. Depressions in the landscape were often attributed to the footprints of these creator spirits. Even the empty desert was assigned to spirits known as *djang*.

According to one of many Dreamtime stories attached to Uluru, the rock rose up when the Sleepy Lizard Women lured two tribes of ancestral spirits away from a special ceremony hosted by the Mulga tribe. Angered by their guests' rudeness, the hosts sang evil songs into the ground, which formed into a terrifying dingo called Kurpannga (now said to prowl the top of Uluru). Kurpannga descended upon the tribes, and a great battle ensued that ended in the deaths of both tribal chiefs. Rising up in grief, the earth became Uluru and wept red tears.

Another myth attributes the rock's dramatic red hue to the lizard spirit Adnoartina and the dog spirit Marindi, who were continually fighting over prey. Because they were equally matched, neither succeeded in vanquishing the other. However, one day they fought

▼ Ayers Rock is linked directly to Dreamtime.

DREAMTIME In Aboriginal mythology, the beginning of creation is known as the Dreamtime, an era when spirits gave form to the land and stocked it with animals and plants. Physical features have spiritual potency, which the Aboriginals call its "Dreaming." Mystical trails known as songlines connect a huge web of sacred sites, and the Dreamtime is kept alive through storytelling, dance, art, and rituals. By reciting the myths associated with these places, Aboriginals can navigate their way across Australia's vast interior.

just beneath Ayers Rock. As darkness fell, Marindi proposed they wait until the following day to settle their fight, but Adnoartina refused, and the fight continued. Eventually, Adnoartina grasped Marindi by the neck and throttled him. He then dragged Marindi's body to the top of the rock to eat him. As he tore at the flesh, Marindi's blood streamed down the sides of the rock, turning Uluru red in the setting sun.

Throughout Australia it was thought that if people followed the exact rituals accorded to the sacred place or site, they would also have direct communication with the spirits. Many rituals and taboos connected with Uluru seek to do this, with parts of the rock reserved for ritual use, especially rites of passage for young men. Anangu people consider it sacrilegious to climb Uluru, which draws them into conflict with tourism at Uluru. The surprisingly large number of accidents, including fatalities, among the tourists who climb Uluru is often interpreted as punishment exacted by the Dreamtime spirits. ◆

▲ Aboriginal art is almost always inspired by landscape and Dreamtime myths. Earth colors, such as red and brown, feature prominently as do white (for sky) and black (for water).

▲ A flying saucer spinning above the countryside

UFO HOT

SPOTS

RENDLESHAM FOREST SUFFOLK, ENGLAND

The Rendlesham Forest incident is one of the most famous unexplained incidents in UFO history.

▲ *Rendlesham Forest, 1980* by American artist Micah Lidberg

SOON AFTER MIDNIGHT ON a freezing December day in 1980, American servicemen stationed at RAF Woodbridge in the southeast of England reported seeing strange lights in the sky. At the same time, radars at the twin base of RAF Bentwaters, north of nearby Rendlesham Forest, had tracked an unidentified object.

Lt. Col. Charles Halt and a team of airmen left Bentwaters to investigate the matter. They initially thought the UFO was a downed aircraft. According to Halt's memo, they saw a glowing object that was metallic in appearance, with colored lights. Serviceman Sgt. Jim Penniston later claimed that he saw an alien craft, triangular in shape and 6 to 9 feet (2–3 m) across.

In the days after the incident, the men returned to the site to investigate what had happened. They detected high levels of radiation in the trees, and saw strange lights again appearing in the sky.

The men's claims could not be proved, and some people suggested they had mistaken lights from a nearby lighthouse for a UFO. After the incident, the men filed top secret witness reports. Copies were leaked to the press and public attention turned to the findings. The presence of radiation was enough to convince the authorities that something strange had landed in the darkness of the forest. People still visit Rendlesham today in the hope of discovering the answer. ◆

WHEN TO VISIT

Explore the misty UFO trail at the time of the winter solstice, early in the morning.

WARMINSTER

WILTSHIRE, ENGLAND

Menacing sounds and vibrations in this quiet town presaged a wave of alleged UFO sightings.

O N CHRISTMAS MORNING, 1964, Mrs. Marjorie Bye was walking to Mass in the town of Warminster when she suddenly felt an oppressive, vibrating energy descend upon her. When shock waves began pounding her head, neck, and shoulders, she huddled against the church in fear, looking up at the sky but seeing nothing.

Over the next few months, many other people reported similar experiences, including nine cases that featured on the front page of the local newspaper, the *Warminster Journal*. Many people not only reported experiencing strange sensations, but also claimed that they had seen curious objects in the sky.

The UFOs were said to be silent, stationary, and cigar-shaped, and covered in winking bright lights. In September 1965, a family in a nearby village claimed they witnessed a brightly glowing, cigar-shaped object remain motionless in the skies for 30 minutes. Arthur Shuttlewood compiled a large dossier of cases, including his own report of seeing a UFO from his home.

> The UFOs were said to be silent, stationary, and cigar-shaped, and covered in winking lights.

Meanwhile, a teenage boy called Gordon Faulkner took a now famous black-and-white photograph of a UFO, which he passed to Shuttlewood, who in turn handed it to a national newspaper. Soon thousands of people from all over Britain and beyond were flooding into the town, hoping to view the strange phenomenon.

Reports of UFO sightings above Cradle Hill, on the outskirts of Warminster, continued for another ten years. It became one of the most popular skywatching sites in England in the 1970s. ◆

▼ Warminster is considered a UFO hot spot.

BERWYN MOUNTAINS SNOWDONIA, WALES

In the 1970s, the inhabitants of a remote Welsh village became convinced they had witnessed a UFO.

O N A COLD, WET EVENING in January 1974, a violent earth tremor ripped through the Berwyn Mountains in Snowdonia National Park, reaching 4.5 on the Richter scale. No one was sure if it was an earthquake or the force of an object from outer space hitting the planet. Some people suspected a meteorite had fallen to earth, but not long after the tremor died down unusual lights were seen in the sky. Rumors spread that a military aircraft or a secret space rocket had crashed.

Local residents later claimed their furniture moved, buildings vibrated, lights dimmed, and pets howled or cowered under the table during the incident. Some witnesses reported seeing glowing red lights streak across the sky, and then disappear into the atmosphere, as if an armada of spacecraft were chasing each other.

▼ The remote Berwyn Mountains, where the disturbances took place

One resident, Pat Evans, feared a terrible plane crash had occurred and volunteered to help find the site. As she made her way to the affected area, she saw a large, glowing sphere pulsating in the distance, changing color from red to yellow to white. Later, she recalled seeing small white lights on either side of the object.

As the rest of the track was inaccessible due to the bad weather, Pat returned to the village, just as the police search party arrived. They were later joined by military personnel and the area was declared a no-go area while the wreckage was recovered. Rumors spread that alien bodies had been found and the British government had covered up the truth of a UFO crash landing. ◆

▲ Was it a meteor shower or something more sinister that streaked across the sky on a dark night in 1974?

DECHMONT WOODS LIVINGSTON, SCOTLAND

For many, an alleged close encounter between a forestry worker and a giant sphere has the ring of truth.

WHEN FORESTRY WORKER Robert Taylor parked his truck on a forest trail off the M8 highway one November morning in 1979, his mind was on the day's tasks. However, when he walked up the heavily wooded slope with his dog and reached the top, he stopped dead in his tracks. In the clearing he claimed he saw a dark, spherical object made of a rough metallic material, with a band around the outside. It was about 20 feet (6 m) across.

As he moved cautiously forward to get a better view, he claims two spiked spheres dropped from the object. About 3 feet (1 m) wide, and similar in appearance to mines, they rolled toward him in unison, then stopped either side of his legs. His dog began to bark as the spikes hooked into his pants and pulled him toward the spheres.

> The dog barked as the spikes hooked into his owner's pants and pulled him toward the spheres.

He remembers hearing a hissing sound and smelling an acrid but invisible gas that made him choke.

The next thing he knew, he was regaining consciousness, face down on the grass with his dog nearby, his legs aching, and his pants torn. The strange objects had apparently disappeared from the clearing. He managed to crawl back to his truck, but it would not start, so he stumbled back to his home in Livingston on foot.

Taylor later revisited the site with the police. They found marks in the soil where he claimed the craft had been, and tracks from the spiked spheres. Although they found nothing else, many have viewed this eyewitness account from a normally skeptical man as a true UFO encounter. ◆

▲ An artist's impression of what Robert Taylor claimed he saw

NUREMBERG BAVARIA, GERMANY

The skies above this north German town turned into a celestial battlefield one morning in 1561.

▲ The woodcut by Hans Glaser records the sky battle over Nuremberg.

AS DAWN ROSE OVER NUREMBERG on April 14, 1561, local citizens woke to an inexplicable terror. Seemingly, the skies above the town flashed, rumbled, and raged not with storm clouds but with objects. Thousands of solid crosses, rods, and spheres purportedly flew across the heavens. Many citizens thought the strange spectacle was an act of God, intended as a lesson to sinners.

According to those who left witness accounts, the events of that morning lasted more than an hour. The contemporary artist Hans Glaser recorded the scene: His woodcut shows cylinders launching numerous blue and black spheres, red crosses, and flying disks. Large rods flew toward the sun, and several objects crashed to earth, vanishing in a thick cloud of smoke.

A local pamphleteer reported that a dreadful apparition, possibly sent by God, had filled the morning sky with cylindrical shapes. From these shapes, which today might have been referred to as spaceships, emerged black, red, orange, and blue-white spheres that darted erratically around the sky. He reported seeing a black, spear-like object slash through the clouds and darken the sky as the spectacle drew to a close.

It seems that the battle in the sky ended as suddenly as it had begun, leaving the citizens of Nuremberg convinced they needed to repent their sins. ◆

WHEN TO VISIT

Go in early spring, when some say the night skies fill with the ghosts of past UFOs.

WALLONIA BELGIUM

In 1990 two supersonic F-16 jets chased a suspected spacecraft through the skies over Belgium.

FROM OCTOBER 1989 through most of 1990, reports of flying objects in the skies over Belgium numbered in the thousands. Some 13,500 people witnessed the phenomena—the majority in Wallonia—including 2,600 people who filed statements describing what they had seen. Most claimed to have seen triangular-shaped aircraft.

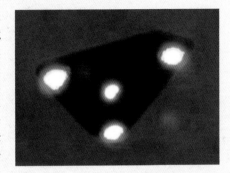

Local police on patrol near the town of Eupen were among the first to file a report. They described how a triangular craft, stationary in the air, illuminated the ground with three powerful beams. These came from circular areas on each corner of the craft; a gyrating red beacon shone from the center of its base.

In March 1990, events took a new turn when the Belgian air force gave chase to one of the craft, using supersonic F-16 jets tracked by airborne and ground radars. The pilots reported that the flight path and trajectories were too extraordinary to explain. Even the air force's 1,250-mile-an-hour (2,000 kph) jets were too slow to keep up when the craft accelerated from 170 to 1100 miles an hour (280 to 1,800 kph) in less than a second and came to a dead stop once they were out of range.

Sightings of similar UFOs over Belgium continued throughout 1990. According to witness statements, the mysterious spaceships made no noise other than a low humming sound. Like the earlier jets, they hovered in the air and then accelerated at very high speed. Many of these civilian sightings were confirmed by Belgian air force pilots, as well as by police officers and air traffic controllers. ◆

▲ Witness reports were consistent in describing the suspected UFOs as triangular with four bright lights.

▼ Most of the UFO sightings were reported in the region of Wallonia.

HESSDALEN SØR-TRØNDELAG, NORWAY

The regular appearance of strange orbs in this Norwegian valley confounds even hardened UFO skeptics.

LOCALS HAVE RECORDED seeing lights of unknown origin in this meandering valley below the icy peaks of the Forollhogna Mountains since the 1940s. Reports peaked between December 1981 and the summer of 1984, with up to 15 or 20 cases each week. Curious tourists soon flocked to the valley, clamoring to spend the night here in the hope of seeing the lights.

The Hessdalen light is described as bright, white or yellow, and standing or floating above the ground. Sometimes, it is said, the light can be seen for more than an hour, along with other unexplained lights radiating from the same valley.

Scientists have put forward various explanations for the lights, including a combustion process involving dust clouds from the valley floor. Another theory is that witnesses are mistaking aircraft, headlights, or astronomical debris for UFOs. In the summer of 1983, local organizations established Project Hessdalen to investigate the phenomenon with the help of scientists and students from Norwegian universities. The investigators carried out a field study in early 1984. They recorded 53 light observations but made no progress in determining how or why the bizarre lights appear.

People still report strange light activity in the valley, though the number of incidents has decreased. Reports now number between 10 and 20 each year. ◆

▲ Could a combination of landscape, atmosphere, and climate be responsible for the lights?

SPOOK LIGHTS Eerie spirit lights feature in most European folklore. The legendary will-o'-the-wisp (right), a dancing golden light, also known as a spook light or jack-o'-lantern, is said to be either a spirit doomed to haunt marshes and wasteland or a fairy who stalks roadsides in order to lead unwary travelers astray.

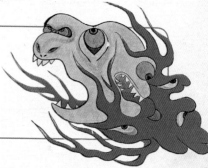

ISTANBUL TURKEY

In 2008 disk-like objects hovered silently over the Sea of Marmara before scurrying across the sky.

OVER THE COURSE of several days and nights in mid-2008, reports of UFOs flooded in from residents living alongside the Sea of Marmara in Istanbul. The objects appeared as glowing orange ovals or cigar-shaped disks with red pulsating lights in each corner.

The sightings were documented and videotaped by Yalcin Yalmin, a security guard at the Yeni Kent Compound, a holiday village in the resort of Kumburgaz. He used a high-spec video recorder with a zoom lens. Considered to be one of the best UFO videos to come out of Turkey, it showed a large amount of detail at high resolution.

The guard took the footage during the early hours of the morning on moonlit nights between the months

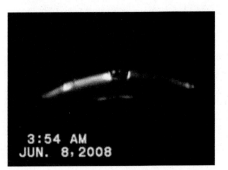

3:54 AM
JUN. 8, 2008

of May and September. The video shows close-range shots of metallic-looking UFOs floating over the sea. Some footage even appears to show occupants peering through a cockpit in the center of one of the alleged spacecraft.

The Scientific and Technology Board of Turkey and the National Observatory reviewed the footage in an attempt to prove the incidents were a hoax, but they were unsuccessful. Experts in Japan, Russia, Brazil, and Chile also examined the film. To date, the aerial objects remain unidentified. On a clear moonlit night in 2009 another sighting was filmed. ◆

▲ Footage of the UFO appears to show a kind of cockpit in the center of the craft.

▼ The Sea of Marmara, the scene of reputed UFO sightings, stretching out beyond Istanbul

SHAG HARBOUR NOVA SCOTIA, CANADA

Strange lights over the harbor preceded the arrival of a glowing craft of unknown origin.

ONE NIGHT IN OCTOBER 1967, residents in Nova Scotia noticed strange orange lights in the sky above the harbor. Not long afterward they heard a whistling sound like a bomb, a "whoosh," and then a loud bang following a bright flash. At least 11 people watched as a low-flying object crashed into the harbor.

Thinking that it was a terrible plane crash, witnesses telephoned the Royal Canadian Mounted Police. One of the constables, Ron Pound, had already seen the strange lights and was making his way to the harbor.

When Pound and three other officers arrived at the crash site,

they noticed an object floating on the water about half a mile (1 km) from the shore. It glowed a pale yellow color and left a trail of yellow foam as it drifted on the icy waves.

Coast guards and local fishing boats rushed to the site. By the time they arrived, the light had disappeared, but the rescuers could still see yellow foam, suggesting that the craft had submerged. The following day, the Rescue Coordination Centre in Halifax filed a report with Canadian Forces Headquarters in Ottawa. It stated that something of "unknown origin" had hit the water that night in Shag Harbour. ◆

◀ Fishermen reported seeing strange lights above the water.

MAURY ISLAND WASHINGTON, U.S.A.

In June 1947, an eyewitness to a UFO incident claimed he was silenced by a "man in black."

SEAMAN HAROLD DAHL claimed he saw strange objects flying in the sky while out looking for driftwood with his son, two crewman, and his dog, just off Maury Island. Dahl reported seeing six large metallic objects appear suddenly and silently above their heads. He estimated that the donut-shaped disks were flying about 2,000 feet (600 m) above sea level. Each craft had a hole in the center and rows of windows around the outer side of the ring.

Dahl claimed five of the UFOs circled the sixth, which seemed to be in difficulty. He described how he and his son saw one of the objects collide with another, causing it to lose control and explode, and then

fall to earth in fragments. Most of the debris landed in the bay, but some landed on the beach. Dahl recovered a section of the white lightweight metal.

Dahl claimed that on the morning following the incident, a man in black arrived at his home and invited him to a nearby diner. As they ate breakfast, the man warned him never to disclose what he had seen. Believing this to be a threat to his family, he changed his story and said the sighting was a hoax. Later, however, he told newspapers that the sighting had been real, but he had retracted his story for fear of reprisals. ◆

▲ Harold Dahl claimed a donut-shaped craft exploded above his boat.

FLATWOODS BRAXTON COUNTY, WEST VIRGINIA, U.S.A.

Of the many reports of aliens in 1950s America, the "Flatwoods Monster" is perhaps the most famous.

ON SEPTEMBER 12, 1952, four boys were playing football at Flatwoods School, Braxton, when they saw a bright fiery ball fall through the sky and land on a hill not far from the school. The boys ran to the home of one of the boys and excitedly told his mother, Mrs. Kathlyn May, what they had seen. The boys and the woman set off to investigate, accompanied by a family friend who was a member of the National Guard. As they approached the site, they could see a glowing, hissing object and smelled an acrid, metallic odor.

According to the story they later told, they came upon a monstrous 15-foot (5 m) being with a red face, orange eyes that glowed, and green clothing that hung in great folds. They described the creature's body as being humanoid, though other accounts record that

> They came upon a monstrous 15-foot being with a red face and orange eyes.

the creature had no visible arms, while others describe it as having stubby arms with claw-like fingers. As the creature floated toward them, the group fled.

Their sighting was verified by other witnesses. They too had seen a fiery object crashing to earth not far from Flatwoods School. When the police investigated the site they found no physical evidence except some track marks, which they attributed to a car, but they did smell the sickening odor that had been reported and detected an unusual heat in the air.

After the incident, many people in the area became sick with respiratory problems thought to be caused by the acrid fumes or some kind of radiation. ◆

▲ Kathlyn May discovers the Flatwoods Monster on a hillside near Flatwoods.

SEDONA ARIZONA, U.S.A.

This energy hot spot in the Arizona desert attracts all kinds of New Age mystics and, some say, UFOs.

SET AGAINST A SPECTACULAR backdrop of red rocks and wide-open skies, Sedona is the New Age capital of the United States. It is famous for its unusually powerful magnetic field, vortexes, and "energies," and it cultivates a reputation for mysticism and spiritual questing. Visitors and residents frequently report seeing UFOs in the area. A thriving UFO industry includes tours, stores, and conferences.

In January 2012, a camera recorded a large, bright green object flying from the south and traveling at high speed toward the Navajo-Hopi reservations. The same month, an identical flying object was seen near the Secret Canyon area.

Such sightings may have begun 20,000–50,000 years ago, when a meteorite crashed in the surrounding desert,

> Lenticular clouds are said to form when spacecraft dip into the atmosphere.

scattering fragments all around Sedona. Most purported UFO activity seems to happen above Bell Rock, a strangely shaped hill south of Sedona that is said to possess a concentration of alien or "higher-dimensional" energy.

Lenticular clouds—lens-shaped formations resembling flying saucers—are often visible during the day. According to local myth, this type of cloud forms when spacecraft dip into Earth's atmosphere.

Many UFO enthusiasts believe Sedona is an entrance and exit ramp for extraterrestrial visitors. The red rock, composed of crystal silicon and iron oxide, gives off a subtle but powerful light, making it a visible landmark from space. ◆

▼ When a meteorite fell to earth many thousands of years ago, it created a crater to the northeast of Sedona.

GULF BREEZE FLORIDA, U.S.A.

This well-documented UFO incident has so far defied scientific attempts to prove it a hoax.

IN THE WINTER OF 1987, many witnesses reported an unusual flying craft in the skies above Florida. Ed Walters, a building contractor in Gulf Breeze, recorded a series of sightings over a three-week period, producing hundreds of high-quality photographs.

It began on the night of November 11, while he was working late in his living room. Looking up from his papers, he noticed a strange glowing object shaped like a child's spinning top outside the front of his house. He walked outside to investigate and noticed that the craft hovered just above the surface of the road. He could see windows and portals and a glowing ring around the bottom of the craft. He quickly found his Polaroid camera, and took photographs. As he did so, a blue beam

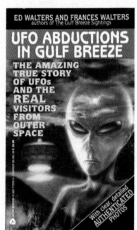

from the UFO lifted him off the ground and pinned him to the wall. A disembodied voice said, "We will not harm you." The next thing he knew, he was waking up on the ground outside his house.

On December 2, Walters claimed he received another extraterrestrial visit, this time by a small creature with large black eyes in his back garden. The figure fled, and he tried to give chase, but once again he was immobilized by a blue beam. Over the next three years, some 200 witnesses came forward with reports, videos, and photographs of similar close encounters, including 30 residents who lived near Walters. ◆

◀ The small town of Gulf Breeze hit the headlines with its extraterrestrial tales.

CLEVELAND OHIO, U.S.A.

A sighting of an unexplained orb in Cleveland is not the first time the city has been visited by UFOs.

IN APRIL 2013, a massive orb was seen in the skies above Cleveland, Ohio. Multiple witnesses filmed the strange circular object as it hovered above the city. Unusually for UFO sightings, it was the middle of the day.

That night, a resident of Cleveland caught the object on a night vision camera while he was filming jets. As he watched, a glowing sphere suddenly accelerated to great speed and then vanished into space. Unlike the jets, it produced no vapor trail. The video of the sighting has since been analyzed by UFO experts, but no conclusions have been drawn so far.

The episode was the latest of several UFO sightings in Cleveland over the years. One of the best known is the Coyne Helicopter Incident. In October 1973, four men in an Army Reserve helicopter flying from Columbus to Cleveland noticed a bright light coming toward them at tremendous speed. Just as the pilot lowered his altitude to avoid a collision, the object stopped and hovered above them. A green beam then swept over the helicopter's windshield, enveloping the cockpit in green light. ◆

▲ The city of Cleveland is associated with several unexplained UFO sightings.

5 UFO HOT SPOTS IN THE AMERICAN SOUTHWEST

The dramatic geology and wide-open spaces of America's Southwest lend themselves to UFO activity—imaginary or real—making it one of the top spots for sightings.

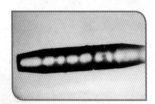

1 MARFA, TEXAS: On a desert plateau in western Texas, the town of Marfa is known for the Marfa Lights—reddish-orange spheres that are 3 to 6 feet (1–3 m) in diameter and travel at high speed. They are said to glow like a distant star at first, then brighten to the intensity of a flashlight, sometimes flickering on and off. There is a public viewing platform 9 miles (25 km) east of Marfa, on Highway 90.

2 LEVELLAND, TEXAS: At 11 p.m. on November 2, 1957, patrolman A. J. Fowler took a call from Pedro Saucedo and Joe Salaz. They explained how they had been out driving when a brightly lit, cigar-shaped object had come toward them. As it approached, their engine cut out. Similar calls followed. They all described an egg-shaped craft that changed from orange to a bluish-green color as it landed.

3 PINEY WOODS, TEXAS: In 1980 Betty Cash, her friend, and her friend's grandson were driving home when they came upon a diamond-shaped UFO that was emitting tremendous heat. Military helicopters circled overhead. Back home, they were treated for radiation sickness, and Betty was later found to have skin cancer. The three failed in their attempt to make the government accept liability.

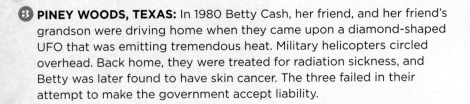

4 TURKEY SPRINGS, ARIZONA: Logger Travis Walton reported being abducted by aliens in the Apache-Sitgreaves National Forest, near Turkey Springs, on November 5, 1975. Six colleagues said they had fled in fear after seeing lights and a disk hovering above Walton. When they returned with police, Walton had vanished. Walton reappeared five days later to tell his extraordinary story.

5 STEPHENVILLE, TEXAS: In 2008 the town of Stephenville made national headlines when local residents reported dozens of UFO sightings. In the early evening of January 8, reports of massive crafts filling the skies poured into police stations. Some claimed they were the size of a football field; others that they were 1 mile (1.6 km) long. Many claimed that they saw military aircraft pursuing the UFOs.

▼ Unusual rock formations, such as these mesas in Arizona, are often associated with UFO activity.

ROSWELL NEW MEXICO, U.S.A.

One of the most controversial UFO incidents in U.S. history began with a storm over New Mexico.

AFTER A HOT AND HUMID day in July 1947, a violent thunderstorm erupted over the state of New Mexico, filling the night sky with lightning, rain, and thunder. On a ranch just outside the town of Roswell, sheep rancher Mac Brazel noticed that the storm seemed different from those he usually encountered. He began to feel uneasy. Suddenly there was an extremely loud crash, but after a while he decided to go to bed for the night and slept through the rest of the storm, unaware of what was happening.

The next morning Brazel went to examine the damage that the storm had caused. Discovering large amounts of debris scattered across his pastures, he took some of the pieces to show his neighbors, and contacted the County Sheriff, George Wilcox.

Wilcox reported the incident to the Army Air Field Office, which arranged for the retrieval of the remainder of the pieces. On July 8, news leaked out that the Air Force had a flying disk, or UFO, in its possession. It is said that many people involved were ordered to cover up the truth by saying the pieces were part of a weather balloon. A few weeks later, a nurse working for the Air Force claimed that she was called to assist in an alien autopsy.

News of the flying disk made international headlines. To this day, there are many people who believe the Roswell incident to be one of the biggest ever cover-ups by the U.S. government. ◆

▲ Roswell has become world-famous for the UFO incident said to have taken place there.

▼ A conceptual image of an alien laid out for autopsy

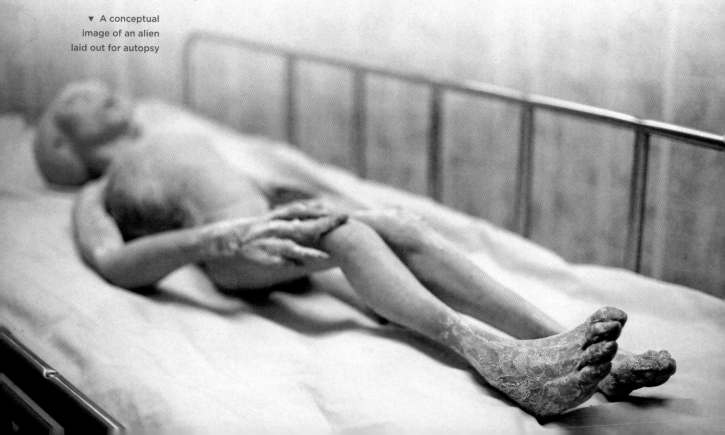

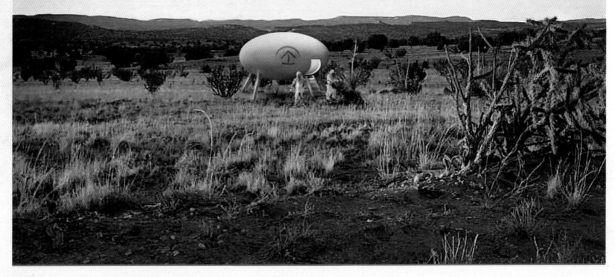

SOCORRO NEW MEXICO, U.S.A.

Government agencies investigated this UFO sighting in Socorro, but their findings were inconclusive.

IN 1964 POLICE OFFICER Lonnie Zamora claimed he had been chasing a speeding car when he heard a thunderous roar and saw a bluish-orange flame in the distance. He stopped his car and began to walk slowly toward a shining, egg-shaped object that was the size of a car. It had red markings on its side.

According to the account Zamora gave in interviews to the U.S. Air Force and the FBI, as he approached the object, two small humanoids clad in white coveralls turned toward him and then disappeared behind the object. As Zamora moved forward, a large engine roared into life, and blue flames shot out from the underside of the craft. Thinking that the object was about to explode,

Zamora fell to the ground to protect himself. When he lifted his head, he saw the object rise from the ground and disappear into the distance. Police reinforcements arrived too late to see the departing craft, but they recorded indentations and burn marks on the ground.

Other witnesses reported similar sightings that night. Paul Kies and Larry Kratzer, who were driving into Socorro from the southwest, reported seeing flames and clouds of brown dust as an oval object shot off over the horizon. Five tourists from Colorado claimed a low-flying oval object passed directly over their car.

▲ The witnesses described seeing an egg-shaped craft.

THE DULCE COMPLEX Beneath the Jicarilla Apache Indian Reservation, a secret government installation is said to house an alien genetics laboratory. Here, captured extraterrestrials are reputedly held for cloning and other experimental purposes. Those operating on this mission may have worn an NRO military patch indicating the classified nature of their work (right).

See Also: Roswell, p. 194

AREA 51 NEVADA, U.S.A.

Could scientists at this secret U.S. airbase have been experimenting on captured UFOs and aliens?

An engineer claimed he worked alongside an extraterrestrial being.

▼ The government chose Area 51 for its remote location. Official maps do not include it.

Deep in the Nevada desert, about 80 miles (130 km) from Las Vegas, lies Area 51, a dusty airbase surrounded by mountains. Although the base was founded in 1955, it was not until 2013 that the CIA even acknowledged its existence. The U.S. government still maintains a high level of secrecy about the site, and the surrounding area is permanently off-limits to both civilian and ordinary military air traffic.

So what goes on in this installation? The extreme secrecy has led to many bizarre theories. Some people even say that aliens occupy the base and are creating a human-alien hybrid here.

A favorite theory among ufologists is that the base was set up to examine crashed UFOs and to store captured alien spacecraft, including debris from the highly publicized 1947 Roswell crash, which many believe was extraterrestrial in nature. Some people claim that government agencies study dead and living aliens here, or use it to hold secret meetings with aliens. Another popular theory is that the U.S. government faked the 1969 moon landing here.

GETTING CLOSER UFO hunters identify three classes of close encounters with extraterrestrial beings. Sighting a UFO within 150 yards (150 m) is a close encounter of the first kind; close encounters of the second kind are when a UFO leaves some form of physical evidence such as a burn mark at the site; close encounters of the third kind are sightings of an alien associated with a UFO. The ufologist and astronomer Josef Allen Hynek, who worked on a study of UFOs for the U.S. Air Force, coined this terminology. The third category was popularized by the 1977 blockbuster movie *Close Encounters of the Third Kind*.

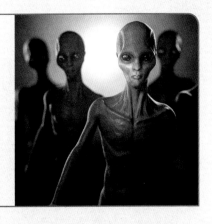

Most Air Force representatives publicly deny such rumors, admitting only to military weapons and conducting tests on Soviet aircraft at the base, but some ex-employees claim to have witnessed strange goings-on. In 1989, for example, the scientist Bob Lazar said he had worked on deconstructing a captured flying saucer at a related facility close to Area 51. Likewise, a mechanical engineer who claimed he worked at Area 51 during the 1950s said in a documentary film that he had helped develop a flying disk simulator at the base, working alongside an extraterrestrial being named J-Rod. Another former employee, Dan Crain, declared that he had also met J-Rod and cloned alien viruses while there. ◆

▲ Humankind has been fascinated with extraterrestrial life for decades, manifested in many popular movies.

SAN CLEMENTE MAULE, CHILE

Could a mysterious stone pavement in the Andes be an ancient landing strip for alien spaceships?

▲ There have been more than 100 reports of UFOs in the area around San Clemente since the mid-1990s.

WHEN TO VISIT

Reports of UFOS are said to peak during December— high summer in the Andes.

IN THE SHADOW OF THE ANDES, the once peaceful town of San Clemente is the UFO capital of Chile, a country where UFO sightings receive regular coverage in the media, and an annual program of conferences on extraterrestrial themes attracts UFO hunters from all over the world.

Reports of strange lights and unidentified craft in the skies above San Clemente increased during the 1990s. In 2008, in response to the multiple sightings, the government created a 19-mile (30 km) UFO trail through the Andes, linking the places where inhabitants claimed to have experienced UFO activity. The trail crosses El Enladrillado, a large area of volcanic blocks that form a pavement high above the Rio Clara Valley. No one knows who formed El Enladrillado, but two of three standing stones on the plateau align with the magnetic north, while the third aligns with the midsummer sunrise. Some people maintain that aliens created El Enladrillado in order to land their spacecraft.

Among the UFOs sighted near San Clemente are shining spheres that hover low over the land and then disappear into wooded areas or water. They are sometimes seen in conjunction with white and purple beams that are 6 to 9 feet (2–3 m) across. There have also been reports of lights flying in unison over the town at night and then disappearing into the darkness. Chile's government has not offered any explanation for the phenomena. ◆

MARACAIBO ZULIA, VENEZUELA

When an intense light appeared over a home in Maracaibo its occupants fell violently ill.

ONE STORMY NIGHT IN 1886, a family living on the outskirts of Maracaibo endured a harrowing experience. The chilling story includes evidence of radiation poisoning almost a decade before radioactivity was known about.

An intensely bright light woke the family of nine during the night of October 24. Assuming a fire had taken hold in the neighborhood, the family left their home in search of safety. Once outside, however, they realized the light emanated from an object hovering above their house. It hummed a dull, continuous sound.

With no knowledge of unexplained aerial phenomena, the family believed the end of the world was coming and decided to pray. As they fell to their knees, they became violently ill with vomiting, and their upper abdomen, face, and lips began to swell. Over the days that followed, their hair fell out and sores developed on their skin.

The victims attributed their injuries to a curse from God; in reality, they were symptomatic of severe radiation poisoning. Nearby farm animals also became ill, and vegetation and trees withered and died.

Detailed accounts of this bizarre incident circulated, and the U.S. consul issued a report. Some say that the bright light hovering above them was an alien spacecraft that had malfunctioned, and that it expelled radioactive energy as it tried to recover. ◆

> Their injuries were symptomatic of severe radiation poisoning.

▲ Could the mysterious, bright hovering light, which emitted radiation, have been a UFO?

PUMAPUNKU TIWANAKU, BOLIVIA

Intriguing theories about extraterrestrials attempt to explain the origins of this enormous structure.

PUMAPUNKU FORMS PART OF A LARGE TEMPLE COMPLEX known as the Tiwanaku site, believed by the Inca to be where the world began. Predating the Inca, it consists of an earthen mound with a stone terrace approximately 20 by 125 feet (6 x 38 m), paved with gigantic stone blocks with joints so precise that not even a razor blade fits between many of them.

Mystery surrounds the purpose and building of Pumapunku. Some believe that Tiwanaku was once a great port on Lake Titicaca (see p. 150)—now some 15 miles (24 km) away—and the terrace is the remains of a wharf where ships once docked. Others believe that the engineering involved in transporting and working with such large blocks—one of which weighs an estimated 400 tons—suggests technology far in advance of that used in Tiwanaku in A.D. 500, the date usually given for Pumapunku's construction. Furthermore, the quarry for these giant blocks lies on the western shore of Titicaca; it is unlikely that the simple reed boats in use in the sixth century could have transported them, and could people have heaved them so far and so high?

One theory is that Tiwanaku's inhabitants discovered the abandoned stone wharf long after it was constructed. An early 20th-century adventurer named Arthur Posnansky claimed Pumapunku was built as an ancient seaport in around 13,000 B.C., when, he calculated, two pillars on the site would have aligned with the rising and setting sun when viewed from the center of the plaza. To support his theory, he pointed to the many images of extinct Pleistocene animals on the stones, traces of an ancient shoreline, the presence of marine fossils, and the paradox of a seaport existing at an altitude of 12,500 feet (3,800 m) above sea level.

> Two pillars on the site would have aligned with the rising and setting sun.

▼ The precisely cut stones of Pumapunku

BUILT BY ALIENS? Throughout the world there are many ancient sites that some contend must have been built by aliens. Among these is the fortress of Sacsayhuaman overlooking the city of Cusco in Peru. Its massive walls fit together so precisely that a piece of paper cannot fit between some of the stone blocks. In Lebanon, the temple of Baalbeck is built on three stones that form the largest building blocks in the world, each weighing around 800 tons—seemingly impossible for humans to move without machinery.

According to Posnansky's theory, the great shift in Earth's axis that ended the Pleistocene period around 11,700 B.C. caused a great uplift in Earth's crust, leaving the once booming seaport stranded in the middle of the mountains far from the sea, and scattering its enormous stone building blocks.

Posnansky's theory led to claims that extraterrestrials built the ancient seaport, using their superior technology to transport and cut the huge stone slabs, and construct buildings on the favorable shores of the sea. The extraterrestrials then either abandoned the ruins, or were wiped out, leaving Pumapunku to be discovered thousands of years later by the Inca. ◆

▲ Some cite Sacsayhuaman's vast size and precise engineering as evidence of extraterrestrial origins.

HANGZHOU ZHEJIANG PROVINCE, CHINA

An object in the skies over Hangzhou closed the airport and brought citizens onto the streets.

At about 8:40 p.m. on July 7, 2010, a flight crew was preparing for descent into Hangzhou when they saw a UFO hovering in the skies over the airport. Passengers on the plane, who had also spotted the object, later stated that it looked like a twinkling spot. Soon afterward, air traffic control grounded outbound planes and diverted inbound flights to nearby airports. They closed the airport for over an hour. People who were stuck there later recalled a fearful silence around them as the authorities tried to pass off the episode as a military flyover that had been badly timed.

Residents of Hangzhou also noticed the strange goings-on in the sky that day. In the afternoon, hours before the airport was closed, many people photographed a hovering object bathed in golden light, with a comet-like tail. They recalled that it pulsated and moved in the sky and then suddenly disappeared without trace. In the hour before the airport was closed, other witnesses claimed they saw a flying object emitting red and white beams of light toward the ground. One local resident was out on an evening stroll with his wife when they both saw a beam of light flash above their heads. Looking up, the couple saw a streak of bright, white light flying across the sky, and they quickly took photographs.

To this day, no one is able to give a clear or convincing explanation of the event witnessed by so many citizens. Local authorities maintain that what the general public and airport officials reported seeing that day was probably just sunlight reflected from aircraft. ◆

> No one is able to give a clear or convincing explanation of the event.

▲ Many Hangzhou residents took photographs of the object as it streaked across the sky.

HARASHAGAHAMA
HITACHI PROVINCE, JAPAN

An early 19th-century document details one of the oddest close encounters recorded in the Far East.

A DOCUMENT FILED in Japan's archives includes illustrated accounts by Japanese fishermen about being lost at sea and finding themselves in strange new lands. But one story is different. It relates how, in the spring of 1803, near the village of Harashagahama, the tide washed a strange-looking craft onto the shore. The vessel, measuring about 9 feet (3 m) tall and 15 feet (5 m) wide, appeared to be made from red sandalwood bound by metal strips. It was bowl-shaped and had windows made of glass or crystal.

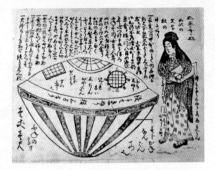

The appearance of the vessel created such a stir that the villagers rushed down to the shore, curious to see the strange craft for themselves. It became known as Utsuro Bune, or the hollow ship. The original drawing that accompanies this tale confirms the shape of the craft.

Inside the ship, people saw symbols and writing in an unknown language and style. But there was something else inside the craft that was even more astonishing—a young woman, with pale skin and red eyebrows and hair. The accounts state that she was about 18 years old and spoke in a strange language. In her arms, she held a wooden box that she would not let anyone touch. As she tried to tell them about her journey, the craft drifted away on the evening tide.

Over the next few months, drawings depicting the same bowl-shaped craft and woman appeared in other regions of Japan. Theories sprang up that the craft was a spaceship and the woman an extraterrestrial being in human form who had visited Earth to tell about another world. ◆

▲ One of the documents recording the strange craft

▼ Did a spring tide in 1803 bring a spaceship to the shores of Japan?

BANDIAGARA ESCARPMENT MALI

In the oral history of the Dogon people, an ancient race of extraterrestrials came to Earth from Sirius B.

THE DOGON PEOPLE OF MALI'S BANDIAGARA ESCARPMENT have a complex culture that is quite different from the cultures of other people in the region. It includes an ancient creation myth involving a race of extraterrestrial people known as the Nommos, who they believe visited Earth from the Sirius star system many thousands of years ago.

According to the Dogon's oral history, the Nommos, an alien race of amphibian creatures, came from a companion star of Sirius, the brightest star in the night skies. Now known as Sirius B, this star is invisible to the human eye and was not discovered by Western astronomers until the mid-19th century.

According to the Dogon, the Nommos landed on Earth in an ark that spun like a top and descended through the air, causing a thunderous storm and a terrible wind. Some who believe that the Dogon are of ancient Egyptian descent point to images and references to similar amphibian beings in Babylonian, Akkadian, and Sumerian myths. The Egyptian goddess Isis is also linked with Sirius, and alignments with the star governed many ancient Egyptian ceremonies.

The Dogon claim that the Nommos not only gave them their knowledge of Sirius B but also told them about other astronomical features long before Western scientists and astronomers discovered them. These included the four major moons of Jupiter, the rings of Saturn, and the fact that the planets orbit the sun—a claim that later landed the 17th-century Italian astronomer Galileo Galilei under permanent house arrest for heresy.

Recent astronomical discoveries echo Dogon myths.

▼ Dogon rock paintings on the Bandiagara escarpment, an area of sandy cliffs

ALIEN EVIDENCE According to British conspiracy theorist David Icke, Italian journalist Peter Kolosimo, and Swiss author Erich von Däniken, intelligent aliens visited Earth in ancient times and left evidence of themselves in rock paintings, carvings, and structures such as Stonehenge (see p. 122). In his 1968 book, *Chariots of the Gods*, von Däniken claimed that extraterrestrials directed the creation of the Nazca Lines (see p. 152) for use as a landing base. Most archaeologists believe there is no truth to such claims.

The Dogon story was first brought to popular attention by Robert K. G. Temple in a book called *The Sirius Mystery*, published in 1977 and largely based on fieldwork among the Dogon in the 1930s by the French anthropologist Marcel Griaule and his student Germaine Dieterlen. With a 400-year-old Dogon codex depicting the Sirius configuration, and ceremonies known as *sigui* held every 60 years to mark the Sirius cycles recorded since the 13th century, there are many who believe the Dogon people's accounts of past contact with intelligent aliens can only be true.

Recent astronomical discoveries also echo Dogon myths, fueling further speculation that there might be some truth in the stories. According to one Dogon legend, Sirius B orbited a third star in the Sirius system. In 1995 two French researchers, Daniel Benest and J. L. Duvent, wrote an article entitled "Is Sirius a Triple Star?" in the respected international journal *Astronomy and Astrophysics*, suggesting the existence of a small third star in the Sirius system—a possibility that has not yet been disproved. ◆

▲ The figures in these prehistoric rock carvings in Val Camonica, northern Italy, resemble modern-day astronauts.

PRETORIA
GAUTENG PROVINCE, SOUTH AFRICA

In 1965 two normally skeptical patrolmen near Pretoria witnessed something they could not explain.

SHORTLY AFTER MIDNIGHT on September 17, 1965, two policemen, John Locken and Koos de Klerk, were patrolling the highway between Pretoria and the town of Bronkhorstspruit, 30 miles (50 km) to the east. Suddenly, their headlights illuminated an unusual object ahead of them—a disk-shaped craft. Neither of them had ever seen such an object before.

Leaving their vehicle, the two patrolmen went to take a closer look. They noticed that the object was copper in color and about 30 feet (9 m) in diameter. Suddenly, without warning, the craft sped away as flames roared out of long metallic tubes from the base of the craft. Constable Locken said the liftoff was quicker than anything he had seen before. The flames, which rose 3 feet (1 m) above the road, continued to burn the asphalt surface for some time. Investigations later revealed that parts of the road had caved in, as if under the pressure of an immense weight, and there were severe burn marks in the road.

The government took the incident seriously and analyzed samples from the site. However, they never released the results of their tests and never explained the incident. ◆

◄ The object shot off suddenly and burned the asphalt below.

TASSILI N'AJJER PARK
ALGERIA

Did extraterrestrials who visited Earth thousands of years ago leave a clue in the Sahara desert?

WHEN HENRI LHOTE (1903–1991), a French explorer, ethnographer, and expert in prehistoric cave art, discovered more than 800 magnificent works of rock art in a remote region of the Sahara desert, he was more than excited. Lhote believed in alien astronauts, and was convinced that the images were evidence of ancient alien contact.

Lhote came across the ancient rock paintings on an outcrop of isolated rocks on an expedition he made just after World War II. They included prancing antelopes, galloping horses, lions, and elephants, and red-colored human figures—male and female—wearing fringed tunics and elegant dresses.

As he looked closer, he noticed that one of the paintings included unusual-looking larger figures, one of which later became known as the Great Martian God. The press publicized Lhote's belief that the painting depicted a prehistoric encounter with extraterrestrials. The Swiss writer Erich von Däniken (see p. 205) later cited Lhote's conviction in his own claims that alien astronauts once visited Earth. ◆

▲ The Great Martian God, the rock painting that convinced Lhote that the rock art was inspired by aliens

BOUZNIKA CHAOUIA-OUARDIGHA, MOROCCO

When a vortex of cold air forced a car off a quiet road in Morocco the motorist was left in shock.

ON THE EVENING of September 15, 1954, a man named Guitta was driving near the coastal town of Bouznika when he saw a dazzling metallic object in his rearview mirror. He gripped the steering wheel and ducked instinctively. A few seconds later, the object passed him at high speed, followed by a gust of cold air.

Alarmed by a sensation that the wind was sucking up his car, Guitta braked sharply, and the car skidded onto the shoulder. As he got out of his car to inspect his punctured tires, he saw the metallic object disappear toward the southeast horizon. Guitta shivered, surprised to find an intense chill in the air. Little did he realize that people on the Ivory Coast were about to have a very similar experience.

On the same evening as the Moroccan sighting, a party gathered for cocktails in the courtyard of the French ambassador's house in Danane. Among the guests were government ministers and men and women from the growing expatriate community. They all witnessed a luminous red object, described as circular and silent, and silhouetted against a dark but clear evening sky. The object remained motionless for more than 30 minutes before changing to an elliptical shape and disappearing over the horizon at high speed.

A little later witnesses recorded a similar observation in the town of Soubré, 155 miles (250 km) northwest of Abidjan. An object flew toward the town at high speed, stayed still for several minutes, and then took off, quickly disappearing into the distance in a cloudless sky. The many witnesses included the chief administrator of Soubré. ◆

> **They witnessed a luminous object silhouetted against a dark but clear evening sky.**

▼ A drive home turned into a terrifying experience.

See Also: Lascaux Caves, p. 127

KIMBERLEY AUSTRALIA

Do rock paintings in this remote region of Australia depict mythical creator spirits or extraterrestrials?

IN 1838 AN EXPEDITION PARTY led by Captain George Grey stumbled across some caves near the Prince Regent River in the Kimberley district of Western Australia. Deciding to take a closer look, the men dismounted from their horses and set off to explore. Inside the caves, they found extraordinary paintings of strange humanoid forms covering the walls. The figures appeared to be wearing spherical helmets.

According to Aboriginal mythology, the Wandjina made the paintings. They were powerful cloud and rain spirits that came down the Milky Way to create Earth, bringing with them thunder, lightning, and monsoon rains. By controlling the weather they maintained Earth's fertility. However, when the Wandjina first opened their mouths, torrential rain poured out, destroying everything in its path.

> Eventually, their mouths vanished because they had no use for them.

Then, according to the myth, the Wandjina re-created the world, vowing never to open their mouths again. Eventually, their mouths vanished because they had no use for them.

According to Aboriginal oral history, the Wandjina spirits made the paintings after creating Earth. They laid down on the rocks to rest and left their imprints there. The heads of the Wandjina figures are often out of proportion to their bodies, with huge dark eyes and no mouths.

Some commentators have compared the rock painting figures to aliens. If the Wandjina are offended by this, it is said they will take their revenge by striking the offender dead with lightning or whipping up a cyclone to devastate the land. ◆

▲ The figures have large eyes and big heads.

WESTALL MELBOURNE, AUSTRALIA

More than 200 students and teachers watched in awe as a UFO hovered above the playing fields.

ON APRIL 6, 1966, SHORTLY AFTER 11 a.m., a mass sighting of a UFO occurred in two public schools in Westall, Melbourne. Pupils at the high school had just finished a sports class when they saw a silver-gray, saucer-shaped craft in the sky. The unknown object was twice the size of a car and seemed to change shape at times. They watched as it descended toward a field, hovered over the edge of the neighboring junior high school, and then disappeared from view.

Soon more than 200 people had gathered outside the schools, scanning the sky. Suddenly, the object came back into view and witnesses watched it for about 20 minutes. It then rose suddenly and streaked through the sky, pursued by five unidentified aircraft.

Two UFO organizations—the Victorian Flying Saucer Research Society and Phenomena Research Australia (P.R.A.)—investigated the incident. Brian Boyle, a member of the P.R.A., accompanied army investigators to the site, took witness statements, and collected samples from the surrounding area. The incident remains unexplained to this day. ◆

◀ Westall was considered one of Australia's biggest UFO incidents.

BURRAGORANG VALLEY BLUE MOUNTAINS, AUSTRALIA

Rumblings in the earth and strange objects in the sky have earned this valley a spooky reputation.

THE BURRAGORANG VALLEY in Australia's Blue Mountains is a wild and beautiful area. But there is much speculation that this tranquil valley lies on top of a secret military base built to investigate and exploit alien technology. In the last 50 years or so, there have been many reports of unusual happenings in the area, including sightings of more than 600 UFOs, as well as claims of alien abductions. Local residents have long reported seeing saucer-shaped aircraft, red and green orbs, and flying yellow disks.

In the spring of 1977, three young campers heard a loud grinding sound coming from deep below the floor of the valley. The ground began to vibrate. The boys searched the area, worried that it might be an earthquake. They found nothing, but the rumblings continued, and the next morning the boys left.

In 1990 a group of high school students hiking in the valley claimed they had seen a silver sphere with spikes projecting from its sides making fast, darting movements above their heads. They said the sphere hovered about 9 feet (3 m) above the track ahead of them before shooting off over the trees. ◆

▲ Wild and remote, the Burragorang Valley has a reputation for UFO incidents.

▲ A 15th-century painting of St. George slaying the dragon

MYTHS &

LEGENDS

LOCH NESS   SCOTTISH HIGHLANDS, SCOTLAND

Many people believe that Scotland's deepest lake contains a prehistoric long-necked monster

AROUND 20 MILES (32 km) long, 1 mile (2 km) wide, and more than 700 feet (200 m) deep, Loch Ness forms a freshwater scar in the Scottish Highlands. It is world-famous for the legend of the "Nessie" monster.

The first recorded sighting was by St. Columba and his followers in the sixth century A.D. When walking next to the lake, the saint asked one of his men to swim out and retrieve an abandoned boat. As the man entered the water, a huge beast rose up and let out a mighty roar. St. Columba held up his cross and shouted at the beast, commanding it to do no harm. According to the story, the monster swirled around and plunged back into the lake's dark depths.

Tales of a Loch Ness monster proliferated in the 1930s. In April 1933, a Scottish couple, Mr. and Mrs.

> She saw a huge creature rolling and plunging through the surging water.

Mackay, were driving alongside the loch when Mrs. Mackay noticed a disturbance in the water. She initially thought it was a duck fight, but, as she looked closer, she saw a huge creature in the middle of the loch, rolling and plunging through the surging water.

By 1934 photographs of the Loch Ness Monster began to appear in the press. Many were clearly staged, but a picture taken by London doctor Robert Kenneth Wilson, showing a creature with a small head and long neck, captured the public's imagination, and reports and photographs of this infamous creature proliferated. They continue to surface. Many believe Nessie to be a descendant of an ancient plesiosaur. ◆

▲ A classic image of the Loch Ness Monster, apparently showing a creature with a small head and a long neck.

DOON HILL ABERFOYLE, SCOTLAND

A creaking pine tree on this wooded hill is said to contain the soul of a clergyman who hunted fairies.

MANY LOCALS PREFER to avoid Doon Hill for fear of the fairies that are said to have imprisoned the soul of Reverend Robert Kirk there in 1692. Kirk was minister of Aberfoyle parish. A fascination for local folk tales led him to publish a book about the "land of the fairies" in which he claimed Doon Hill was the gateway to a secret fairy land. He claimed he had visited the hill daily and eventually found his way through a magical portal that led to the innermost fairy court.

According to local myth, the Doon Hill fairies were angry about the intrusion into their sacred world and decided to imprison Kirk if he ever returned. One night in May, Kirk walked to the hill dressed only in his nightshirt. He collapsed at the top of the hill and was not found until the next day. His rescuers took him home, but he died soon after and was buried in his own churchyard. It was believed that the fairies took Kirk's body, filled his coffin with stones, and then imprisoned his soul in a huge pine tree at the top of Doon Hill.

Visitors to Doon Hill write their wishes on pieces of white silk, which they tie to branches of the trees both to placate and petition fairies. It is also said that if you run around the great pine tree seven times, the fairies will appear. ◆

▲ *Dancing Fairies*, a painting by Swedish artist August Malmström

THE COTTINGLEY FAIRIES In 1917 two young cousins, 16-year-old Elsie and 9-year-old Frances, allegedly took a series of five photographs depicting their encounter with fairies at the bottom of their garden in Cottingley, England. The writer Sir Arthur Conan Doyle used them to illustrate an article on fairies in 1920, and was convinced they were evidence of the paranormal.

See Also: Glastonbury Tor, p. 216

CAMELOT SOMERSET, ENGLAND

King Arthur and his knights are said to sleep under Cadbury Hill deep in the Somerset countryside.

ACCORDING TO LEGEND, the Iron Age hill fort on Cadbury Hill, near the market town of Yeovil, is the site of Camelot, court of the mythical King Arthur.

The 16th-century historian John Leland, adviser to Henry VIII, was the first to link Cadbury with Camelot. He called it Camalat. Archaeologists believe it may have gained this reputation because, in the sixth century, it was the base of a warrior leader, possibly called Arthur. An archaeological investigation of the 18-acre (7 ha) site in the late 1960s revealed that it had been massively fortified during the sixth century at the time when King Arthur is said to have flourished.

It is said that King Arthur and his men sleep still in a cave in the hill, ready to fight for their country. The entrance to the cave is guarded by an iron gate, which, according to legend, opens on Midsummer's Day once every seven years so that Arthur and his warriors can ride out to hunt. They are said to gallop toward a spring near Sutton Montis church to water their weary horses.

So well known is the story of the sleeping king and his knights that when a group of 19th-century archaeologists visited the district, an inhabitant asked whether they had come to "dig up the king." ◆

▲ View toward Cadbury Hill, the site of the mythical Camelot

EXCALIBUR King Arthur's sword, Excalibur, was attributed with magical powers. Various legends tell of how he came to possess it; some say he drew it from a stone, others that it was given to him by a sorceress known as the Lady of the Lake. Dozmary Pool in Cornwall is one of several watery locations where it was said that she gave the mystical sword to Arthur (right).

CASTELL DINAS BRAN DENBIGHSHIRE, WALES

This ruined castle in the hills of Wales harbors legends of knights, a giant, and a secret cache of gold.

BUILT ON THE SITE OF AN Iron Age hill fort, Castell Dinas Bran, or Crow Castle, was already a ruin by the 13th century, believed by locals to be haunted by evil spirits. No one had the courage to stay in the castle until a proud and vain knight called Payn Peveril decided to challenge local wisdom.

Peveril and 15 knightly followers made a pact to spend the night in the castle, signing their oath in blood. That evening, after much feasting and drinking, they settled down to sleep within the crumbling walls.

According to local legend, before long a storm swept across the castle hill, rousing an evil, mace-wielding giant named Gogmagog, who set upon the castle's unwanted visitors. Peveril defended his men and fatally stabbed Gogmagog with his sword. As the giant lay dying, he told the story of his rival, King Bran, who had built Castell Dinas Bran in a vain attempt to defend himself against the giant. The king had eventually admitted defeat and fled the castle, leaving the giant free to occupy the fortress and terrorize the land.

As the giant grew weaker, he told Peveril that a stash of treasure lay buried beneath the walls of Dinas Bran, including gold and precious jewelry. Before he could reveal the location, however, the giant died, and the treasure was never discovered. ◆

▲ Gogmagog was said to be a giant of giants. He features in numerous British folk tales.

▼ The romantic ruin of Castell Dinas Bran, once the home of a famous Welsh giant

See Also: Camelot, p. 214

GLASTONBURY TOR — SOMERSET, ENGLAND

This conical hill near Glastonbury is a place of reverence and magic linked to the legends of King Arthur.

GLASTONBURY TOR WAS ONCE surrounded by swamps and fenland, and washed on three sides by the River Brue. According to legend, the tor is associated with the island of Avalon, where the enchantress Morgan le Fay took the wounded King Arthur after his final battle. The chronicler Gerald of Wales reported the alleged discovery of King Arthur and Queen Guinevere's labeled coffins in Glastonbury Abbey in 1191.

A resurgence of interest in Celtic mythology in the 19th century led to the tor's association with Gwyn ap Nudd, King of the Fairies. The hill was also cited as the entrance to Annwn, the otherworld of Celtic mythology—a timeless, formless mirror of the mortal world, which was inhabited by spirits and demons. According to *The Mabinogion*, a book of Celtic myths, Arawn, joint ruler with Hafgan of

> The tor is said to be an entrance to Annwn, the otherworld of Celtic mythology.

Annwn, decided to trick the shape-changing Pwyll, Lord of Dyfed, in order to swap places with him for a year. Arawn planned to use Pwyll's strength to destroy Hafgan and become sole ruler of the Otherworld.

One day, while out hunting, Pwyll's hounds chased off Arawn's hounds in the middle of a kill. As recompense for losing the prize stag, he persuaded Pwyll to rule the Otherworld for a year while he ruled over Dyfed. During his reign Pwyll killed Hafgan, making Arawn the kingdom's sole ruler when he returned. According to the *Book of Taliesin*, a 14th-century collection of poems, King Arthur and his knights traveled through Annwn in search of the Cauldron of Plenty—the eternal source of otherworldly delights and immortality. ◆

▼ The atmospheric Glastonbury Tor is marked by the ruined tower of a 15th-century church.

ROSSLYN CHAPEL MIDLOTHIAN, SCOTLAND

Carvings of pagan gods, fallen angels, and medieval knights fill this ancient chapel near Edinburgh.

OWNED BY THE ST. CLAIR FAMILY since 1446, Rosslyn Chapel captures the imagination of all who visit it. The chapel is steeped in legends about the Knights Templar and their quest for the Holy Grail, the chalice used by Christ at the Last Supper. The final chapters of Dan Brown's bestselling novel *The Da Vinci Code* suggest that the Holy Grail is hidden beneath Rosslyn Chapel, having been taken there by the Knights Templar when they fled France for Scotland.

Mystery shrouds the chapel's vaults where male members of the St. Clair family were once buried without coffins, in their full knightly regalia. Modern-day excavation of the vaults failed to reach one section of the underground complex, while a survey in the 1980s revealed metal objects sealed inside the vaults' walls.

Intricate carvings incorporating mysterious symbols fill the chapel. In the 18th century, an apprentice mason is said to have produced the elaborately carved Apprentice Pillar while his master was in Rome. On his return, the master flew into a jealous rage and killed the apprentice. The 213 mystical symbols carved into the stone ceiling have confounded historians for generations. Music scientists believe the lines and dots represent vibrations caused by sound, forming part of a musical notation system or code. ◆

▲ The crypt of Rosslyn Chapel

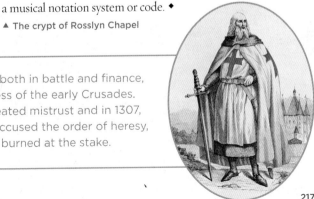

THE KNIGHTS TEMPLAR Known for its prowess both in battle and finance, this Christian military order was integral to the success of the early Crusades. However, rumors about the knights' secret rituals created mistrust and in 1307, Philip IV of France, deeply in debt to the Templars, accused the order of heresy, fraud, and obscenity, and had the main protagonists burned at the stake.

SHERWOOD FOREST NOTTINGHAMSHIRE, ENGLAND

A former lord turned outlaw once roamed this royal forest in Central England, setting wrongs to right.

ROBIN HOOD, A WELL-KNOWN character of English folklore, was a fugitive who roamed Sherwood Forest, stealing from the rich to give to the poor. He was helped by his exemplary archery skills and band of Merry Men—fellow outlaws who wanted revenge on the greedy Sheriff of Nottingham.

According to legend, Robin exercised compassion when robbing his wealthy victims. If they told the truth about their fortune, he let them go. He even showed mercy to the infamous sheriff.

Was Robin Hood a real person? Some say he may have been a young noble forced into a life of robbery by the dastardly murder of his father and the appropriation of his rightful inheritance. A grave at Kirklees Priory in

> Robin may have been a young noble forced into a life of robbery by the dastardly murder of his father.

West Yorkshire is inscribed with the words "Here lies Robard Hude," and some claim Robin died at the hands of a prioress who poisoned him while purporting to treat an illness. Before he died he told his faithful companion Little John to shoot an arrow from the priory window. Wherever the arrow landed was to be the site of his grave.

An early reference to Robin Hood in a poem of 1377, *Rymes of Robyn Hude*, was the first of more than 200 poems, stories, and ballads about Robin Hood to appear by the early 18th century. Since then, there have also been countless movies, television series, and plays. ◆

▲ The heroic bandit appeared in many movie adaptations, including *Robin Hood: Prince of Thieves* (1991).

CHALK GIANT   CERNE ABBAS, ENGLAND

A mighty giant carved into Dorset's chalk hills is the focus for ancient fertility rites and ceremonies.

NOT FAR FROM THE Dorset village of Cerne Abbas, a spectacular figure of a giant covers the side of a west-facing hill. Legends about the mysterious giant and how he came to be there are legion. Some claim he was a real Danish giant who terrorized the locals and ate their sheep. According to this story, the people of Cerne Abbas mobbed and killed the giant while he slept on the hill one night and then dug a ditch around his body, marking him out forevermore. In one version of the legend, the giant comes alive at night and stumbles down to a nearby stream to drink.

With his huge phallus and testicles, the Cerne Giant features in numerous fertility rites and ceremonies. In the past, locals would raise a maypole on the grass above his head, and childless couples would dance around the pole to stimulate fertility. It was also thought that infertility could be cured by having intercourse on top of the figure. There are many stories of infertile women conceiving a child after sleeping near the giant's phallus, and of virgins ensuring their lover's fidelity by walking three times around the giant.

Historians believe the giant could be an image of the Greek-Roman god Hercules, who was amalgamated with a local pagan god around A.D. 180–193. ◆

▲ The mysterious giant is 180 feet (55m) tall.

> **THE UFFINGTON HORSE** On the edge of the Berkshire Downs, this highly stylized prehistoric figure is formed from deep trenches filled with crushed white chalk. Some archaeologists believe it to be a symbol of equine veneration created by the inhabitants of the nearby Iron Age hill fort, Uffington Castle. It is one of several similar horse figures in England.

BLARNEY CASTLE COUNTY CORK, IRELAND

Why do visitors flock to this castle to hang backward over the battlements and kiss a magic stone?

For many visitors to Blarney Castle, the chief attraction is a stone set at the top of the castle walls. It is said that those who kiss the stone will receive the gift of eloquence—the "gift of the gab" as locals like to say. To touch the stone with one's lips, it is necessary to walk to the top of the battlements and lean backward over the parapet's edge, a precarious maneuver that requires assistance from castle staff and demands the precaution of safety rails.

Some say the stone is half of the Stone of Scone in Edinburgh Castle. Traditionally, Scottish kings were crowned while sitting above the Stone of Scone—also known as the Stone of Destiny—in the belief that it would bequeath divine power.

> The goddess told McCarthy to kiss the first stone he found on his way to court.

Legend attributes the magical power of the Blarney Stone to a former owner of the castle, Cormac McCarthy, the king of Munster, and Clíodhna, the Celtic goddess of love and beauty. According to the story, McCarthy asked Clíodhna to help him win a lawsuit. The goddess told McCarthy to kiss the first stone he found on his way to court in the morning. He followed the goddess's advice, and went on to plead his case with exceptional eloquence. He won the lawsuit by deceiving without offending—the very essence of "blarney." In recognition of his success, McCarthy incorporated the stone into the parapet of the castle. ◆

▼ Blarney Castle is set in beautiful wooded countryside, but the main draw for visitors is a curious stone.

GIANT'S CAUSEWAY COUNTY ANTRIM, N. IRELAND

An extraordinary stone staircase off the coast of Northern Ireland is said to be the work of giants.

BELOW THE CLIFFS near the town of Bushmill, some 40,000 interlocking columns, some of them more than 40 feet (12 m) tall, form a descending staircase into the depths of the North Atlantic.

The steps are said to be the remains of a causeway built by giants. According to legend, the Scottish giant Benandonner, the Red Man, challenged the Irish giant Finn MacCool to a fight. Accepting the combat, Finn built a causeway between Scotland and Ireland so that the pair could meet on neutral ground.

As Finn watched Benandonner approaching across the causeway, he realized his opponent was much bigger than he had imagined. In some stories Finn defeated the Scottish giant, but in others he ran home to hide, and his wife disguised him as a baby. When Benandonner knocked on Finn's door, he was so astonished to see the tremendous size of the "baby" MacCool he beat a hasty retreat, believing the baby's father must be a giant among giants. Escaping from the house, he fled across the causeway to Scotland, causing it to fall apart and crash into the sea as he thundered over it.

Across the sea off the coast of Scotland, the Isle of Staffa (see panel) contains similar basalt columns—a lasting testament to the clash between the foes? ◆

▲ The hexagonal blocks fit together like a honeycomb.

FINGAL'S CAVE Like the Giant's Causeway, the walls of this cave on the Isle of Staffa in Scotland are also composed of hexagonal basalt pillars, which are 72 feet (22 m) tall. Named after Fingal (Finn MacCool in Scottish legend) and known in Gaelic as Uamh-Binn, or the "Cave of Melody," the cave inspired the composer Felix Mendelssohn to write the overture *The Hebrides*, or *Fingal's Cave*.

KNOSSOS CRETE, GREECE

Tragedy struck when an Athenian prince slayed a monstrous bull in the Minoan palace of Knossos.

In 2000 B.C., Crete was the center of the Minoan civilization. According to Greek mythology, King Minos kept the Minotaur, a monstrous half-bull, half-man creature in a dark labyrinth, designed by Daedalus, under the palace at Knossos. The labyrinth was so complex that the Minotaur could never escape.

According to the story, when the Minoans won a great victory over the Athenians, King Minos demanded that the Athenian king send seven boys and seven girls to Crete at nine-year intervals to be sacrificed to the Minotaur. On the third occasion of this ceremony, the Athenian king's son, Theseus, volunteered to slay the monster. Taking the place of one of the youths, he set off with a black sail, promising to return with a white sail if he succeeded.

When Theseus arrived at Knossos, Ariadne, the daughter of King Minos, fell in love with him. She gave Theseus two gifts—a sword to kill the Minotaur and a ball of thread. She told Theseus to fasten one end of the thread to the entrance of the labyrinth so that he would be able to find his way out. Theseus plunged into the labyrinth and stabbed the beast.

Using the thread to escape, he fled to the beach with the other Athenians, Ariadne, and her sister Phaedra. However, on the beach, the goddess Athena told Theseus to leave Ariadne and Phaedra behind. In his distress at losing his love, Theseus forgot to hoist the white sail on his return to Athens. Seeing the black sail, his father thought his son was dead, and threw himself off a cliff. ◆

▲ Theseus and the Minotaur mural at the Palace of Knossos

▼ The mythical Minotaur was said to live in a labyrinth under the palace at Knossos.

DELOS CYCLADES, GREECE

A nymph gave birth to divine twins on Delos—a "floating" island conjured up by the god of the ocean.

IN GREEK MYTHOLOGY, when the nymph Leto fell pregnant by Zeus, his wife, Hera, consumed by jealousy, ordered the Earth to deny the nymph shelter wherever she tried to rest. Poseidon, the god of the ocean, pitied the fugitive and offered Leto Delos—a floating island that was not anchored to the ocean floor. Because the island was in motion, Hera's edict did not apply.

The nymph took refuge in a cave in Mount Cynthus on Delos, and over the course of nine days and nights gave birth to the divine twins—Apollo, the god of light and beauty, and his sister, Artemis, the huntress.

Delos means "visible," and according to legend, after the birth of Apollo, four columns rose out of the sea to secure the island so that it could be seen in the same place forevermore. A crack in Mount Cynthus was said to house the first oracle of Apollo, who also made an altar to himself from the horns of goats killed by Artemis when the twins were just four years old.

The island became a major center for the worship of Apollo, Leto, Artemis, and Dionysus from 900 B.C., and from the fourth century B.C. an annual festival with dancing and athletics was held in their honor. ◆

◀ Poseidon, the god of the ocean and savior of Leto

DELPHI NEAR MOUNT PARNASSUS, GREECE

Apollo himself was said to speak through the oracle at Delphi, the chief oracle in the Greek world.

WHEN HERA, the wife of Zeus, discovered her husband's paramour Leto had given birth to the divine twins Apollo and Artemis, she sent the monstrous snake-dragon Python to hunt out Leto and destroy her. To protect his mother, Apollo cornered the serpent in the cave at Delphi and killed it.

According to Greek mythology, Delphi is the center of the Earth, identified by Zeus when he commanded two eagles to fly toward one another from the eastern and western extremities. Mythology claims Apollo built his own oracular temple there, aligning its axis to the midsummer sunrise and midwinter sunset, and marked the center of the Earth with a stone known as an *omphalos*.

The Greeks named the prophetess who delivered the oracle Pythia, after the slain serpent. Intoxicated by vapors rising from a chasm in the rock, Pythia spoke nonsense that priests interpreted as prophecies from Apollo.

Delphi became the most important oracle site in the Greek world. The name may be connected to Apollo, who took the form of a dolphin to guide Cretan sailors to his new temple. It is thought that the omphalos was a meteorite that had fallen to earth. ◆

▲ Pythia pronounces the oracle of the god Apollo, attended by the temple priests.

223

AKROTIRI SANTORINI, GREECE

The hunt for the lost city of Atlantis centers on Santorini, where a great Minoan city once flourished.

WRITERS, GEOGRAPHERS, CLASSICAL SCHOLARS, and archaeologists have long disputed the location and even existence of Atlantis—the lost civilization mentioned in the dialogues of Plato in 360 B.C. The Greek philosopher described Atlantis as a powerful naval city with fabulous temples and shrines situated on an island paradise. Many archaeologists think the description fits the great Minoan city of Akrotiri on ancient Thera (now known as Santorini), which was destroyed by a volcanic eruption in 1627 B.C.

The source of Plato's Atlantis story was the sixth-century B.C. poet and legislator Solon, who in turn heard it from temple priests in ancient Egypt during his travels there. In Plato's account, Atlantis is the domain of Poseidon, god of the ocean. Poseidon fell in love with Cleito, a mortal woman who bore him five pairs of male twins. The eldest of these, Atlas, was made king of the ocean and given the mountain of Atlantis and the surrounding islands as his kingdom. Atlas's brothers also received territories.

Poseidon, Plato states, carved the mountain into a palace and enclosed it with three circular moats of increasing width. The Atlantians then built bridges northward from the mountain, making a route to the rest of the island. They dug a great canal to the sea, and alongside the bridges carved tunnels into the rings of rock so that ships could pass into the city around

> Atlantis sank into the ocean "in a single day and night of misfortune."

▼ Most archaeologists think that the lost city could have been on Santorini.

PLATO'S ATLANTIS Two aspects of Plato's account confuse Atlantis hunters—mention of the Pillars of Hercules, generally believed to be the Strait of Gibraltar at the mouth of the Mediterranean, and his claim that Atlantis was larger than Asia and Libya. It may be that the "pillars" were eastern Mediterranean landmarks that have since disappeared and that Plato's text was misinterpreted and actually meant between Asia and Libya.

the mountain. Gates and towers guarded every passage into the city, and a wall surrounded each of the city's rings. The walls were constructed of red, white, and black rock and studded with precious metals.

According to Plato, as Atlantis grew more powerful, it expanded into a great empire. Some believers in Atlantis theorize that the Atlantians may have passed on their know-how to the ancient Egyptians and even the Maya. Plato tells how the Athenians resisted invasion by the Atlantians and liberated all the conquered lands, after which a period of catastrophic earthquakes, volcanoes, and floods ensued. According to Plato, Atlantis sank into the ocean "in a single day and night of misfortune." ◆

▲ An ancient map showing the island of Atlantis. An eruption in 1627 B.C. destroyed Akrotiri and may have triggered a tsunami.

MYCENAE PELOPONNESE, GREECE

Myth and reality interwine at Mycenae, where the mighty Agamemnon launched the Trojan War.

In the second millennium b.c., Mycenae was a major center of Greek civilization. Its armies dominated southern Greece, and its history later inspired Homer's *Iliad*, the cornerstone of Greek mythology.

Tyndareus, the mythical king of Sparta, had two daughters, Clytemnestra and Helen. Clytemnestra married Agamemnon, who became king of Mycenae, and Helen married his brother Menelaus, who went on to inherit Sparta's throne. Regional relations were stable until Helen eloped with Paris of Troy.

Agamemnon waged a ten-year war against Troy to win Helen back for his brother. In one of his last campaigns against the Trojans, Artemis, goddess of the hunt, becalmed his warships in revenge for the killing of a stag. To appease the goddess, Agamemnon sacrificed his daughter, Iphigenia. He regained the necessary wind power and went on to win the war.

After the war, Clytemnestra and Aegisthus, the lover she had taken in her husband's absence, murdered Agamemnon in his bathtub in revenge for sacrificing Iphigenia. Agamemnon's son Orestes then murdered Clytemnestra and fled to Athens to evade justice. He eventually returned to Mycenae to kill the illegitimate son of Clytemnestra and Aegisthus and seized the throne. ◆

▲ The entrance to Mycenae

HELEN OF TROY Described by the 16th-century English playwright Christopher Marlowe as "the face that launched a thousand ships," Helen was said to be the most beautiful woman in the world, immortalized in countless works of art (right). Forty-five suitors competed for her hand in marriage. After the fall of Troy, some accounts state that she returned to Menelaus, others that she was murdered on Rhodes.

RENNES-LE-CHÂTEAU LANGUEDOC, FRANCE

A quiet village on the edge of the French Pyrenees brims with esoteric mysteries and riddles.

IN THE LATE 19TH CENTURY, the village priest Bérenger Saunière discovered coded parchments concealed inside a pillar while restoring his church. Seeking assistance in deciphering their contents, he went to Paris where a young priest with knowledge of such mysteries helped him to unravel the code.

On his return from Paris, Saunière began receiving large sums of money that may have been connected with his discovery. He used these to refurbish the church and build the neo-Gothic Tour Magdala. Saunière died in 1917, leaving the secret of his considerable wealth with his housekeeper, Marie Dernaud. Marie was to reveal all on her deathbed, but a stroke left her unable to speak.

Speculation on the source of the parish priest's money was rife. Was it a lost treasure, or was the priest blackmailing the church with a terrible secret contained in the parchments? Some say Saunière uncovered treasure of the Knights Templars, Cathars, or King Solomon's Temple. Others linked the parchments to the Holy Grail (see page 217) and said they revealed that Mary Magdalene was Jesus' wife and the mother of his children.

> Saunière's confession was so shocking that the priest denied him absolution.

It is said that Saunière's confession before his death was so shocking that the priest who heard it denied him absolution and the last rites. Adding to the mystery is a series of parchments found by his cleric in 1891. One message reads: "This treasure belongs to Dagobert II king and to Sion and he is there dead." Dagobert was a murdered seventh-century Frankish king but no one knows who Sion refers to. ◆

▲ The Tour Magdala was built by Saunière in 1901.

HORSELLOCH CAVERN
THURINGIA, GERMANY

This cave in the Thuringian forest has been described as a gateway to hell and the seat of Venus.

In the beautiful Harz mountains of Thuringia stands Mount Hörselberg, emerging from its largely verdant surroundings like "a vast stone sarcophagus." Through the heart of this peak runs a river that has hollowed out the rocks into a network of caverns, including the mysterious Horselloch Cavern, inaccessible to all but the most intrepid explorers.

As the water rolls and tumbles through the long natural tunnel, it produces a cacophony of noises, which may, some thought, be the sounds of the souls of the damned being tormented in hell.

Others believed that the sounds arose from orgies taking place in the *Venusberg*, the subterranean pleasure palace of the goddess Venus, who seduced the legendary knight and minstrel Tannhäuser and kept him in her cave.

After seven years he tried to escape and confess to a local priest who sent him to the pope. His sins were so grave, the pope said, that forgiveness was as unlikely as the pope's staff blossoming with flowers. Tannhäuser returned to Venus, thinking he was doomed, but the staff did bear flowers. ◆

◄ A 16th-century woodcut showing a scene from the Tannhäuser legend.

TEMPLE OF CASTOR AND POLLUX
FORUM ROMANUM, ROME, ITALY

A temple in the Forum celebrates a great victory won with the help of the divine twins.

The Temple of Castor and Pollux honors the triumph of the infant Roman Republic over the Latin League at the Battle of Lake Regillus at the end of the fifth century B.C. According to legend, the divine twins Castor and Pollux appeared on the battlefield in support of the republic, dressed in full armor and mounted on their steeds. Afterward they watered their horses in the healing Spring of Juturna near the Forum and proclaimed the republic's victory.

The sons of Zeus and his lover Leda, the twins were conceived when Zeus disguised himself as a swan in order to seduce her. The same night Leda slept with her husband Tyndareus, King of Sparta, and produced twins from each union—Castor and Clytemnestra, and Helen (who became Helen of Troy) and Pollux.

The Romans inherited the cult of Castor and Pollux from the Greek culture of southern Italy. According to legend, Rome was founded by the Roman equivalent of Castor and Pollux, Romulus and Remus. The legend claims that Romulus killed Remus in an argument over who would rule the city. He then named it after himself. ◆

▲ The ruined columns of the Temple of Castor and Pollux.

MOUNT ARARAT

AGRI PROVINCE, TURKEY

For centuries people have searched for evidence of Noah's ark on the snowy peak of Mount Ararat.

THE STORY OF NOAH'S ARK is common to the Torah, the Bible, and the Quran. It is a redemption story in which a disillusioned God decides to undo Creation by flooding the earth. He wants to drown the sinners and begin again, using two members from each species. He selects the patriarch Noah to build an ark and carry out his plan, and installs lions to guard Noah's family from the envious sinners who try to climb aboard as the floodwater rises. After one year, Noah's family and the animals go forth to repopulate the earth.

According to the Bible, the ark came to rest on Mount Ararat. People have searched for evidence of the ark on the mountain since the third century A.D. In 1876 the British historian, diplomat, and explorer James Bryce found a slab of hand-sawn timber at a height of around 13,000 feet (4,000 m), well above the tree line, which he believed was from the ark. In 1955 the explorer Fernand Navarra recovered a 5-foot (1.5 m) beam that was buried under one of Ararat's glaciers, which researchers from the Forestry Institute in Spain say is around 5,000 years old. More recently, in 2010, Chinese explorers uncovered seven large wooden compartments buried below snow-covered volcanic debris near the peak. They claim that they are conclusive evidence of the ark. ◆

> In 1876 British explorer James Bryce found a slab of hand-sawn timber well above the tree line.

▲ *The Animals Entering the Ark*, oil painting by 17th-century Flemish painter Jacob Savery

BERMUDA TRIANGLE ATLANTIC OCEAN

This vast expanse of water has long been known for unexplained disappearances of aircraft and ships.

KNOWN TO SOME AS THE DEVIL'S TRIANGLE, the Bermuda Triangle lies between Miami, Puerto Rico, and Bermuda in the North Atlantic. Christopher Columbus was the first to record unusual occurrences in the area. A copy of his logbook of 1492 states that his crew suffered navigational difficulties around the Sargasso Sea. They spotted many land birds and seaweed, but found no land. In his log, Columbus explained how, among other strange happenings, his compass began to give erratic readings, and the sea suddenly changed from being as calm as a lake to high and treacherous, even though there was no wind. The ship was lost in the Caribbean seas for more than a week before the crew finally sighted land.

> **Many believe that a powerful vortex of energy causes ships and aircraft to disappear.**

In the last 100 years, aircraft as well as ships have gone missing in the area. In 1945 five military air planes and a rescue plane disappeared after leaving for a training mission east of Fort Lauderdale. The planes never returned to base; a search and rescue aircraft was sent to look for them but that disappeared too, along with its 13-man crew.

Many believe that a powerful vortex of energy causes ships and aircraft to disappear. Some say the triangle is even the site of the lost city of Atlantis (see p. 224), and that the remnants of energy crystals used to fuel the lost city interferes with the electronic equipment of ships and planes. Recent discoveries of ancient sphinxes, tombs, and pyramids in the North Atlantic have perhaps made claims of a submerged city not as far-fetched as they seemed. Others claim

▼ Ships have foundered in the waters of the Bermuda Triangle for centuries.

THE
BERMUDA
TRIANGLE
an incredible saga
of unexplained
disappearances

Charles Berlitz

that the Bermuda Triangle houses a downed alien aircraft that interferes with technology, or that it serves as a portal for extraterrestrial beings.

In 1970 pilot Bruce Gernon and his father were flying to Bimini Island in the Bahamas when they suddenly faced a strange cloud that expanded at immense speed before suddenly morphing into a whirling tunnel. Before they could grasp what was happening, they were flying through the rotating tunnel and then emerging in a thick fog of storm-like energy. At this point, their compass spun wildly. When the fog settled, Gernon found himself miles from where they expected to be. He was also farther away than he would have been if he had flown by plane during the time that had passed. This experience led to speculation that the Bermuda Triangle could be a time-travel tunnel. ◆

▲ Berlitz was fascinated by stories of the paranormal. He believed in the existence of Atlantis as well as of the Bermuda Triangle, and tried to link the two.

BADLANDS SOUTH DAKOTA, U.S.A.

A place of both dread and fascination, the Badlands have a large stock of terrifying legends.

SCULPTED BY TURBULENT wind and rain, the Badlands is an area of buttes, pinnacles, canyons, and strange rock formations. Native American tribes inhabited the area for more than 10,000 years, eking out an existence in the inhospitable landscape, surviving the intense heat of summer and the snow of winter.

In the 1870s, European settlers moved into the area, forcing out the indigenous people. Members of an expedition led by General Custer had discovered gold in the mountains and the gold rush was on. In consequence the Badlands are steeped in Native American legends,

augmented by the superstitious tales of the cowboys and miners who tried to conquer the landscape.

Near the butte known as Watch Dog, a favorite hiding place for rattlesnakes, a desert banshee is said to howl and cry out omens of death. Some say the ghost of a shape-shifting spirit can be seen and heard at night on a hill, a mile or so south of Watch Dog. In the day, her hair blows wild in the wind as she transforms from a spirit to a snake or coyote to prey on the unwary travelers crossing the desert plain. ◆

◀ Beware the shape-shifting rattlesnakes that hang around Watch Dog butte.

KILAUEA VOLCANO HAWAII, U.S.A.

Hawaii's most volatile volcano is said to harbor a passionate and dangerous goddess.

PELE, THE HAWAIIAN GODDESS of fire and volcanoes, is said to live in Halemaumau, a crater inside Kilauea, the most active of Hawaii's volcanoes, where she mourns the loss of her mortal lover, Lohiau. From time to time the goddess erupts in terrible anger, throwing lava down the mountainside.

According to Hawaiian mythology, Pele is diverted from this continual torment when Hog-man comes to court her. Hog-man is a shape-shifter who can transform into a pig, a man, or a fish. Delighted by his affectionate teasing, she becomes increasingly enamored by Hog-man and their flirting grows dangerous and passionate. Sometimes she overwhelms him with her

flames and lava, and he retaliates with fog and rain, sending pigs scuttling across the land to churn up the increasingly sodden earth. As the rain falls, everything turns to mud and Pele's fires are eventually extinguished.

At this point, according to the myth, the other gods grow worried that their sacred fire-sticks might be doused with water. They intervene and give Pele gulleys and ravines in which her lava can flow without ill effect. At the same time, they give the Hog-man lush valleys, where mists can roll and rains fall at a safe distance from the volcanic path. ◆

▲ Effigy of Pele, Hawaii's temperamental goddess of fire and volcanoes.

NIAGARA FALLS

ONTARIO, CANADA / NEW YORK, U.S.A.

As the water pounds over this landmark, the Maid of the Mist rises from her cave wreathed in rainbows.

OVER THE CENTURIES, many legends have sprung up about the Niagara Falls. One tale concerns the Ongiaras, a peace-loving Native American tribe that lived beside the Niagara River, whose people were dying for mysterious reasons. They believed the only way to save their people was to appease the thunder god, Hinum, who was said to live with his two sons behind the waterfalls.

The tribes sent canoes filled with fruit and flowers behind the falls, but still their people fell sick. In desperation, once a year they sacrificed one of their most beautiful maidens, but death and disease continued to plague the tribe.

One year, Lelawala, Chief Eagle Eye's daughter, was chosen as a sacrifice. Wearing a wreath of white flowers, she stepped into a white birchbark canoe and plunged over the falls to her death. According to the tale, Hinum's

Once a year they sacrificed one of their most beautiful maidens.

sons caught Lelawala in their arms and fell in love with her. She told them she would stay with the one who could explain why her people were dying. The younger brother told her of a giant snake that lived at the bottom of the river. Once a year, he said, it grew hungry and entered the village to poison the water and then eat the dead. Lelawala convinced the youngest son to let her go back to her tribe in spirit form to tell them about the snake.

The next time the snake returned to the village, the tribe attacked it. Almost dead, the snake slid to the edge of the falls, but as it tried to escape it caught its head on one side of the river and its tail on the other, creating the Horseshoe Falls. Meanwhile Lelawala's spirit returned to the cave to be with her lover. She was known forever after as the Maid of the Mist. ◆

▼ The magical landscape of Niagara Falls

TEOTIHUACÁN NEAR MEXICO CITY, MEXICO

The Aztecs revered this ancient city of their predecessors, believing the gods created the universe here.

LOCATED ABOUT 30 MILES (50 KM) NORTH OF MEXICO CITY, the ruins of Teotihuacán are among the most remarkable examples of Mesoamerican civilization. The site was inhabited from around 200 B.C. until its collapse almost 1,000 years later. No one knows the true origin of the first Teotihuacán people, nor what language they spoke. By the time of the Aztec, the city had been abandoned for hundreds of years, but the Aztec revered it as a sacred place and named it Teotihuacán, meaning the "place of the gods."

According to Aztec legend, the gods gathered at Teotihuacán at the end of every great age to re-create the universe. With each cycle, a new god served as the sun. In all, there were five generations of sun, each of which ended in great destruction and darkness. When the fifth sun was chosen, the gods gathered at Teotihuacán to decide who would sacrifice themselves in the fire to become the sun and moon. Two gods were chosen—Tecciztecatl, the god of the earth's riches, to become the sun, and Nanauatl a poor, hermit-like god, to become the moon.

With the approaching ritual, the gods made offerings to purify themselves. Tecciztecatl offered expensive gifts while Nanauatl gave his blood and acts of penance. As the massive bonfire grew and became ready for the final offering, Tecciztecatl strode up to throw himself on the pyre. As he got closer, however, he felt the intense heat and was suddenly afraid. After four attempts his courage failed him. The rest of the gods, disgusted at Tecciztecatl's cowardice, called Nanauatl. He quietly stood up, walked to the platform, and without hesitation threw

> In all, there were five generations of sun, each of which ended in great destruction.

▼ The ceremonial center of Teotihuacán

THE OLMEC The first great Mesoamerican civilization to flourish in Mexico were the Olmec (1500–400 B.C.). Their pantheon of gods, identified by archaeologists from Olmec carvings, included the Dragon, Feathered Serpent, Bird Monster, Fish Monster, and Were-Jaguar, as well as gods connected to maize and rain. When cataclysmic climate change or volcanic eruptions forced the Olmec to abandon their cities, their civilization merged with others. Aspects of their culture, such as ritual ball games—which sometimes involved human sacrifice—were incorporated by the Maya and Aztec.

himself into the flames. Tecciztecatl, embarrassed that this lowly god could show such superior courage, then ran up and threw himself in as well.

At first, the world remained in darkness. But then two small sparks of light grew in intensity, until there were two great orbs lighting up the sky. The other gods became worried—what would happen to the world with two suns burning brightly?

Eventually one of the gods became angry with Tecciztecatl's lack of courage. Grabbing a rabbit, he threw it directly in Tecciztecatl's face, dimming his light forever. Tecciztecatl became the moon, doomed forever to follow the sun, but never burn as bright. Meanwhile, Nanauatl stood still in the sky, lacking the power to move by himself. The wind god then sacrificed the rest of the gods to create enough wind to blow the sun around the world. ◆

▲ The Olmec are renowned for their artifacts, particularly their huge stone heads with staring eyes.

CHICHÉN ITZÁ YUCATÁN, MEXICO

Did a serpent's shadow set in motion a chain of events that led to the fall of this once mighty city?

WHEN THE TOLTEC PEOPLE MOVED to Chichén Itzá in A.D. 1000, they merged their own cosmology with the Maya system, resulting in the towering Pyramid of Kukulcan. It was built so that the sunlight would fall along the northern staircase to create the shadow of a serpent (known as Kukulcan) slithering down the steps during the spring and autumn equinoxes.

No one knows what happened to the Toltec people, or why the civilization ended so abruptly. According to legend, their fate was set in motion when a beautiful Maya princess called Sac-Nicte traveled to Chichén Itzá to attend the equinox celebration. As she stood beside the pyramid, watching the descent of the serpent, her eyes met the adoring gaze of Canek, the prince of Chichén Itzá. However, Sac-Nicte was promised to Ulil, the prince of neighboring Uxmal. One of the princess's soothsayers told Canek that Sac-Nicte would wait for him among green flowers one day, but he would first have to fight for her hand.

On the day of Sac-Nicte's marriage to Ulil, Canek arrived with 60 of his best warriors and stole the princess. Enraged, Ulil launched a war against Chichén Itzá. In terror, the peace-loving Itza people abandoned their homes and temples, and followed Canek and his beloved Sac-Nicte. ◆

▲ The Pyramid of Kukulcan

MAYA FUNERARY RITES The Maya people feared and respected death. Those who died in childbirth, or were sacrificed, were believed to go straight to heaven. Maize was placed in the mouths of the dead as food for the underworld, and distinctive jade masks (right) were used in elaborate funerary rituals. The Maya civilization ended in the ninth century A.D.

ANGKOR WAT NEAR SIEM REAP, CAMBODIA

The epic sagas of Hindu legends are told in the sumptuous carvings of the great Angkor Wat.

ANGKOR WAT, MEANING "temple mountain," was built for the Hindu god Vishnu during the Khmer Empire, which dominated Southeast Asia from the 9th to the 15th century. Its elaborate architecture and host of ornamental carvings tell hundreds of stories from Hindu mythology.

One of the most celebrated scenes, on the eastern gallery of the temple, illustrates a myth known as the "Churning of the Sea of Milk," in which the wise man Durvasa offers a garland of flowers to Indra, the king of the gods. When Indra places the garland around Airavata, his white elephant, the animal tramples on the flowers, insulting Durvasa. The wise man then curses the lesser gods, or Devas, causing them to lose their divine immortality. Distraught by the loss of their powers, the Devas approach Vishnu for help.

Vishnu tells them they must find and drink the nectar of immortality to regain their glory. To do this, they must churn the ocean of milk with a mountain and the tail of the serpent Vasuki. The Devas are too weak to churn on their own, so they enlist the help of a rival band of gods, the Asuras.

Mount Mandara is used to do the churning, but the force required is so great that the mountain begins to sink into the milk. Taking the form of a turtle, Vishnu bears the mountain on his back so they can continue churning. Eventually the nectar of immortality pours forth, but the deceitful Asuras steal it. Vishnu then tricks the Asuras by transforming into the beautiful enchantress Mohini, who retrieves the nectar. The Asuras see through the trick too late, and Vishnu gives the nectar to the Devas who regain their immortal powers. ◆

▲ Vishnu has his spiritual home at Angkor Wat.

▼ The intricately carved walls of Angkor Wat

5 MYSTIC SOUTHEAST ASIAN LEGENDS

Thwarted love, crimes of passion, a wall-scaling monster, and a dragon twin sister pepper a rich repository of legends in the countries of Southeast Asia.

① MOUNT KINABALU, BORNEO: Cloaked in swirling mists or topped by puffs of cloud, this mountain changes aspect daily. Some say its name means "place of the dead," after the spirits that are believed to dwell here. Others claim it means "Chinese widow," after a heartbroken Kadazan woman who turned to stone when her lover, a Chinese prince who had climbed the mountain to find a giant pearl, returned home.

② LANGKAWI, MALAYSIA: The tomb of Makam Mahsuri is a popular tourist attraction in Langkawi. According to legend, Makam was stabbed with her family's dagger for alleged adultery. As she lay dying, white blood flowed from the wound, signifying her innocence, and she cursed Langkawi with seven generations of bad luck. Soon afterward, the Siamese conquered the kingdom and her curse came true.

▼ Dawn rises through the mists of Borneo's rain forest.

③ SISTERS' ISLANDS, SINGAPORE: According to legend, Minah and Linah lived by the coast of Singapore. One night Linah was abducted by a pirate who had fallen in love with her. Weeping over the loss of her sister, Minah swam after the pirate ship and drowned. Desperate to escape her captor, Linah dived into the sea and met the same fate. The next day, the islands sprang up where the girls had drowned.

④ MELAKA, MALAYSIA: In the 1960s, the women of Melaka were alarmed over reports of an *orang minyak*—oily man, a monster said to abduct virgins at night. According to a newspaper report, one eyewitness saw it crawling up the wall of a house and then jump from house to house. Some believed it to be a supernatural creature, others a warlock who coats himself with grease as black as his soul.

⑤ KOMODO ISLAND, INDONESIA: An ancient myth explains why the Komodo dragon made this island its home. A princess called Putri Naga had twins—a boy named Si Gerong and a female dragon called Orah. The boy never knew about his sister, but years later, while out hunting, a dragon came out of the forest. As Si Gerong took up his spear, a princess appeared and told him the dragon was his sister.

WEDDED ROCKS ISE, JAPAN

Two rocks in the sea off Ise symbolize the union of the creator gods Izanagi and Izanami.

▲ The two rocks are linked by a rope bridge made of rice straw.

WHEN TO VISIT

Come at sunset, when the twinkling town lights add to the mysterious atmosphere.

IN SHINTO MYTHOLOGY, THE FLOATING BRIDGE OF HEAVEN hung high above the primordial ocean. Izanagi, the creator, dipped his jeweled spear into the nothingness and stirred the water. As he pulled it out, drops fell into the air and created an island. Izanagi lived on this island with his consort, Izanami. Their first creation was an ugly, bloodsucking leech child so horrible they put it in a boat and left it to drift on the ocean. Their next creations were the seasons, the eight islands of Japan, trees, and animals.

Their last creation was the fire spirit. However, Izanami died giving birth to fire and descended to Yomi, the Shinto underworld. Beside himself with grief, Izanagi went down to Yomi to beg her to return, but Izanami warned him neither to look at her nor speak to her until she had negotiated her departure with the underworld spirits. Izanagi was impatient at this, and with a magic comb from his hair lit up the underworld. In the light he saw Izanami's rotting corpse.

Compelled to be the goddess of death forevermore, Izanami chased Izanagi out of Yomi, vowing to devour 1,000 people every day for what he had done. Izanagi retorted that he would create thousands more. With the creation of the living and dead finished, Izanagi built himself a gloomy house on the island of Ahaji and lived as a hermit forevermore. ◆

HACHIMAN SANCTUARY KAMAKURA, JAPAN

Shoguns and samurai once frequented this Shinto shrine to the mighty god of war.

DEDICATED TO THE GOD of war, Tsurugaoka Hachiman-gu is perhaps the most important Shinto shrine in Kamakura. Built by Minamoto Yoritomo, founder of the Kamajura Shogunate (military government) during the rise of the warrior clans known as samurai, it was once a place of murderous power struggles and political intrigue. A 1,000-year-old ginkgo tree, which until recently stood to the left of its great stone stairway, was said to be a hiding place for assassins and was nicknamed *kakure-ich*—hiding away tree.

As god of war, Hachiman was also the divine protector of Japan. Some say the god is based on Emperor Ojin, a fourth-century military leader who was said to possess supernatural powers, including the power to change the tides to prevent invaders from landing.

With the spread of Buddhism in Japan, the Hachiman shrine in Kamakura doubled as a Buddhist temple, remaining so until the mid-19th century, when the two religions were formally separated. During this time Hachiman became a syncretic deity (combining different beliefs), often portrayed in the guise of a Buddhist monk.

Continuing a long-standing tradition, young men come to the temple to mark their passage into adulthood, often leaving *emas* (prayer wishes) on small wooden plaques beside the shrine. Hung where the *kami* (spirit) can read them, they usually incorporate an image of a horse—*ema* literally meaning "horse picture." Wealthy merchants once offered real horses in exchange for blessings. ◆

▲ Hachiman incorporated Buddhist and Shinto characteristics.

▼ Pilgrims bring their offerings to Hachiman.

BAGAN MANDALAY, BURMA

On a bend in the Irawaddy River, the Bagan kings built an extraordinary center of spirituality.

▲ Thousands of temples, monasteries, and pagodas dot the landscape as far as the eye can see.

WHEN TO VISIT

Travel between November and February to avoid the torrential monsoon rains.

BAGAN SPREADS ACROSS A FERTILE PLAIN covered in palm and tamarind trees—a vast city of temples and pagodas built by the kings of Bagan between A.D. 1057 and 1287. Yet within 100 years of this astonishing architectural flowering, most of the Bagan kingdom had been swept away by earthquakes and invading Mongol armies. Around half of the original 4,500 temples survive. They contain frescoes, carvings, and countless statues of Buddha in bronze and gold.

The great Ananda Temple was completed in 1105. The story of its building is a tragic one. Eight monks had approached the Bagan king Kyanzittha, seeking alms. During the course of their meeting, they mentioned how their own Nandamula Cave temple was so much more beautiful than the temples in Burma. Curious to find out more about this sumptuous temple, the king invited the monks to the palace to learn more from them. Overwhelmed by their host's lavish hospitality, the monks described every detail of their Himalayan temple's decoration, stonework, shape, and size, and even drew up architectural plans of a replica of the Nandamula. The king then asked the monks if they would build the temple in the middle of the Bagan plain, and they enthusiastically agreed. However, once they had overseen the building of the main structure, the king murdered the monks to ensure no similar temple would ever be constructed again. ◆

XANADU MONGOLIA

An opium-induced dream about this magical summer palace inspired the poet Samuel Taylor Coleridge.

THE 13TH-CENTURY VENETIAN explorer Marco Polo called Xanadu the city of Chandu, built by the Khan. He described a city that formed a vast square, with an outer city and an inner city that included the palace of the Kubla Khan. This was made of the finest marble and decorated with paintings of beasts, birds, trees, and flowers that delighted and astonished visitors.

Polo also mentioned a portable palace made of gilded and lacquered cane in the grounds of the marble palace. It rested on gilded columns, each of which was topped by a golden dragon, its tail attached to the column while its head supported the architrave. Kubla Khan lived in this cool cane palace during the height of summer, and returned to the marble palace in August, when the cane palace was taken down.

Polo's description inspired the English Romantic poet Samuel Taylor Coleridge to write the poem "Kubla Khan," describing a mystical, "stately pleasure dome." In the preface Coleridge tells how he wrote the poem one night in 1797, following an opium-induced dream he had had after reading Polo's description of the palace. ◆

◀ The "stately pleasure dome"

IFUGAO RICE TERRACES PHILIPPINES

Governed by a large cast of rice deities, the Ifugao Rice Terraces form a green stairway up to heaven.

CARVED INTO THE MOUNTAINS of Ifugao 2,000 years ago, the Ifugao Rice Terraces are an ancient irrigation system that draws on the water in the cloud-wreathed rain forests above. Described by locals as the Eighth Wonder of the World, the terraces start from the base of the mountain and spiral to a height of several thousand feet. It is said that if the steps of the terrace were placed end to end, they would encircle half the globe. According to local mythology, Ifugao refers to the rice grain given to them by their chief god, Matungulan.

Legend also states that a pair of siblings called Bugan and Wigan took refuge in this mountain during the 40-day deluge that inundated world. As the only survivors, they became the ancestors of the Ifugao people.

The Ifugao cosmos has six regions—four float above earth, one is earth itself, and the sixth lies beneath earth. Numerous deities govern daily life. Twenty-three different gods preside over the art of weaving alone, including Monlolot, the winder of the spindle, and Mamiyo, the stretcher of skeins.

Eleven gods help stamp out rice pests. Bumigi is in charge of worms and Lumadab has the power to dry up the rice leaves. Ampual controls the transplanting of rice and expects gifts in return for his blessings. Wigan is the god of good harvest while Puwok controls the dreaded typhoons. In the underworld, Yogyog and Alyog cause the earth to quake. ◆

▲ A 15th-century figurine of a rice god from Ifugao

243

PLAIN OF JARS XIENG KHOUANG, LAOS

Some say an ancient race of giants left these enormous jars scattered over the mountain plateau.

HIGH IN THE MOUNTAINS of Laos, numerous ancient jars lie half-buried in sand like shells on a beach. When archaeologists first discovered them, they were filled with black soil embedded with glass beads, burned teeth, and human bone fragments, often from more than one skeleton. Scattered around the stone jars were more bones, pottery fragments, iron and bronze objects, ceramic weights, and charcoal.

The jars lie in clusters, some comprising just a few and others several hundred. Some of the jars are 10 feet (3 m) tall. The vast majority are undecorated, but a few are carved with human faces or animals.

Most archaeologists believe the jars date from around 500 B.C. to A.D. 500 and were used for ancient burials or cremations. However, local villagers subscribe to a legend

> **The jars were filled with black soil embedded with human teeth and bone fragments.**

that involves giants. According to this story, a race of giants inhabited the hills and mountains of Laos, ruled by a king giant called Khun Cheung.

One day, after a victorious battle in a long and brutal war, Cheung decided to throw a party for his people and ordered jars for storing rice wine. The larger jars were intended for the more important giants, and the biggest one was to be reserved for Cheung himself.

Tradition states that the jars were made using natural materials such as clay, sand, sugar, as well as animal products (in fact, they are made of sandstone). This led locals to believe that a nearby cave served as a kiln in which the huge jars were fired. ◆

▲ The megalithic site of the Plain of Jars is an atmospheric spot that fascinates visitors.

HIMALAYA NEPAL / TIBET

Many claim that a fearsome ape-like creature roams the Himalaya, leaving giant footprints in the snow.

TALLER THAN A HUMAN and covered in hair, the yeti came to the notice of Western culture at the end of the 19th century. By the 1920s, explorers were searching high into the Himalaya for the elusive beast.

In 1921 the British explorer Charles Howard-Bury reported finding footprints of a loping, wolf-like creature while he was crossing the 21,000-foot (6,400 m) Lhakpa-la. His Sherpa guides told him that the tracks belonged to the Wild Man of the Snows, a deity from pre-Buddhist times. The Lepcha people once worshipped a "glacier being" as god of the hunt, and followers of the Bon religion were said to use the blood of the wild man in ceremonies.

In 1925 N. A. Tombazi, a photographer and member of the Royal Geographical Society, sighted a huge, human-like creature at about 15,000 feet (5,000 m) near Zemu Glacier. He watched it for about a minute from a distance of 200 yards (183 m). Two hours later, Tombazi and his companions descended the mountain and saw the creature's prints, which resembled those of a human.

Western interest in the yeti peaked in the 1950s. While climbing Mount Everest in 1951, British mountaineer Eric Shipton took photographs of large prints in the snow at 20,000 feet (6,000 m). Many experts have scrutinized these images. Some say they are the best evidence yet of the yeti's existence. In 1954 the English newspaper *Daily Mail* claimed expedition teams had obtained hair specimens from an alleged yeti scalp found in the Pangboche monastery. The hairs were black to dark brown in color in dim light, and fox red in sunlight. ◆

▲ Is the yeti a myth or reality?

▼ The snowy peaks of the Himalaya, where Sherpa guides have long asserted the existence of the yeti.

JIUNDU SWAMPS ANGOLA / CONGO / ZAMBIA

A flying dinosaur is said to plague the Jiundu swamps, capsizing small canoes and attacking locals.

THE KONGAMATO, MEANING "breaker of boats," flies above the vast swamps of western Africa, swooping so quickly that its victims never see it coming. Some believe it may be the very large and peculiar saddle-billed stork or even a giant bat, but almost all accounts say it is a reddish-black creature resembling a pterodactyl.

Local people have returned from the swamp with deep wounds that they avow are the result of Kongamato attacks. Eyewitness accounts say the creature has leathery wings, razor-sharp teeth, a beak, and claws. When British scientists showed drawings of pterosaurs to local people, they reeled back from the images and pointed to the sky.

> The Kongamato flies above the swamps, swooping so quickly that its victims never see it coming.

Many stories and legends have sprung up about the creature. One tells of a strange beast rising up from the water like a cormorant, then diving straight down to upset a canoe, driving its sharp beak through the belly of a fisherman.

The Kaonde people of Zambia used to carry protective charms called *muchi wa Kongamato*. They described the creature as a huge red lizard with bat-like membranous wings that were 5 feet (1.5 m) across, teeth, and a huge beak. In the 1930s, the coelacanth, a deep-sea contemporary of the pterodactyl, was discovered off the coast of Africa. It seems likely that flying dinosaurs do still exist after all. ◆

▼ The flying creature resembles a pterodactyl.

WONDER HOLE RICHTERSVELD, SOUTH AFRICA

It is said that a man-eating serpent uses this sinkhole to slip into a tunnel and slither to the sea.

▲ Legends often explain sinkholes as entrances to an underworld or the lair of monstrous creatures.

KNOWN BY THE NAMA PEOPLE AS HEITSI EIBIB, meaning "emptiness," this limestone sinkhole was named the Wondergat, or Wonder Hole, by European settlers exploring the Richtersveld in the 19th century. The sinkhole plunges straight down into the earth. At 15 feet (4.5 m) across, and almost perfectly circular, it descends 65 feet (20 m) before veering into a tunnel that allegedly travels more than 40 miles (64 km) to the sea.

The *grootslang*, or great snake, is an African monster said to live in the Wonder Hole. Some say it transforms into a young maiden in order to lure men to the sea and then drown them. The indigenous San people believe the snake can kill with its breath alone. In the 19th century, a well-known gold prospector called Fred Cornell encountered a large snake-like creature scaring his pack mules here. He threw several sticks of dynamite into the Wonder Hole in an attempt to kill it, but the dynamite never blew.

According to legend, when the nomadic Nama people arrived in the Richtersveld from Namibia across the border, the snake turned them into half-human trees so they could never leave. It is said that the "heads" of these trees always face north, longingly gazing toward the beloved land that the Nama left behind. Now rare, these trees grow on the southern slopes of the Richtersveld mountains. From a distance, the trees look like human figures staring toward the north. ◆

WHEN TO VISIT

Arrive at sunrise in May or June and take the hiking path leading up to Cornellskop.

BAAL'S PALACE UGARIT, SYRIA

A cache of clay tablets uncovered in Syria relates the adventures of the ancient god Baal.

In the 1920s, a Syrian farmer plowing a field in Ras Shamra in northern Syria turned up a strange clay tablet. It transpired that it was evidence of a Bronze Age city called Ugarit buried below a hill on the outskirts of the town. Archaeologists had soon uncovered hundreds of other tablets, most of which recounted the epic stories of Baal, a god in Canaanite mythology. The stories are known as the Baal Cycle.

The cycle begins with Baal overthrowing his rival Yam and seizing his throne. A banquet is held in his honor, but the next day Anat, his sister, lover, and warrior goddess, kills the warriors of the city of Ugarit, and the townspeople run away in fear. Baal complains to Anat that even though he had won the battle with Yam, his father, El, will not allow him his own palace. Anat threatens to make El's gray hair run with blood unless he allows Baal his own court. Earthquakes then erupt at her feet and chase El from his chamber. Believing the quakes to be a sign from the higher gods, El gives the abandoned Ugarit palace to Baal.

The cycle ends with Baal's struggle against Mot, the god of death. To avoid Baal becoming Mot's slave for eternity, the sun goddess Shapash advises Baal to substitute a body in place of his own in his final battle with Mot. Baal hides in the mountains and the gods think Baal is dead. In her grief, Anat searches the underworld for her brother, begging Mot to restore him to life. When Mot laughs at the goddess, she attacks him with a sword, shakes the bones out of his body, crushes his flesh, and throws his remains to the birds. Heartbroken, but avenged, Anat returns to El, and there before her is Baal, finally king of Ugarit. ◆

▲ A bronze and gold figurine of Baal, wielding a thunderbolt

▼ The Bronze Age city of Ugarit

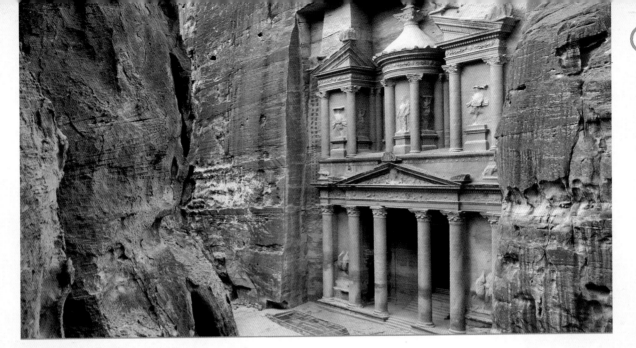

PETRA MA'AN, JORDAN

Spirits known as _djinn_ are said to guard the narrow entrance of this rock-cut city in southern Jordan.

THE STRIKING ROSE-COLORED city of Petra can only be reached through a crevice in the rocks. Known as the _siq_ (gorge), the passage is 1 mile (2 km) long and 10 to 20 feet (3–6 m) wide in places, its walls soaring hundreds of feet toward the sky.

The Nabataeans founded Petra in the sixth century B.C., creating the base of a commercial empire that extended into Syria. Traders would arrive in Petra with their dusty caravans, and unload their cargoes of pungent spices, myrrh, frankincense, precious gems, and silks.

The Nabataeans worshipped the moon goddess Allat, identified with the Mesopotamian goddess of the underworld, Ereshkigal, and later Aphrodite, the Greek goddess of love. According to scholars, the Nabataeans believed Allat was the mother of the pre-Islamic god Hubal, who was worshipped extensively in Mecca.

Spirits known as djinn are said to lurk inside the temples. Mentioned in ancient Islamic texts, they inhabit the netherworld and are made of a smokeless yet scorching fire. The djinn can be good, evil, or neutral. Two large blocks of stone known as the Djinn Blocks flank the entrance to the siq. Some visitors report feeling the blazing heat of the invisible djinn as they pause to admire the monuments. ◆

▲ The city of Petra was entirely carved out of the rocks.

DISCOVERER IN DISGUISE Swiss-born explorer John Lewis Burckhardt (1784–1817; right) discovered Petra in 1812 on his quest to find the source of the Niger River. When he was told of a hidden valley with archaeological treasures guarded by protective locals, he disguised himself as an Arab and said he wanted to honor a tomb at the end of the valley—it was there that he discovered Petra.

See Also: Ayers Rock, p. 176

NOURLANGIE ROCK ARNHEM LAND, AUSTRALIA

Lightning spirits inhabit this ancient rock in the Northern Territory, ready to strike at any time.

LIKE A GIANT SHIP STRANDED in a sea of trees, this sandstone outcrop was left behind as the plateau eroded away. For tens of thousands of years it has been sacred to the Aboriginal tribes of the Kakadu region.

At certain places in the cliff face, ancient rock paintings depict the Mimi spirits, who purportedly taught the Aboriginals how to hunt, prepare kangaroo meat, and create fire. Their elongated bodies are so thin that they threaten to break in the wind. To avoid this, they are said to make their homes in the rock's crevices.

Electrical storms rip through Arnhem Land during the monsoon season, and Namarrkon, the lightning spirit, plays a central role in the region's creation myths.

> Shaped like a grasshopper, he leaps across the stormy skies and hits the clouds with an ax.

Shaped like a grasshopper, Namarrkon leaps across the stormy skies and hits the clouds with an ax to summon thunder. A lightning bolt in the form of a white band links his ankles, head, and hands. When Namarrkon comes to earth he splits trees asunder and slices the roofs off houses.

In mythology, Namarrkon and his wife, Barrginj, who is also depicted in Nourlangie's rock shelters, create a ghastly race of grasshopper children known as the Alyurr. In November, these blue and orange grasshoppers spring across the land as anticipation builds for the dramatic entrance of Namarrkon and the summer monsoon. ◆

▲ Elongated Mimi spirits inhabit the rock's crevices.

BAIAME CAVE
SINGLETON, NEW SOUTH WALES, AUSTRALIA

Ancient paintings in a cave in the Hunter Valley depict the mightly creator god Baiame.

In a shallow rock shelter on a private property at Milbrodale, 17 miles (27 km) south of Singleton, the creator god Baiame spreads out his astonishing snake-like arms. Known as the Sky Father, Baiame is depicted in this 3,000-year-old image as a large figure embracing the tribal territory of the Wanaruah people. The figure has large staring eyes and no mouth.

The Wanaruah are a culturally and environmentally rich group of Aboriginals in the upper Hunter Valley. Their paintings tell the story of how Baiame created the land. According to myth, Baiame came down from the sky to build the rivers, mountains, and forests. He gave the people their laws and culture, and made the kangaroo, wallaby, emu, and all the creatures of the valley. He gave the wedge-tailed eagle, which wheels high above the valley, the role of protecting the land and the tribe.

Baiame also created the first initiation site, known as a *bora*, where boys are traditionally initiated into manhood through the performance of secret rites. Traditionally women were not allowed to see the drawings of Baiame or approach his sites.

According to the creation myth, when Baiame had finished making the world he returned to the sky. As he jumped back to heaven from Mount Yengo, he flattened the mountain's summit. Its flat top can be seen not far from Wollombi Valley. Baiame is said to be married to Birran-gnulu, who is often identified as an emu. ◆

▲ Baiame made the eagle the totem, or protector, of the tribe and the land.

▼ The all-embracing figure of Baiame, framed by two trees

INDEX

PICTURE CREDITS

Every effort has been made to credit the copyright holders of the images used in this book. We apologize for any unintentional omissions or errors and will insert the appropriate acknowledgment to any companies or individuals in subsequent editions of the work.

1 John Gay/English Heritage/Arcaid/Corbis **2** Bule Sky Studio/Shutterstock **4** Julie Dermansky/Corbis **6** Domingo Leiva **9** Archives Charmet/The Bridgeman Art Library, Copyright: SHLP/BPP **10** Last Refuge/Robert Harding World Imagery/Corbis **14** Leslie Garland Picture Library/Alamy **15** Alessandro Colle **16** Andrea Pistolesi **17** Royal Holloway, University of London/The Bridgeman Art Library **18** Lloyd WA Cosway **19** The Bridgeman Art Library **20** Pictorial Press Ltd/Alamy **21 t** Mary Evans Picture Library **b** shieldparanormal.com **22** Bernard Annebicque/Sygma/Corbis **23t** The Marsden Archive/Alamy **b** Giraudon/The Bridgeman Art Library **24** Getty Images **25 t** Alinari/The Bridgeman Art Library **b** Giraudon/The Bridgeman Art Library **26-27** Stephen Cullum **26 t** Burg Wolfsegg, H. Rauchenberger **b** Alfred Schaffer, Panoramio **27 t** sellingpix **c** INTERFOTO/Alamy **b** Sibrikov Valery/Shutterstock **28 t** Wikimedia Commons **b** The Bridgeman Art Library **29** Archives Charmet/The Bridgeman Art Library **30 t** J. T. Vintage/The Bridgeman Art Library **b** Ron and Joe, Shutterstock **31** Wikimedia Commons **32 t** Photo © Civil War Archive/The Bridgeman Art Library **b** Medford Historical Society Collection/CORBIS **33 t** Mary Evans Picture Library **b** Antiquarian Images/Mary Evans **34** Wayne Hsieh **35** Alan Horsager **36** The Bridgeman Art Library **36** San Jose History Museum **37** Pete Ryan **38-39** Axel Koester/Sygma/Corbis **38 t** Getty Images **b** Getty Images **39 t** Moviestore collection Ltd/Alamy **c** Getty Images **b** Michael Nicholson/Corbis **40** Anne Lewis/Alamy **41** Fairfax Media via Getty Images **42t** GeA educatie **42b** Alfred Kubin **43** British Library/Robana via Getty Images **44-45** John W Banagan **45** Werner Forman Archive/The Bridgeman Art Library **46** Wikimedia Commons **47** Wikimedia Commons **48-49** chungking, Shutterstock **49** chungking, Shutterstock **50 t** British Library/Robana via Getty Images **b** Delcampe Auctions **51** Kobus Tollig **52** Lario Tus **53** The Art Archive/Alamy **54-55** GEORGE BERNARD/SCIENCE PHOTO LIBRARY **56** Peter Phipp/Travelshots.com/Alamy **57 t** Lordprice Collection/Alamy **b** batcow.co.uk **58 t** Stefano Bianchetti/Corbis **b** Marco Cristofori/Robert Harding World Imagery/Corbis **59 t** Bildagentur-online/Sunny Celeste/Alamy **b** Archives Charmet/The Bridgeman Art Library **60 t** Mary Evans Picture Library **b** The Art Archive/Alamy **61 t** Getty Images **b** A. W. Cutler/National Geographic Society/Corbis **62** Edmund Lowe Photography **63** The Bridgeman Art Library **64** Daniel Jolivet **65 t** Matteo Borrini **b** De Agostini Picture Library/G. Dagli Orti/The Bridgeman Art Library **66** listverse.com **67 t** Archives Charmet/The Bridgeman Art Library **b** matt griggs/Alamy **68** The Bridgeman Art Library **69 t** Dan Beards **b** LUKE MACGREGOR/Reuters/Corbis **70 t** Adam Sowers **b** Mr TinDC **71** Bettmann/CORBIS **72-73** Julie Dermansky/Corbis **72 t** Lonely, Shutterstock **b** sdominick **73 t** PICTURES IN PARADISE/THE KOBAL COLLECTION **c** Heather Leila **b** V.S. Anandhakrishna **74** Kain White **75 t** Authentic-Originals/Alamy **b** Deviant Art **76** Kevin Schafer/Minden Pictures/Corbis **77 t** Laurence Winram/Trevillion Images **b** Kurt Komoda **78** Topic Photo Agency/Corbis **79 t** Flickr/Kurt Komoda **b** Wikimedia Commons **80-81** Idris Ahmed/Alamy **80 t** V&A Images/Alamy **b** Deviant Art **81 t** ibnlive.in.com **c** Wikimedia Commons **b** Maximilian Weinzierl/Alamy **82 t** Zute Lightfoot/Alamy **b** Jeff J Daly/Alamy **83** Walker Art Library/Alamy **84-85** Heritage Image Partnership Ltd/Alamy **86 t** The Bridgeman Art Library **b** The Daniel Heighton Travel Photography Collection/Alamy **87** English Heritage **88 t** Robert Stainforth/Alamy **b** The Bridgeman Art Library **89** Giraudon/The Bridgeman Art Library **90 t** Mary Evans Picture Library/Alamy **b** The Bridgeman Art Library **91** The Bridgeman Art Library **92-93** The Art Archive/Alamy **92 t** Leemage **b** Laurence Duris **93 t** Mary Evans Picture Library/Alamy **b** Archives Charmet/The Bridgeman Art Library **c** mediacolor's/Alamy **94 t** Wikimedia Commons **b** Mary Evans Picture Library/Library of Congress **95** Giraudon/The Bridgeman Art Library **97** The Bridgeman Art Library **98 t** Bildarchiv Monheim GmbH/Alamy **b** Wikimedia Commons **99** Mary Evans Picture Library **100 t** Getty Images **b** ourinvisiblefriends.com **101 t** The Art Archive/Alamy **b** Alinari via Getty Images **102-103** Mary Evans Picture Library **103** Photos 12/Alamy **104** Radius Images/Alamy **105 t** Mary Evans Picture Library **b** Matthew D White **106** The Bridgeman Art Library **107 t** Mary Evans Picture Library **b** Mary Evans Picture Library **108** Cristián Godoy **109** © Lucinda Lambton/The Bridgeman Art Library **110-111** The Bridgeman Art Library **110 t** Getty Images Europe **b** Jad Davenport/National Geographic Society/Corbis **111 t** Ronald Sumners **c** Photo © Holly Georgia Webster/The Bridgeman Art Library **b** Rolf Richardson/Alamy **112** epa european pressphoto agency b.v./Alamy **113 t** The Stapleton Collection/The Bridgeman Art Library **b** Parth Joshi **114** The Bridgeman Art Library **115 t** Mary Evans Picture Library **b** JTB MEDIA CREATION, Inc./Alamy **116** Kurt Komoda **117 t** David Forman/Eye Ubiquitous/Corbis **b** René Mattes/Hemis/Corbis **118 t** Mary Evans Picture Library **b** Hemis/Alamy **119 t** Kurt Komoda **b** Alex Wallace/www.photonewzealand.com/photonewzealand/Corbis **120-121** © Illustrated London News Ltd/Mary Evans **122** © Charles Bowman /Axiom **123** Mary Evans Picture Library/Grosvenor Prints **124 t** © Look and Learn/The Bridgeman Art Library **b** June Cooper/Alamy **125** De Agostini Picture Library/G. Dagli Orti/The Bridgeman Art Library **126** Gamma-Rapho via Getty Images **127 t** Sisse Brimberg/National Geographic Creative **b** age fotostock/Alamy **128 t** Sylvain Sonnet/Corbis **b** De Agostini/A. Dagli Orti **129** Getty Images **130 t** Leemage **b** imagebroker/Alamy **131 t** Serguei Fomine/Global Look/Corbis **b** Johner Images/Alamy **132** De Agostini/Getty Images **133** The Art Archive/Alamy **134** The Bridgeman Art Library **135** Jim Zuckerman/Corbis **136** trotalo, Shutterstock **137 t** SuperStock/Alamy **b** De Agostini/Getty Images **138** Getty Images Europe **139** Izzet Keribar **140 t** Tom Till/SuperStock/Corbis **b** atlasobscura.com **141** Philip Wallick **142** The Bridgeman Art Library **143 t** Prisma Bildagentur AG/Alamy **b** Michael Durham **144** Rick D'Elia/Corbis **145** Alvis Upitis/Alamy **146 t** National Geographic **b** Glasshouse Images/Alamy **147** De Agostini Picture Library/G. Dagli Orti/The Bridgeman Art Library **148 t** speroforum.com **b** Alain Keler/Sygma/Corbis **149** Martin Araya **150-151** Eric L. Wheater **150 t** Ancient Art & Architecture Collection Ltd/Alamy **b** John Elk **151 t** De Agostini Picture Library/G. Dagli Orti/The Bridgeman Art Library **c** Dr_ATV **b** Hemis/Alamy **152 t** William Albert Allard/National Geographic **b** STRINGER/PERU/X01495/Reuters/Corbis **153** WIN-Initiative **154** Marko Stavric Photography **155** farutac **156** PHOTO BY PRASIT CHANSAREEKORN **157 t** The Bridgeman Art Library **b** Photo © Luca Tettoni/The Bridgeman Art Library **158 t** Luca Tettoni/Robert Harding World Imagery/Corbis **b** The Stapleton Collection/The Bridgeman Art Library **159** Benoy K. Behl/National Geographic Creative **160** aravind chandramohanan/Alamy **161 t** Photo © Christie's Images/The Bridgeman Art Library **b** Tim Makins **162** Flickr Vision **163** Greg Vore/National Geographic Creative **164 t** De Agostini Picture Library/The Bridgeman Art Library **b** Jill Schneider/National Geographic Creative **165** Patrick Horton **166 t** Panorama Media **b** Jochen Schlenke **167** akg-images/Erich Lessing **168** STR/epa/Corbis **169 t** Richard Nowitz, National Geographic Creative **b** Bibliotheque Nationale, Paris, France/The Bridgeman Art Library **170** Sean Caffrey **171** Kenneth Garrett/National Geographic Creative **172 t** Robert Preston/Alamy **b** Robert Harding Picture Library Ltd/Alamy **173** The Bridgeman Art Library **174** Gary Cook/Alamy **175 t** oversnap **176-177** Robert Van der Hilst/The Image Bank/Getty **177** Art Gallery of South Australia, Adelaide, Australia/South Australian Government Grant/The Bridgeman Art Library **178-179** © L. Clarke/CORBIS **180** Micah Lidberg **181** Ben Brain/PhotoPlus Magazine via Getty Images **182 t** Mary Evans/Natural History Museum **b** Vincent Lowe/Alamy **184** Wikimedia Commons **185 b** Niels Melander/Alamy **186 t** Cultura RM/Alamy **b** © David Slater 2010 **187 t** Maistora (Vladimir Dimitroff) **b** Wikimedia Commons **188 t** Mary Evans Picture Library **190** Stocktrek **191 b** Mary Steinbacher/Alamy **192-193** Michele Falzone **192 t** Flickr/Robert Thomson **193 b** Tony Rowell/Corbis **194 t** Stephen Saks Photography/Alamy **b** Chuck Pefley/Alamy **196** Panoramic Images **197** Science Picture Co. **198** Mary Evans Picture Library/Alamy **199** National Geographic Image Collection/Alamy **200** Dmitry Burlakov/Alamy **201** The Bridgeman Art Library **203 b** Mary Evans/Library of Congress **204** Religious Images/UIG **205** Wikimedia Commons **206 t** Mary Evans Picture Library **207** Rostislav Glinsky **208** Lonely Planet Images **209 t** Fer Gregory, Shutterstock **209 b** Keith McInnes Photography **210-111** The Gallery Collection/Corbis **212** Antonino Barbagallo/Corbis **213 t** © Nationalmuseum, Stockholm, Sweden/The Bridgeman Art Library **b** SSPL via Getty Images **214 t** Stephen Spraggon/Alamy **b** Wikimedia Commons **215 t** Illustrated London News Ltd./Mary Evans **b** Mary Evans Picture Library/Alamy **216** The Bridgeman Art Library **217 t** John Heseltine/Alamy **b** Roger-Viollet, Paris/The Bridgeman Art Library **218** AF archive/Alamy **219 t** LatitudeStock/Alamy **219 b** Carys Davies **220** Reed Kaestner/Corbis **221 t** Gareth McCormack/Alamy **b** Jim Richardson/National Geographic Creative **222 t** Ian Dagnall/Alamy **b** Peter Philipp; Harald Jahn/CORBIS **223 t** Interfoto/Sammlung Rauch/Mary Evans **b** Interfoto/Sammlung Rauch/Mary Evans **224** De Agostini Picture Library/G. Dagli Orti/The Bridgeman Art Library **225** Interfoto/Sammlung Rauch/Mary Evans **226 t** RnDmS, Shutterstock **b** © Stefano Baldini/The Bridgeman Art Library **227** The Marsden Archive, UK/The Bridgeman Art Library **228 t** Interfoto/Sammlung Rauch/Mary Evans **b** Bettmann/CORBIS **229** Photo © Christie's Images/The Bridgeman Art Library **230** © Royal Naval Museum, Portsmouth, Hampshire, UK/The Bridgeman Art Library **232** 19th era 2/Alamy **233** Werner Forman Archive/The Bridgeman Art Library **233** The Bridgeman Art Library **234-235** Kari/Alamy **235t** Martin Gray/National Geographic Creative **236 t** Russell Kord/Alamy **b** Werner Forman Archive/The Bridgeman Art Library **237 t** The Bridgeman Art Library **b** Robert Clark/National Geographic Creative **238-239** Louise Murray/RobertHarding World Imagery/Corbis **238 t** BANANA PANCAKE/Alamy **b** Wikimedia Commons **239 t** jolemarcruzado **c** De Agostini Picture Library/A. C. Cooper/The Bridgeman Art Library **b** Mauricio Handler/National Geographic Society/Corbis **240** Dorling Kindersley/UIG/The Bridgeman Art Library **241 t** De Agostini Picture Library/The Bridgeman Art Library **b** Mary Evans /Library of Congress **242** Scott Stulberg/Corbis **243 t** Bibliotheque Nationale, Paris, France/The Bridgeman Art Library **b** The Art Archive/Alamy **244** Aurora Photos/Alamy **245 t** The Bridgeman Art Library **b** Alex Treadway/National Geographic Creative **246** © British Library Board. All Rights Reserved/The Bridgeman Art Library **247** sah/Image Source/Corbis **248 t** De Agostini Picture Library/A. Dagli Orti/The Bridgeman Art Library **b** The Art Archive/Alamy **249 t** Bruno Morandi/Corbis **b** Wikimedia Commons **250** Jason Edwards/National Geographic Creative **251** 19th era 2/Alamy